AND IT CAME TO PASS

Gruinard
Bay

Rubha Ré
Lighthouse
Laide •
• Ullapool
Loch Ewe
Melvaig •
Aultbea
Dundonnell
Loch
Broom
Poolewe •
Inverewe
An Teallach
• Strath
The Gairloch
Gairloch
Loch Maree
Badachro •
Letterewe
Slioch.
Red Point •
Loch Torridon
Ben Alligan
Beinn Eighe
• Kinlochewe
Isle of
Rona
Diabaig
• Torridon
Achnasheen

Loch Monar

• Applecross

Loch Monar

Loch Mullardoch

Loch Carron
Stromeferry
Kyle of
Lochalsh

Loch Affric

Kyleakin
• Dornie
Loch Duich

Isle of Skye
• Glenelg

WESTER ROSS

N

Sound of Sleat

Loch Clunie

Scale approx. 12 miles to inch

AND IT CAME
TO PASS

BY

BEE JAY

BARKER JOHNSON
STRATH · GAIRLOCH · ROSS-SHIRE
1962

PRINTED IN GREAT BRITAIN
BY R. & R. CLARK, LTD., EDINBURGH

FOREWORD

TIMES were when it seemed everyone was writing a novel. Nowadays mostly it is the writing of an autobiography by some personality of our age. However, this is *not* an autobiography, nor is it a travelogue, nor even a love story (though it could well have been), but merely a pleasing, readable, 'chatty' account—with many anecdotes, legends and the like—of the wonderful folk one comes across in the Highlands of Wester Ross; of a lifetime's desire to eventually live amongst them and the grandeur of their mountains, hills, lochs and savage coastline associated with Ross-shire; and of the journey one needs to take to Gairloch, which, hamlet, village or parish—call it what you will—extending all round the Gair Loch itself, is the focal point on which the various stories revolve.

It is not written by a Scotsman, but simply by one who has known both the folk and the country they inhabit, work and toil, for nearly half a century; and by one who now has a setting —a share—in their beloved land.

It is hoped it will be of much interest to the many thousands of visitors who come to these parts in the summer months, and of particular benefit to our American and Commonwealth cousins who want to know all about everything in Scotland— historically and otherwise—in a matter of a couple of days. If they read this book, so gaining intimate knowledge of this faraway county, they can return home and safely tell their friends they can now 'do Scotland' in one day instead of two! The Scottish Tourist Board may accordingly view this literary effort with a certain degree of discomfort, for it may deprive some hotels and guest houses of one day's board!

Apart from Gairloch and other notable places within easy distance of that paradise, *i.e.* Ullapool, Inverewe Gardens, Loch Maree, Torridon (to name but a few), there is a comprehensive guide and account of the Isle of Skye and Bonnie Prince Charlie. Skye, the island that breathes mystery and romance; for the story of noble-hearted Flora Macdonald will never fade, and

one never tires of the episodes and wanderings of her handsome
Prince being told and re-told.

Over 5,100,000 people stayed at Scottish hotels and boarding
houses in 1961, and nearly 600,000 tourists from abroad visited
Scotland that year. Some 10,000 and more came to Wester Ross,
and 200,000 crossed 'over the sea to Skye', and, in 1963, it is
estimated at least £80,000,000 will be spent in Scotland by
holiday-makers. Truly big figures!

There is much humour to be found in this book; and Scottish humour at that. It is informative also; so all told, everyone's
tastes will doubtless be satisfied, and may it well result in bringing Wester Ross and Skye more into prominence?

This is a Scottish book entirely different from any other,
written in an unpretentious style, by a *Sasunnach* (and a Yorkshireman too!) born of partial Cheshire parentage—the county
of 'grinning cats' fame—who has spent most of his life in the
East amidst swaying palm trees and glamorous native girls—
they also swaying ecstatically in their kilt-like grass skirts—and
where much imaginative, inventive spirit is woven and bred.
Some parts, however, are written solemnly and reverently; and
with all due deference to local customs.

So, to one and all, English or Overseas, my glass is raised
with 100° proof Scotch whisky from Glenlivet, but with no
water added (not even Scotch water), and I say *Slàinte Mhath!*

GAIRLOCH   S. B. J.

CONTENTS

CHAP.		PAGE
1	In the Beginning	1
2	The Journey—Destination Gairloch (1)	9
3	The Journey—Destination Gairloch (2)	26
4	Gairloch	40
5	The Great Silence	59
6	The Gairloch Nightingale	64
7	Across the Bay	72
8	Gairloch—Ullapool	87
9	Skye and Prince Charlie	95
10	Fishing and Shooting—Whisky and Haggis	124
11	The Kirk	143
12	The Stone of Destiny—'Lia Fàil'	174
13	Scottish Humour	189
14	The Gaelic—A' Ghàidhlig	194
15	MacBraynes	202
16	Inverewe Gardens	208
17	Christmas and New Year	212
18	Sbruileach—Fragments	217
19	In the End	234

Dedicated
to my old friend Morag
who made it possible for me
to write this book

GAIRLOCH POST OFFICE AND FLOWERDALE BRIDGE

GAIRLOCH SANDS

HIGHLAND CATTLE, PORTREE ROAD, SKYE

BADACHRO BAY

CHAPTER I

IN THE BEGINNING

ALTHOUGH the great Book commences with these words, it is not to say these forthcoming pages try in any way to emulate such greatness ; but the words, as they stand, serve as a starting-point.

As hinted in the Foreword, how does it come to pass that a Yorkshireman should ever come to live in Scotland, let alone in far-away Wester Ross, and above all write about such a district and its people. Why pick on a little hamlet like Gairloch to live ? Why not retire and live near a city, say Edinburgh, with all the facilities it affords in the way of music, theatres, cinemas, club-life, good shops and above all 'people' ? Why go into isolation as some friends say ? Why cut yourself off from civilisation, other wags remark ? You don't know a sheep from a goat, so why live amongst crofters, others tell me. But all the same many of those who raise their eyebrows in wonder have, deep down, a sneaking envious feeling.

My first introduction ever to Scotland was as a boy in my teens, when, having passed from the Grammar School to the Technical College stage studying science, physics, applied mathematics and other complicated subjects, one of the teachers (he would be termed a professor in this year of grace)—quite a young full-of-life Scotsman, believe it or not, named O'Riordan —let out the hint that the best youth in his class would be given the train fare up to Scotland to spend (not at his expense though !) two weeks with himself and his friends in a little village in the Isle of Arran.

I happened to be that lucky fellow, full of energy and vivacity, and when it was so decided (having parents' permission, of course, for we were still living in the Victorian era, though the good old Queen had died a few years before) I had to see the map as to where this place Arran was. It was like going to visit a foreign land.

The arrangement was to travel up by excursion train at night (to save money—for George O'R was paying), then change at Glasgow to catch another train to Wemyss Bay on the Clyde ; and from there step on board an 'ocean liner' (Messrs. Williamson's turbine steamer, the *Queen Alexandra*—considerably altered in later years (1935) and renamed *Saint Columba*) and look out for the pier bearing the name Loch Ranza. I had never been on a ship before. The steamer was nicely fitted out for such short runs down the Clyde—or 'doon the watter' as Glasgow folk called it. There was a German band on board, three musicians, violin, 'cello and piano (which was the custom those days, before radios and loud-speakers were known), and they moved around the decks playing ten minutes here and there, and produced a shell-like contraption for us to drop in the pennies ; no doubt some of these men were spying out the land, and the ports of call, for the Fatherland, ready for the 1914 war.

It was a unique experience. Young, and all alone, with one suitcase bulging and held together by string, in a strange country with people speaking in a foreign tongue, or so it seemed to me. Each time we drew near a pier, I looked for the password, and it seemed many hours went by, until lo and behold ! 'Loch Ranza'. And I was the first to jump off the gangway.

I can remember the scene to this very day.

It was hot and sunny—though I had been told it could rain for months on end in the island—and the bevy of beauty that met my eyes was breathtaking. Girls, girls and more girls, laughing, joking, wearing bright frilly frocks (no jeans or provocative shorts, low-cut blouses or ruby lips in 1909) ; and me, a studious young man who was soon to set out on a career abroad, with no time at all for the opposite sex.

I looked for my 'professor', thinking of far-back Yorkshire where everything was staid and solid ; that surely this could not be the place for him to come to, let alone Bee Jay ! But no, this was it ; the lot, and no mistake, for just on the landside of the barrier (you see MacBraynes made you pay 1d. to get on to the pier) was my friend, waving, grinning, no hat or collar and tanned a nutmeg brown.

'At last!' I said ; and sighed, tired, hot and sticky round my collar and bowler hat, for I had been travelling over twelve hours ; there were no fast-moving diesels then.

Going through the turnstile that squeaked and stuck, needing the oil-can, and giving up my half-ticket, I felt journey's end had come at last to my wearied self.

Greetings over, and introductions galore to all the girls, he said, 'Now we'll push off'. Would I like to go by rowing-boat, or walk ?

Taken aback, I was told the actual rendezvous was 'round the corner' (I found later on, up in the Highlands, if you ask where So-and-so is, the answer is invariably, 'Oh ! just round yon corner'), which turned out to be some 3 miles up the road— a hard, rough non-macadamised road—at a little clachan, a white-washed row of twelve cottages only, to be precise, and known as Catacol ; a peculiar sort of name I thought—but then, every-thing was now peculiar to me.

To make things easier, I am glad to say, one of the party of welcome took my bag in the small boat, whilst we others walked the rough way. Arriving, it was all so quaint but beautiful, and of course I had never seen the like of it before ; sea, Goat Fell (2900 feet)—nothing to do with goats ! it is a corruption of the Gaelic gaoth-ceann, 'windy head'—and other hills and glens in the distance. The landlady, Mrs. Millar (we all lived in the two cottages she owned in the row), was there to greet me—a beaming, well-made, red-faced woman of, I suppose, 60 years upwards, wearing a dress that only fitted here and there, sand-shoes and no stockings ; and soon the smell of Scotch broth, coming from steaming pans where hens were being boiled amongst a variety of vegetables, wafted through from the kitchen ; that, and mutton and rice pudding. Mountains of scones, pancakes, dough-nuts and buttered bread and jam thrown in later on. And we had mutton for every main meal the full two weeks I was there. I think there could not have been any cows on the island ; only sheep ! Plenty to eat, and plenty of fresh air ; breakfast (real oat-meal porridge that you could cut with a knife), lunch, tea and high tea ; and later at night, glasses of real fresh milk and, of course, more mountains of pancakes, scones, doughnuts and real butter—the lot ! And all for 4s. a day ; everything for 28s. a week. 'Nae bad !'

We led a casual open-air life, lolling about doing nothing, taking the boat out (no charge), especially at night when the

midges were troublesome ; and always—always—going down
to the pier each morning to meet the boat in and see if anyone
attractive was arriving that we might possibly 'date' later on.
There was not a single car on the island ; and you never saw a
policeman. The nearest P.C. would probably be across on the
mainland at Campbeltown ; quite a safe distance !

A current (love-sick) song then was, 'If I should plant a tiny
seed of love in the garden of your heart ; would it grow to be a
great big love one day, or would it die and fade away?' I am
sure we all planted in our dreams many a seed in those early carefree days ! And to date this period even more, the hit tune of
the year was 'Alexander's Ragtime Band'.

I have mentioned midges ; of all the insect life, I think the
midge is the most obnoxious. They are always in swarms on
warm, calm evenings June–October. All along the west coast
of Scotland (Ross-shire included !) midges seem to abound, and
they can inflict on a sensitive skin a nasty bite and lump.

> Yes . . . I love the Ross-shire coast and seas
>   And all her mountain ridges ;
>   I love her birch and forest trees
>   But how I loathe her midges !

We took it in turns to walk the 3 miles, at 6.30 a.m., to the
bakers to get fresh rolls and bring them back for breakfast. The
old lady was named Murchie—Miss Murchie—a real spinster and
quite a religious character, with a sphinx-like unchangeable expression, like a piece of Ballachulish slate ! And if she didn't ap-
prove of you, then she had no rolls for you. Just like that. It was
shortly after Mr. Willet had got his Daylight Saving Bill through
Parliament and clocks went on one hour then. But Miss Murchie
never changed her clock or time ; and, of course, we had to remember that, and time ourselves accordingly when going for the
rolls. One day I said to her, 'Miss Murchie, why don't you put
your clock on to the right time ?' She replied tersely, 'That's
the Lord's time, and if it's good enough for Him, it's good
enough for me !'

She was an old skin-flint. There would always be a bit of
string or bacon end, or something 'casual-like' lying on the scale-
pan, and *not* the side where the weights were put, so you always
got a wee bit less weight than you should. No self-calculating,
adjusting machines those days. There was no mad rush or

queuing-up, as nowadays on holiday, for the daily papers. There was not the sale for them as now, and I don't remember ever buying one.

So this was Scotland, I said, and with such pleasant flirting companions, I said to myself, 'B. J., you must cross the border again and again'. The holiday over, the dreary sad journey back began ; garlands and confetti showered upon you as you left the pier ; a riotous proceeding really, and many aching hearts left behind. But we were young. Back to study, the 'professor' too, now a strict disciplinarian, with never a hint of the Arran mixture, or of our many escapades there.

That was how I came to know Scotland.

That was the beginning.

I returned to the old haunts, with ever-growing local experience, three or four more times, and then one day I caught sight of MacBrayne's advertisement ; a week at sea, sailing from the Broomielaw, Clyde, visiting Stornoway and all the little ports of call *en route* to that far-away spot.

I booked for the month of June, on the old *Claymore*, 726 gross tons, built in 1881, and subsequently broken up at Bo'ness in 1931, after doing fifty glorious years at sea.

The year, 1914—the year of the First World War, and the year I left in July to take up a post in Ceylon, where I was to spend (with periods of leave) nearly a quarter of a century of my working life.

The *Claymore* was, of course, a wee bit of a tramp compared to what I was to experience later on in the 20–30,000-ton superliners to the Orient, but it was comfy, and, of course, the cruise was packed full of interest : of places and scenery I had never heard of or seen in my life, and with the Northern Lights thrown in as well, it was enchanting.

As far as I remember, after leaving the muddy Clyde on the evening tide, we put in at Campbeltown, Port Ellen (Islay), West Loch Tarbert, Oban, Tobermory (Mull), up Loch Sunart to Salen, thence rounded Ardnamurchan Point—the most westerly point in Scotland—to Mallaig, Armadale (Skye), Glenelg (the only place in Scotland spelt the same either way), Kyle of Lochalsh, Broadford and Portree (Skye), across to Gairloch, Aultbea, then to Ullapool (the largest fishing village of importance near the northern boundary of Ross-shire), Lochinver—just inside the

Sutherland boundary—then across the Minch to Stornoway on the Island of Lewis. Here the steamer tied up for a whole day and we took a farmer's pony and trap across the 14 miles of the island to Callernish to see the Druid-like stones there (second only to Stonehenge). Returning, we touched at other small piers on the Outer and Inner Hebrides (Hebrid*ees* ; not as I heard only last year a South country visitor call it, *He Brides*!), Harris, North Uist, South Uist, Barra and back to Glasgow and the Clyde.

But of course it is of Gairloch, Ross-shire, that I have to pin-point, at which place we dropped anchor after leaving Skye.

This Gairloch is not to be confused with the Gare Loch on the Clyde, not far from the Holy Loch where the U.S.S. *Proteus* is stationed. There appear to be a number of place names very similar in Scotland, *e.g.* Tarbet (Loch Lomond) ; Tarbet (Loch Nevis not far from Mallaig) ; Tarbert (Loch Fyne) ; West Loch Tarbert (Argyll) ; Tarbert (Harris) ; Loch Tarbert (Jura). There is the Armadale mentioned in Skye, also an Armadale—an industrial town—in West Lothian near Edinburgh. There is the Island of Scalpay off Skye ; and another Isle Scalpay off South Harris.

Gairloch, Wester Ross ; Gairloch, meaning 'the short loch'. Of all the places we touched at—and there were several others besides those I have named (where a rowing-boat would come out to take off any odd person and cargo, and row back again to the little jetties)—it was Gairloch that struck me with its beauty ; the fascinating approach to the Gair Loch itself ; and on going ashore for the few hours we had before darkness (although in June it is hardly ever dark at all on the North-West coast) walked to the Post Office, saw the big house (Flowerdale), later to be at varying times the rendezvous for Lloyd George's wartime Cabinet meetings ; then past the Bank and the tiny golf course, up the hill to the hotel, passing and stopping to look down on the wonderful golden sands of Gairloch bay ; and then onwards to the wee village of Strath and on to the gorgeous extensive beach and clean-washed sands at Little Sands and Big Sands—unrestricted and uncrowded ; and to lazily amble along these miles of foreshore, one felt one was in a special uncharted world.

Retracing my steps to the steamer by midnight on this beautiful clear June evening, I took out my itinerary map and put a X against Gairloch, underlined it and said to myself, this—of all places—is where I would truly wish to live should I ever chance to retire.

Gairloch, 1914. It took me by storm ; and that was some 48 years ago since I first made the wish and laid the plans. Long, long years. The pity is it took so long. It could have been shorter, much shorter, for in 1923 I could have 'staked a claim' a few miles from where I am writing this today. But then I was still keeping the flag flying in the East, and one could never tell what the future had to hold. Who, in 1923, could have foreseen the Second World War ?

These weekly steamer cruises no longer operate. Mac-Braynes no longer tie up at dear old Gairloch pier, although it is a fine substantial affair. Gairloch appears to have been washed out of their itineraries. Their steamers now radiate from Mallaig and Kyle of Lochalsh for the inner and outer Isles ; and from Oban too ; and, of course, for the more or less near-by Clyde ports ; but always, always they omit Gairloch !

They were jolly little steamers in those days. As soon as you went up the gangway, you threaded your way to your *very* small cabin through piles of cargo—crates, sacks, farm implements, cement and the like—all labelled for strange-sounding parts I had never heard of and all breathed of far-away places.

Animals and people were herded together ; no racial discrimination then ! And when the livestock was discharged, the hose pipes were freely used on decks and passengers alike, unless you were quick on foot !

The chief cargo discharged seemed to be crated, and by the look of it, whisky ; and such crates were generally treated and handled with more care than the calves and lambs ! The crates were carried ashore slowly and reverently. By the time the steamer put in again on the return journey, crates had all been unfastened and many of the corks thrown away ; just in case ! 'Hush, be quiet', to quote a Gairloch expression.

At one small, lonely pier I spoke to the 'piermaster', saying it seemed a nice spot, but a long way off the beaten track. 'Yes,' he said, 'it is a bit of a worry.' 'You know,' he said, 'I've got to walk over 3 miles to get a glass of whisky.' 'But,' said I, 'why don't you get a bottle and keep it in the house ?' 'Mon,' he said, 'do ye no ken ; whisky does'na keep !'

The folk on the islands are very different from those on the mainland. The mainlander is always looked on as an 'outsider'. An islander once married a Scotch lassie from the mainland and they lived together for many, many years, when she died beloved by all. But as one islander said to another, 'I hear the foreign woman has died!' A notice is generally fixed on the church door when the minister goes to spend a day or so on the mainland to take a service there, saying, 'No service this Sabbath, the minister has gone abroad'.

And so 'it came to pass'. After all the long years, that is how it began; and I suppose I must thank Messrs. David Mac-Brayne for it; and later on I devote a chapter to their pioneer work of the opening up of the Highlands. Thank goodness for the old *Claymore*. The present-day *Claymore* (1024 tons) is a very different ship from the old one. It is a beautifully lined, seaworthy vessel, spacious cabins lined with polished woodwork; and when I sailed on her three years ago my early tea was brought in by a very chic stewardess! Very much ahead of 1914. But then times have changed these fifty years. Haven't we all?

And so, from far away Ceylon, 7000 miles from England, I planned to return one day to live in Gairloch; and it has truly 'come to pass'. Bearing in mind the old Chinese proverb—'a 1000-mile journey begins with one step'—I had already made seven steps by 1914.

Therefore, to Scotland, and to Wester Ross, I raise my glass; my very best respects; *Slàinte Mhath!*

CHAPTER 2

THE JOURNEY—DESTINATION
GAIRLOCH (1)

PREVIOUSLY I mention being 7000 miles from England, which, in 1914, took me seven steps on my journey back again.

'*Destination Gairloch*' : two crisp words which have the flavour of a box-office winning title of a spy film set in Outer Mongolia.

Yes, I was a long way from Gairloch in 1914 ; Ceylon, where I spent close on twenty-five years, seems now but a dream compared to Wester Ross ; now a living reality.

In the early 20th century when I was in Colombo everything was pro-British ; we were looked upon as a great Colonial power ; when I finally left in 1937 we were being pushed off the pavement. I always think myself fortunate at being East during the time our prestige was highly rated, and that I was able to leave before being knocked off the same pavement. During my life there, Ceylon was a Crown Colony, becoming a fully independent dominion in 1948.

It is a beautiful island, lying between 6 and 9 degrees north of the equator in a longitude of 80 and 82 degrees. Colombo itself (over 200 years old, its name stemming from an ancient Arab name Kalambu—not from Columbus as is widely thought) was 7 degrees off the equator, the mean temperature about 80 degrees and rainfall over 90 inches in the year ; humidity percentage 90 or 95. The Port was known as the Charing Cross of the East, a veritable central meeting-place for passengers to and from the East, Australia, and Africa. The population was made up of Singhalese, Tamils, Indians, Afghans, Burghers, Moors (Arabs), Malays, and just a few Europeans.

The small island, about 270 miles long by 100 miles wide, hangs like a pear-drop from the chin of India only 70 miles away at its northern tip. Although we call it Ceylon, its real name is

9

Lanka, an old Sanskrit name brought down twenty-five centuries ago by the North Indian conquerors, the Sinhalese (meaning 'Lion Race').

Cone-shaped Adam's Peak is its highest mountain. After Adam and Eve were cast out of heaven, says Moslem tradition, they had their choice of all the world's loveliest places for their earthly garden of Eden—and chose Ceylon. Adam's Peak is literally the holiest mountain in the world, revered by countless millions of people because of the foot-shaped impression in the rock at its top. To hundreds of millions of Moslems and Chinese, this is Adam's footprint. To some 400 million Buddhists, the print was made by Buddha on his third and last visit to Ceylon. To Hindus, it was made by their god Siva. To Eastern Christians, it is the print of St. Thomas the Doubter. So you see we have theories in plenty. The Sri Pada (Holy Foot-print) measures 64 inches long, by 30 inches wide.

At Kandy there is the Temple of the Tooth, sacred to all Buddhists, for it is supposed to house a molar believed to have been Buddha's.

Rich in history, Ceylon also contains two fabulous buried cities: one, 'Anuradhapura', founded in 437 B.C. at the time the Parthenon of Athens was being built, had a population of 3 million and ranked with Babylon and Nineveh ; the other, 'Polonnaruwa', about 1000 years younger. Both cities ultimately declined with collapse of political power in those days, and were lost for centuries.

These are but a few items concerning the 'Isle of Delight', just to allow readers to realise that the wish to eventually live at the spot where I had made a cross, 'Gairloch', that fateful day in 1914, was not brought about or hastened in any way by living all those years abroad in an impossible 'dump' of a place. On the contrary, Ceylon, as I have said, was beautiful, and many happy years I spent amongst its oriental wonder and colourful surroundings. But life was very artificial ; there was nothing to it, so to speak, when you took mental stock of everything and everybody. To me it was a means to an end; and the end was 'Destination Gairloch'.

For general easiness I am assuming our American, and Commonwealth cousins, and English folk too, make for Edinburgh when they come to Scotland ; and so it is from that city I start you on the 200-odd mile journey to Wester Ross.

I hope my Glasgow friends will not be annoyed with me ! Tourists will, of course, want to see Glasgow as well, but for the journey north it is far more salubrious to make the start from Edinburgh, so avoiding the bottle-necked-diesel-exhaust, choking fumes you are likely to follow all the 20 miles along the side of Loch Lomond. For once you find yourself behind two heavy transport lorries on 'yon bonnie banks o' Loch Lomond' you are certain to arrive in the 'open' making for Crianlarich looking as though you had been down a coal-mine and feeling anything but friendly even towards your fellow passengers, let alone to anyone else.

So to those coming North it is better to gravitate to Edinburgh ; and although it has been called the fairest city in Europe, it has more often than not been called 'east-windy' and 'west-endy'. But it sure is a fine city, made, of course, by broad Princes Street (Scotland's most fashionable street), with its shops on the one side and on the other side there runs a deep ravine with its gardens, open-air theatre band-stand, floral clock, above all of which the Castle is perched high on the Rock. There is the new Edinburgh and the old Edinburgh. It is a capital city (becoming the capital of Scotland in 1452) with the authentic regality and atmospherics of Holyrood Palace, to say nothing of its name 'Auld Reekie', an affectionate term by which the old-towners call it. I believe the story goes a long way back, in that a devout old man across the Firth of Forth who timed his household's evening prayers by the smoke of Edinburgh, which he could see from his wee house. When Edinburgh started to cook the supper and the smoke (reek) commenced to pour out of its chimneys, he would summon his family, saying it was time to say their prayers and go to bed, for, he said, 'I see Auld Reekie's ganging to her bed too.'

On Castle Rock is the Scottish National War Shrine, designed by Sir Robert Lorimer and opened in 1927. Inside, it is a moving sight ; one of the greatest, perhaps, in this country ; a work of consummate artistry. The casket holding the roll of honour stands on an outcrop of the living rock ; a masterpiece of genius.

At one o'clock each week day a gun is fired from the Castle— a time-signal dating back years. But we must be on the move and leave Edinburgh for our destination, for we have a date in Wester Ross. From Edinburgh via Stirling, where there is another famous Castle perched, like that of Edinburgh, on a rocky eminence, and which was a favourite residence of the Stuart kings and queens. Not far away is the scene of the Battle of Bannockburn, which I feel sure overseas tourists will wish to see, where Robert Bruce vindicated the independence of Scotland by routing the army of Edward II in June 1314 ; the only important battle ever won by the Scots over the English.

Stirling is always called the 'gateway to the Highlands'. As a motorist I would call it the 'bottle-neck to the Highlands', unless you happen to go through on a Sunday when you can pass through the main street with ease and comfort. The Wallace Monument, crowning a wooded crag, can be seen for miles around, and is at the junction of the Dunfermline and Bridge of Allan road. The monument is built close to the battlefield where Wallace defeated De Warenne in 1297. Very war-minded these Scots ! Stirling is renowned for its historical background and steeped in the traditions of centuries, and has long been a centre of Scottish life and culture. In 1962 it held its 5th Festival of Music.

From Stirling onward to Callander ; overshadowing this beauty spot is Ben Ledi (2875 feet)—the Hill of God—which invariably carries a covering of snow on it, even till early summer. I always think once you are at Callander you are really on the move to Highland scenery and glens, and you begin to breathe in a special tang of air ; you feel you are getting into a great country, quite unknown to England's characteristic standards.

Callander to bonnie Strathyre via the Pass of Leny, through which, at the Falls of Leny, you see a wonderful cascade of water in a setting of birch and heather. Off by Strathyre is Balquhidder where Rob Roy the outlaw and his wife and sons are buried in the churchyard there (1734). Still onwards you soon reach Lochearnhead, a pretty hamlet at the western end of Loch Earn. Through Glen Ogle, reaching a point almost 1000 feet above sea-level, you soon come to the road junction to Killin (right), to Crianlarich (left) ; and we take the left, through Glen Dochart past Luib. Crianlarich (which means 'The Aspen site') is, in the main, a railway junction, and it would be here in the centre of this village you would arrive if you had taken the road from

Glasgow via Loch Lomond. You here see the huge mass of Ben More (3845 feet).

A few more miles, through Strath Fillan, we are at Tyndrum (pronounced Tyne-drum), meaning the 'House on the Ridge', and then for Glencoe via Bridge of Orchy, Black Mount, Rannoch Moor (one of the largest and most desolate stretches of boggy moorland in all Scotland), Kingshouse (where a ski-slope has been constructed, and a ski-lift operates) ; thence through Glencoe itself—one of the most awesome passes in Scotland in wintry weather—a landscape without mercy as was the case of the scene of Scotland's most dastardly clan massacre (the Campbells butchering the Macdonald's—Papists and Jacobites—who were their hosts. Thirty-eight people including two women and several children were killed in cold blood in the early hours of that morning of 13th February 1692 ; and the rest, about 150 men, women and children, fled into the mountains to perish in a snow-storm.) All under 70 years of age were to be put to the sword was the order. Guests murdered hosts ; it was without doubt Highland barbarism at its worst.

After Kingshouse and before entering into Glencoe proper you pass the 'Three Sisters of Glencoe' on the left, or 'Faith, Hope and Charity'—the Gaelic names being Aonach Dubh, Gearr Aonach and Ben Fhada.

We then arrive at South Ballachulish, 34 miles from Tyndrum, a slate-quarrying village of world renown in former days ; but little is quarried nowadays ; in fact the whole place looks as though the plague had visited it, so empty and void it looks and feels. Instead of going across the ferry (and in the season you would probably be held up for several hours) just as you come out of Glencoe you should turn to the right (instead of left to Ballachulish) and go round Loch Leven—an inner arm of the great sea-loch Loch Linnhe—19 miles, reaching North Ballachulish, which is the point where the ferry would have landed you after a few minutes' crossing from South Ballachulish. It is a pleasant 19-mile run, high up on the south side, then dropping down to Kinlochleven, a village and factory created by the British Aluminium Company in 1909 for the production of aluminium. The water-power is obtained from the Blackwater Reservoir some 8 miles long in the hills above, formed by making a dam a little over half a mile long and 30 yards high. One is really impressed to see such a hive of industry operating and tucked away in such an isolated area ; it is all so unexpected. Kinlochleven is set in a deep bowl of the mountains, cut off from the sun for much of the year.

We are therefore across the ferry, either by boat or the alternative 19-mile road, and will soon be at Fort William, the head of Loch Linnhe, and the start of the Caledonian Canal through Loch Lochy, Loch Oich and Loch Ness ; and you feel you are really nearing the Highlands of Wester Ross, mile by mile.

The Caledonian Canal is 60 miles in length, but only about 20 miles of the total waterway are artificial, the rest being composed of the three lochs named above ; natural freshwater lochs of great depth extending the run of the valley. The Canal has twenty-nine small locks, controlled by the Ministry of Transport, and was surveyed by James Watt and constructed by Telford, 1803–1847, the cost being nearly 1½ million pounds. The main object was to save fishing craft the slow and sometimes perilous journey right up the west coast of Scotland to the top of Caithness through the Pentland Firth (twixt the Orkneys and Caithness) and down to the east coast ports.

Fort William owes its name to a vanished fort rebuilt in William III's time. Fort William, like Fort Augustus 32 miles further up the Canal, was built in the 18th century to subdue the Highlanders, and nestles under 'the Ben'—Ben Nevis—the highest mountain in Britain, 4406 feet high, nearly 850 feet higher than Snowdon, and is a vast bare mass of granite, and snow generally lies on 'the Ben' all the year round. I would not say Fort William is in any way an attractive town, but it serves as a very good tourist centre. There is a West Highland Museum which is most interesting with all its Jacobite relics, including a lock of Bonnie Prince Charlie's hair !

Pressing on we soon come (along General Wade's military road) to Spean Bridge, a junction spot for either Inverness (up the Canal) or via Glen Spean and Loch Laggan to Newtonmore, Kingussie, Aviemore and so on along the central Scottish great north road passing between the Cairngorms on the right and the Monadhliath mountains on the left, to Inverness also. Around Spean Bridge every crag and cave in the hillsides is associated with memories of the tragic days of 1745–46. Here the first shots of the rising were fired, and two companies of government troops and their officers were taken by a handful of Highlanders led by Macdonell of Keppoch.

Not far away on the left, near the end of Loch Lochy, is Achnacarry, the seat of Cameron of Lochiel, near to which stands the venerable ruins of the old castle, the home of the famous Lochiel who, following the dictates of his heart, sponsored the Stuart cause ; for his loyalty he lost all his estates and became an exile from his country. Near by is the 'Dark Mile', an avenue of beeches planted by Lochiel long before joining the 1745 rebellion. This avenue is so intense in verdure, and so closely are the branches of the trees knit and entwined that the sun scarcely penetrates this stretch ; hence its name. In this dark, sombre avenue Bonnie Prince Charlie sought refuge as a lonely chevalier then in hiding from his pursuers after Culloden.

Carrying on by the shores of Loch Lochy and crossing the Canal at the top of that Loch, we travel up the second of the three freshwater lochs of the Canal system via Loch Oich, narrow and the highest of the three lochs ; only 4 miles long but a beautiful one studded with small tree-clad islets ; and we so arrive at Invergarry, where there is another road junction ; to the left takes you through some exceptionally fine country via Tomdoun, Shiel Bridge, Dornie to Kyle of Lochalsh ; to the right our road alongside the canal to Fort Augustus and Loch Ness.

Near Invergarry is a curious old monument known as 'The Well of the Heads' standing by the shore of Loch Oich, which marks the spot where the heads of the seven murderers of the young Macdonells of Keppoch were washed by the avengers before being presented to the older Glengarry. The story which it perpetuates is one of greed and avarice. After sending his sons to be educated in France, Keppoch died leaving the management of his affairs and his lands in the hands of several of his kinsmen. Upon returning, the sons, who would in due course have taken over control of the estates, were cruelly murdered by their traitorous relatives. The bard of the Keppoch family urged Macdonell of Glengarry, the Chieftain, to avenge this act. And so 'it came to pass'. The inscription engraved upon the monument relates the story in brief, in English, Gaelic, French and Latin ; thus wise :

. . . As a memorial of the ample and summary vengeance which, in the swift course of feudal justice inflicted by the orders of the Lord M'Donell and Aross, overtook the perpetrators of the foul murder of the Keppoch family, a branch of the powerful and illustrious clan of which his Lordship was the chief, this monument is erected by Colonel M'Donell of Glengarry XVLL Mac-Mhic-Alaister His successor and representative in the year of our Lord 1812. The heads of the seven murderers were presented at the feet of the noble chief in Glengarry Castle after having been washed in this spring ; and ever since that event which took place early in the 16th century it has been known by the name of 'Tobar-nan-ceann' or 'The Well of the Heads'.

At Invergarry the ruins of the castle of this famous chieftain can still be seen standing upon a rocky promontory.

Leaving here, and crossing the Bridge of Oich at the northern end of Loch Oich, we wend our way and soon reach Fort Augustus. It is a neat, pleasant little village, breathing brimful of restfulness.

The original fort was built by General (then Marshal) Wade in 1729, for after what is known as the first Jacobite rising in 1715, and the defeat of the Stuart cause, the Hanoverian Government thought it desirable to select some central spot in the Highlands for the establishment of a garrison, and thus overawe the warlike clans that had organised the rebellion ; and General Wade named the Fort after William Augustus, Duke of Cumberland, youngest son of George II, the subsequent victor of Culloden. It was capable of accommodating 300 men. During the 1745 Jacobite rebellion, the fort sustained a two days' siege at the hands of Prince Charlie's forces as they were marching northwards before engaging with Cumberland at Culloden. This was in March 1746. Two months after, when the Stuart cause had been completely vanquished, the victorious Hanoverian forces once more resumed ownership.

In 1853, at the outbreak of the Crimean War, the garrison was withdrawn, and after a period of abandonment the fort was sold in 1867 by the government to Simon, 13th Baron Lovat, the representative of the reinstated Frasers of Lovat, who secured the buildings and adjoining lands for £5000. For many years the dismantled fort was occupied by various small tenants, a portion being reserved to the owner to serve as a shooting lodge.

In 1876 the Benedictine Fathers of the English Congregation of the Order, who were desirous of establishing a monastery in Scotland, accepted the offer of a 999 years' lease of the fort and its surrounding land. The monastery, therefore, now stands on the site once occupied by the fort of sinister memories, and is tucked away amongst a charming locality.

Apart from the Abbey itself there is a boys' boarding school, founded in 1878, where practical as well as theoretical knowledge is obtained ; also there is a spacious hall with a large stage which is used for meetings and social affairs.

The crowning feature of the Abbey school is the Tower, 110 feet in height, containing the great clock and carillon of nine bells. Under one of the windows in the school is a plaque with an inscription recording the thanks of the government to the abbey, for fitting up the school as a convalescent hospital during the Great War.

This school now accommodates about one hundred pupils and enjoys a growing and well-founded reputation for proficiency both in study and in sport.

The handsome church was completed in 1917 after forty years' labour. The whole of the monastery is built round a quadrangle, the four buildings, the College, Monastery, Hospice and Scriptorium, being connected by cloisters, designed in Gothic style.

Whilst visiting the monastery a few years ago, and seating myself in the church one evening, looking around admiring its loftiness and superb architecture, a monk came quietly along and sitting down at the keyboard of the organ commenced to play— without a word of music—sacred and classical works. Seldom have I seen or heard an organ played with such affection, sweetness and delicacy of touch. At the end of about twenty minutes, he stopped, rose off his seat and left ; just like that ; saying nothing to anyone, nor looking at anyone. His music I am sure, must have ascended right up high into the skies ; for I am certain he was thinking of, and playing to, the skies ; and they alone. Very solemn, very impressive, very moving ; and I felt I had received, at first hand, a lesson in humility.

Later in this book I refer, in more than one instance, to taking off one's hat. If I had had one on then, I would have surely raised it, not only in fitting reverence, but in admiration and thanksgiving, for the thundered chords and diapasons.

This great organ, originally built (in 1875) by Bryceson for a mansion house in Regent's Park, London, was removed to the old Albert Palace in Battersea Park, London, in 1884 ; and when the Palace was demolished ten years later, it was purchased by Fort Augustus Abbey, transported thither by rail and steamer, and stowed away for another twenty years in the largest room in the monastery.

In 1914 the building of the choir of the church was begun, and a part of the organ was installed on the north side, and brought into use. In 1936–38 the entire instrument was rebuilt and electrified by Lawton (Aberdeen) and is now in daily regular use. Over 10 miles of wire have been used in the action alone of this gigantic organ, which contains 4200 pipes, 4 keyboards on the console, and 100 stops in all—many of them of rare and extraordinary beauty. And all this at the beginning of the Highlands overlooking Loch Ness in the peaceful stillness of Fort Augustus. Small wonder the Loch Ness monster (should there be one) has its habitat near this godly village.

It is worthy of note that the Benedictines, whose motto is the Latin word PAX (Peace), should have come into possession of what was, in its day, a centre whence spread devastation, oppression and bloodshed, with all other attendant horrors of warfare.

Leaving Fort Augustus, we now travel up the 24-mile length of Loch Ness. This loch always seems to attract more attention of the general public than its two sister lochs, Oich and Lochy. It is never greater than one mile wide, so you can never but think of it other than a loch, and not that of a sea-loch. It is deeper than the deepest part of the North Sea and three times deeper than the Falls of Niagara. Although it has never been thoroughly charted as to its depth, even by tough divers, at certain spots the water is some 135 fathoms, about 800 feet, deep ; black, inky-black, cold (its temperature only varies a degree or so summer or winter), dark, evil-looking peaty water on a storm-cast day. And yet a young 19-year-old student girl—who incidentally was the first woman to swim Ullswater in the Lake District—attempted to swim it end-to-end in midsummer of 1961. She was plucked unconscious from the bitterly cold water after only covering 2 miles of the 24, and when she 'came-to' said 'no one will ever swim that loch' ; and one old local grandad muttered, 'Loch Ness is not meant to be swum : there is evil in them dark waters'.

This loch is, of course, millions of years old, older than the hanging gardens of Babylon ; it holds about 1¾ million million gallons of water, the greatest volume of water in the country. No one seems to know what the word 'Ness' means in Gaelic ; 'from below' appears to be the generally accepted meaning ; and in one very, very old book, Mackay's *History of Inverness-shire*, it is referred to as the 'Loch of the Seven Wells' ; and the story goes like this :

. . . The bed of Loch Ness was at one time a great fertile valley, in which there were seven wells, the largest being in the middle. From the beginning of Time the valley folk were warned they must never draw water after sunset and that the wells must never be left uncovered. One day a young married woman had gone to draw water from the largest well, when her thatched cottage caught fire. She dropped her water and bucket and fled to her house to save her baby. An old man cutting hay in the meadow shouted out 'go back and cover the well'. But she was too bent on saving her baby boy. Looking back over her shoulder as she ran she could see the water was already rising over the rim of the well, but on she ran to save her son and save him she did. When she came out of her cottage the water was up to her feet, and the people were taking to the hills. Legend has it that all were drowned.

That is the story of the seven wells ; sometimes also referred to as the 'Loch of the Careless Woman'.

The 'monster' first hit the headlines in 1933, and overnight it became world-famous; and over 10,000 cars drove round the loch side one week that August just in case they could see 'her'. Despite the scepticism, derision and allegations of purely tourist advertisement, there is such a wealth of lore on the subject that those living in the area cannot deny outright its possible existence. If it is an hallucination, then it is a truism to say that many people of distinction have been subjected to the experience. Far be it for me to say yea or nay. I would rather have the colourful and imaginative legend or fact left as it is—nebulous.

Carrying on up the loch side, the next hamlet we pass is Invermoriston, another picturesque district. From here the road veers left also on its way to Kyle, like the one from Invergarry ; both roads meeting at Cluanie Bridge *en route* to Shiel Bridge and Dornie. Next we come to Drumnadrochit, a real Scottish name to retail to your English friends !

A mile or so before you pull in to Drumnadrochit is Urquhart Castle, a ruined shell, which was built under Edward I ; one of the curtain-walled castles built to dominate the Great Glen. It is

in the bay here that once echoed the roar of the late John
Cobb's speed-boat. The few villagers still speak sadly of him,
the man who dared the loch. Around here is the driest place in
the north, the average rainfall being only 18 inches. Lower
down the canal, at Invermoriston, they can easily record 44 inches
a year. At Drumnadrochit, because of the unusual angle of a
glen some miles away, the wind blows the unwary backward
one minute and with its next puff sends the unbalanced pedestrian
almost flat on his face. Nobody knows why. It may be a north-
east wind tearing down Loch Ness one minute ; the next a south-
west. The loch seldom gives up its dead ; many have been
drowned in it, few recovered.

Nobody knows why in a storm every seventh wave on the loch
is bigger than the others ; nobody knows why lots of strange things
take place on this loch. To some of the old inhabitants of these
lonely clachans, Loch Ness could be the ninth wonder of the world.

Drumnadrochit used to be a favourite retreat in the summer
for Prime Minister Neville Chamberlain, and I have many times
stayed at the hotel when he and his fishing party were in
residence. He would be out all day in a boat and come back
looking tired, his gaunt-like face deep in thought ; whether it
was of the one that got away, or of the nettle he had clasped
firmly, which was the metaphor he used when he returned from
Munich, I couldna' say. He was certainly not holding up and
waving a piece of paper saying he hoped it was 'Peace with
honour, and Peace for our time', as was his official declaration in
1938 when he touched down at London Air-port.

From Drumnadrochit you can turn left for Cannich and Glen
Affric, but at Milton, a village a mile along, turn sharply up a
hair-pin bend and over the moors, 12 miles to Beauly ; or should
you carry on direct from 'Drum' northwards, you reach Inverness, 14 miles away.

In journeying to Ross-shire I always cut out Inverness by
turning off left at 'Drum', so eliminating the two sides of the
triangle (a saving not only of 13 miles, but of a wearisome traffic
jam during the season that exists in, and close to, Inverness).
Besides that, I have little interest in towns, for I am making for
Gairloch, but in this instance I will wait for you, whilst you pay
Inverness a visit ; then out you come the 11 miles to join me at
the Beauly junction where I had arrived from over the moors *ex*

Drumnadrochit ; and where the town of Beauly is but a mile or so away.

Inverness. I always thrill as I enter Inverness, for there to greet the incoming motorist, printed on a board, in big letters, is 'Inverness, *ceud mìle fàilte*' ; and underneath (should you not know the Gaelic !) 'a 100,000 welcomes'. It is an even better feeling than when, coming up from England via Carter Bar, you see the sign-board 'You are now in Scotland'—for at Inverness you are only 74 miles from Gairloch.

Inverness, Queen of the North, is the capital of the Highlands ; it really is the only town of any size in the North of Scotland. It prides itself on its speech, its purity and intonation ; and I agree.

Inverness has the advantage over Edinburgh in that it has a broad, lovely river flowing through it. There are pretty walks round the river Ness, and pretty islands too, several joined to the bank by foot bridges.

There is a fine, wide, vehicular traffic bridge which takes you out of the town going North ; a real credit to the town and the contractors. This new bridge was completed in September 1961, and was formally opened by Provost Allan Ross, deputising for former Scottish Secretary Mr. Tom Johnston, on the 28th of that month, amidst pouring rain.

The Ness bridges have been dogged by ill-luck.

Bridge No. 1 went up in flames in 1411, when a fierce clan chief, Donald of the Isles, passed through on his way to the Battle of Harlaw.

Bridge No. 2, known as 'the great wooden bridge of Inverness', collapsed in 1664 while being repaired.

Bridge No. 3, a stone-built seven-archer, stood for a century and a half before being swept away in 1849.

Bridge No. 4 was the suspension bridge which this latest structure has replaced, and the trouble with that bridge lay, not so much in keeping it up, as in getting rid of it !

As the Second World War clouds gathered, the flagmen allowed only one vehicle at a time to cross, and at last a contractor started preparatory work for this new Ness bridge. But the war came and soon the bridge had to cope with convoys of tanks and heavy army lorries. Despite many arguments and discussions the suspension bridge held on through the post-war years, until it was finally closed in May 1958.

Turning now from bridges to cemeteries!

Tomnahurich (Hill of the Yew Trees) is a most renowned cemetery in Inverness ; a hill of death, when in the stone age torrents burst their way seawards, this hill opposing them stood firm, and the waters passed by on either side ; and Inverness has made of it a most beautiful cemetery. Many an old local would feel it an honour to be buried and lie peacefully at rest in Tomnahurich.

There is a very interesting small book I heartily recommend to readers, viz. *The Prophecies of the Brahan Seer*, who was undoubtedly imbued with second sight. He was one Kenneth Mackenzie, better known as Coinneach Odhar Fiosaiche, the Brahan Seer, who was born in the Island of Lewis, in the parish of Uig, about the beginning of 1600, and became possessed of a stone in a remarkable way by which he could reveal the future of man and mankind. He no doubt predicted a great many things ; among these may be placed his prophecy, 150 years beforehand, of the making of the Caledonian Canal and that ships would sail round the back of Tomnahurich Hill. In point of fact a paragraph appeared in the *Inverness Advertiser* in 1859 (*i.e.* before Tomnahurich had been made a cemetery) and reads thus :

> Tomnahurich, the far-famed Fairies' Hill, has been sown with oats. According to tradition, the Brahan prophet who lived 200 years ago predicted that ships with unfurled sails would pass and repass Tomnahurich, and further that it would yet be placed under lock and key. The first part of the prediction was verified by the opening of the Caledonian Canal, and we seem to be on the eve of seeing the realisation of the rest by the final closing up of the Fairies' Hill.

This, mark you, was in print before the prediction was fulfilled. The Seer's prediction was that the day would come when Tomnahurich, or as he called it, The Fairy Hill, would be under lock and key and the fairies secured within. A unique cemetery on the top of a hill and the spirits (of the dead) chained within. It is, in all, a remarkable book and well worthy of reading, for it is connected mainly with North of Scotland predictions ; and the Brahan Seer was the keenest-eyed of all Highland prophets.

Of course, in talking of Inverness one must naturally mention its Castle, situated on a high mound overlooking the flowing river Ness, a veritable watch-tower of the Highlands. The Castle stands on or near the site of Macbeth's Castle, several times destroyed and rebuilt in the course of the troubled and eventful history of the Highlands, when sometimes it was in possession of the English and at other times of the Scots ; although the modern structure of today serves only as the administrative centre of the county. It is supposed the first castle on this site was built in 1057. During the 1715 rising the Castle was, for a short time, in the hands of the Jacobites, but was recovered for George I by Rose of Kilravock, and Simon, Lord Lovat.

On the mound standing in front of the Castle entrance is the statue of Flora Macdonald, whose name (as readers will shortly learn after reading the forthcoming chapter on Skye) is so linked with Bonnie Prince Charlie.

The inscription on the monument is in Gaelic and English, and reads :

> As long as a flower grows on a field
> So long will the fame of the maiden endure.

Very sweet ; very touching. Poor Flora ; poor Flora indeed.

Bringing events more up to date it may be worth recalling that in September 1921, His Majesty's Cabinet met in the Town Council Chambers to discuss the Irish question, and a framed document bearing signatures of Prime Minister Lloyd George and other members of the Cabinet hangs upon the wall of the room.

And so we say farewell, *slàn leat*, to Inverness and take the road out across the river northwards to Beauly (12 miles). Shortly before entering Beauly one catches a glimpse of Beaufort Castle, built in 1882 (and is the thirteenth to be built on the site), the modern seat of Lord Lovat, chief of the Clan Fraser. Beauly takes its name from the French *beau lieu*—beautiful place. The country around differs in its scenery ; the mountains to the south-east are clothed with verdure ; those to the north and west are bold, heath-covered and craggy.

There is a pretty legend that Mary Queen of Scots was responsible for the name. She stayed at the Priory House for one night in the course of a journey to Dingwall in 1564, and it is said that on waking up in the morning she looked out on the vista from her window and exclaimed *'c'est un beau lieu'*—it is a beautiful place. This legendary link with the ill-starred pearl of the

Scottish monarchy appeals to the romantic in us all, and no doubt the Queen did in fact so describe the inspiring view which greeted her eyes that morning, but history, in that case, can only give the incident the credit of a charming coincidence.

The Brahan Seer, mentioned before, prophesied of Beauly (over 350 years ago), 'The day will come, however distant, when "Cnoc na Rath" will be in the centre of the village'. This was, in the Seer's day an absurd suggestion, for the village then stood at a place south of the present railway station, called in Gaelic *Bealaidh-Achadh*—or the Broom Field—quite a mile from Cnoc na Rath. This prophecy has, however, been fulfilled, for the last building to be put up—a public school—is within a few yards of the Cnoc.

Although I have stated the name Beauly is generally supposed to have been derived from the French *beau lieu*, there is perhaps a Celtic origin. The village then being originally at Bealaidh-Achadh and so-called when the present Beauly was non-existent, it is natural to suppose the inhabitants carried the original name of their wee village along with them, resulting in the Gaelic *Bealaidh*, anglicised into Beauly.

The main road passes through the wide square of the town, where a monument commemorates the raising of the famous Lovat Scouts at the time of the Boer War. Now a busy market centre, Beauly still contains the red-stoned ruined Priory of St. John Baptist, founded in 1232 by Sir John Bisset of Lovat, for a French religious order. Set amongst stately elms and sycamores, it is a reminder of the simple lives of the French monks who once lived there in contemplative peace.

Continuing on our drive to 'Destination Gairloch', we soon pass Muir of Ord, and in doing so, cross from Inverness-shire to Ross-shire. At Muir of Ord a road runs eastwards to the Black Isle : Fortrose, Rosemarkie and Cromarty. Like many 'isles' in Scotland, it is really a peninsula, a very fertile peninsula, the shores of which are bounded on one side by the Cromarty Firth, and on the other by the Beauly Firth, both merging into the large Moray Firth. The reason why this peninsula is called the 'Black Isle' is because snow never lies there. It is famous for its crops and cattle.

From Muir of Ord, taking the west, not the eastward, road, we make straight across country to Contin, instead of going up (again) two sides of the triangle to Dingwall (the county town of Ross-shire) and Strathpeffer, for it is a pleasant run through Strath Conon avoiding main-road traffic and towns and is a direct route to where we are destined for, Gairloch. Thereafter from Contin, in a mile or so, we pass the Falls of Rogie, a famous beauty spot where the Black Water and the Rogie Burn meet in a wild gorge and the water crashing over the black rocks in a spectacular fall. Viewed when salmon are leaping in their efforts to ascend the falls, the scene cannot easily be forgotten ; all in a setting of rock, heather and birches. (I refer to these falls in a later chapter.) To the east of these falls and south of Dingwall and Strathpeffer is Loch Ussie, into which loch it is said the Brahan Seer cast his divining-stone.

The Black Water loops north-west from these falls and soon, following the curve of Loch Garve, we reach the tiny village of Garve itself, set in the colourful wonderland of the north-west, among waters and heights (Ben Wyvis 3430 feet, and rarely free from snow, to the north-east) and moorland ; unbelievably an astoundingly different country from that we have come from only a mile away at Contin.

Here at Garve, with a lovely 'snug' hotel of fishing and food renown and wonderfully managed, the whole scenery changes like a flash ; precipitous mountains loom ahead midst rugged beauty ; moorland stretching upon moorland, and if it should be September, the heather for as far as the eye can see, takes on a colour of spilt claret. One word, and one word only can describe it all, 'fabulous'. Loch Garve with its wooded shores presents an incomparable picture ; everything now is so different ; you seem to be entering a completely new world, a break-away from the old ; and as such, I too, will break away, starting with Garve as part 2 of the journey 'Destination Gairloch'.

CHAPTER 3

THE JOURNEY—DESTINATION
GAIRLOCH (2)

So we are at Garve ; now only two hours from 'home' ;
although it is only 46 miles, motorists from south of the
border would say 'Two hours ? more like under one hour'
—but then you show complete ignorance of Wester Ross and its
tortuous-narrow-blind-cornered roads ; not only that, but should
you travel it in the season it might well take you three hours on
account of stopping at the many 'passing places' to allow other
cars to pass you on *their* way back home. I put 'passing places'
in inverted commas for that is what they are there for, *not* 'parking places' or 'lay-bys' for you to stop and look at the scenery
or have a picnic there, so making it difficult at times of heavy
traffic to pass on one's way ; or should you meet a car trailing a
caravan that has got stuck in the wet ditch—which very often
happens—you might be lucky if you make it that same day ! So
you need to be prepared, and as remarked in another corner of
this book, once you pass Garve nobody hurries ; nobody.

In the old days there were no recognised planned passing
places at all ; you just chanced coming across a bit of the road
that was wider than usual, got out, signalled frantically with your
handkerchief to the other on-coming car ¼ mile away to come on ;
and that was that. Nowadays the passing places are numerous
and easily marked that you can see them well ahead and some of
them treated with luminous paint which is most useful for night-
time driving indeed. One lady remarked on making the journey
for the first time 'What a large number of bus stops there are on
this lonely uninhabited road !'

26

Although there are dozens of passing places one still may have to 'back' one's car 30 or 40 yards at times. There are many motorists coming up this way who have no idea whatsoever of backing or reversing their cars any more than a yard or two ; in and out of their own garage at home, or parking in a street and manœuvring and reversing 2 or 3 feet only. When they come along these roads and have to reverse 40 or 50 yards and those being far from dead straight, they simply cannot do it ; and looking at you like a spaniel, beg of you to reverse *your* car to the far off passing place you have put behind you many many yards off.

I met a car with a woman driver and her lady companion at a bend once on the Loch Maree road and as it was obviously 'her move' to go back, I got out and enquired the why and the where-fore she didn't, only to be told 'I am so sorry, I really can't reverse ; do you mind obliging and going backwards yourself that 100 or so yards ? Many thanks' !

You *must* be able to reverse and manœuvre your vehicle, no matter what type it may be and to reverse it many yards at a time, and to be sharp about it also, for in the season if you hold up for a few minutes or so, you find cars galore piled up behind you that seemed to have come from nowhere, all having to reverse; and if you are in a jam and have to reverse it can be very annoying and irritating even though you *are* past Garve ! Oh ! yes, it can be great fun travelling these roads ; you *must* keep your eyes focused well ahead, not just 50 or 60 yards ; $\frac{1}{4}$ mile in some places, watching the on-coming bends and traffic. And yet you meet such irresponsible drivers, 'tearing' along regardless ; and I have frequently had near misses although I was travelling slowly, and in low gear.

With all due respect to the fair sex, I find there are two sets of women drivers who can be, and are, a menace up in these parts. One, the youngish girl drivers, careering along with a lighted cigarette between their ruby-painted lips, smoke getting into their eyes—and generally in an open sports car given them by 'Father'—looking round at the scenery, or their boy friend, laughing and driving with 'carefree' abandon, never keeping a straight eye on the road, thinking there cannot possibly be any-one else on such roads and in such a distant land ! The other, the elderly women-drivers, although knowing the roads are 'tricky', grasp the steering wheel like grim death, but who—on account of their age—are very slow to react to any sudden emergency. Neither sets seem to realise they are sitting at the wheel of a vehicle that can have lethal possibilities in any split-second of its journey.

Back again to the 'old days', the roads then were but cart tracks ; and not always good tracks either. Today they are all tar-macadamised with good surfaces and the County Council are always attending to strips here and there needing repairs, making it easier for the tourist. The road engineer has a very large area to cover, hundreds and hundreds of miles, so we should remember that, and not take umbrage at any small stretch of road surface we might come across as not being perfect to our town city'ss andard.

He has a fine body of men working for him, mostly crofters in the particular locality ; for I have seen and talked to many of them.

General Wade is the man who constructed most of these Highland roads after the "Fifteen' ; military roads they were termed and you can see his little 'hump-back' stone bridges all over the north.

There is a little rhyming couplet I learnt when I first came north long years ago. It is very cryptic and very true—

> If you saw these roads before they were made,
> You'd go down on your knees and bless General Wade !

Now, as I have said, all this is changed and I would like to record my own tribute in verse as—

> To come up here a decade or so,
> Was more than a venture, as some of us know ;
> But now over roads, a pleasure to drive on,
> We should take off our hats and thank Willie Bannermon !

Garve, with its cosily-tucked-in hotel, and its cheerful, friendly owner, Miss Helen Mackenzie of the third generation from when the hotel was built in 1856 ; of the days of stage-coaches and carriers, when it took two or three days sometimes to get the mails through from Garve–Ullapool (32 miles) ; and if it had been heavy snow, then perhaps a week or ten days. Today by mail-van it is only a matter of an hour non-stop, for the road is wide and straight for miles, something akin to the M1 standard. The

Inn, being an old posting-house, was used by the drovers of those days when journeying to and from the Dingwall stock sales.

From Garve then, we really commence on our true journey to Wester Ross. A mile out, at the hamlet Gorstan, one road turns right—to Ullapool by Strath Garve and the course of the Black Water river and the vast forests which cover this strath (Strathvaich in particular), the haunts of the red deer ; the other straight on is *our* road to Gairloch. From Garve to Loch Maree by way of Strath Bran is our way, and you are now embarking on seeing landscapes of the wildest, high mountains, rock-streams, moors, lochs and glens ; colours galore made either by the setting sun or rain, or both with the attendant rainbows caressing you and the roadway you follow. No towns ; only villages, hamlets or clachans, consisting mostly of scattered crofts and homesteads with a church and a post office—clachans, in fact. A 'clachan' may be said to consist of a school, a church and an hotel ; or as the old saying went 'Education, Salvation and Damnation!'. Hotels few, roads narrow, winding and hilly ; no garages to speak of, certainly none boasting first-class repairs. That is the picture, the glorious panorama in Technicolor as the film people would say ; and I feel sure when you do reach journey's end you will say I have not exaggerated ; that it is even more spectacular than words can describe.

Leaving Garve we make for Achnasheen (Field of Storm) 16 miles, the one and only road, twisting and turning, passing the long 6-mile Loch Luichart, utilised in the hydro-electric scheme, the magnificent power station being at Grudie Bridge. Should you be interested to view the power house, and visitors are welcome (you are asked to sign the book on leaving), you should take a look to see if your shoes are clean ; or even take them off as though you were entering a mosque, for as soon as you enter its portals you would think you were in some beautiful stately home, with red polished floors and not a speck of dust to be seen anywhere. There were two men using a Hoover polisher on the floors when I made an unexpected entrance ; and this in a building, an industrial building, at the back of beyond ; polishing the station floor and wearing soft slippers so as not to mark their handiwork! It is, however, a beautifully built house blending well with the hills and valleys, the dense foliage and fast running burns. Oh yes! very spick and span and elaborate indeed ; and its erection and upkeep has no doubt put 'nought point something' on to the cost of current production *ex* Grudie.

Thence by Loch Achanalt, Strath Bran (already named), to Achnasheen, a road and country packed full of breathtaking interest.

From Achanalt by the banks of the river Bran the mountains tower on either hand, hemming in the verdure-fringed river which winds its way through this rugged stretch of country. On the left is Sgurr Vuillin, 2845 feet high ; and ahead Fionn Bheinn, 3060 feet, its lower slopes rising abruptly from the shores of Loch Rosque.

As for Achnasheen it is only 'noted' for its railway station, a very busy one ; for there, goods and mail to Gairloch and the north-west are unloaded ; the main line carries on to Kyle.

From Achnasheen our journey is even more exciting than before. The road to the left just out of Achnasheen takes you via Loch Carron to Strome Ferry and Kyle ; to the right is our way. The road for three miles travels alongside the north bank of the desolate Loch Rosque. It then mounts 800 feet and descends Glen Docharty 1 in 12. Just past the summit and shortly passing the A.A. box, suddenly coming round a bend without warning, there comes into view the majestic panorama of Loch Maree and the country for miles beyond.

Should you be privileged (and you will all your life consider it a privilege) to have a nice bright day, you will look down on this famous watershed open-mouthed, with miles of apparently clear glass reflecting the morning's sun, with—it seems—scores of fir-clad islands floating on its waters, the haunts of much bird-life, gulls and grey geese whose homes are sheltered by the feathery trees rising from the loch itself ; you will look down on all this and look up to Slioch on the right (3217 feet) and Beinn Eighe (Ben Eay) to the west (3309 feet)—a white quartzite mass. It is a dazzling view, this silvery setting, the more so I think because you are looking 800 feet down on everything. You can search the dictionary from end to end for all the superlatives you can find ; search your mind for all the appropriate epithets, but none I feel sure can adequately or justly describe the sudden and terrific impact of the occasion. Nothing short of seeing it for yourself will suffice. It is not as though you are on the edge of a precipice looking sheer down ; nothing so frightening as that, but you are looking down and across to the great expanse of the west and what it has to offer. Of all the countless lochs in Scotland, none possess this commanding, arresting approach ; none.

Kinlochewe, a thoroughly Highland village, contains the old burial-ground of Culinellan. The neat little church was erected in 1878 by public subscription. There is a large grove of tall ash trees in the burial-ground and a colony of rooks appear to nest each year there. A little to the north of the church is the hillock called 'The Hangman's Hill', where some of the Mac-Leods are said to have been hanged. Kinlochewe means 'at the head of Loch Ewe'. There is a very nice cosy, well-managed hotel here ; with food at its best. The bridge at Kinlochewe was built in 1843.

From Kinlochewe we now travel the road that skirts the romantic Loch Maree. Ten miles to Loch Maree Hotel is our next important stop, where there is much demanding attention.

Loch Maree, a gem if there ever was one ; a real Highland loch over 12 miles in length, 30 feet above sea level. Embracing beauty, romance, superstition, and of course—salmon and trout ; mostly the latter.

We stop at the hotel, which was built in 1872.

This hotel claims distinction on account of the visit of Her Majesty Queen Victoria who occupied the house from 12th to 18th September 1877. This visit called forth the reverential loyalty of all in Gairloch parish.

As we enter the doorway and look up we see a plaque bearing the translation of the Gaelic words on a boulder, 'Torridon Red' sandstone, Sir Kenneth Mackenzie, Laird of Gairloch, caused to be carved to mark the occasion, and which is to be seen just across the roadway from the hotel door.

The Gaelic inscription is as follows :

AIR AN DARA LATHA-DEUG DETH MHIÒS
MEADHONACH AN FHÒGHAIR, 1877, THÀINIG
BAN-RIGH BHICTORIA A DH'FAICINN LOCH-MARUIBHE,
AGUS NAN CRÌOCHAN MU'N CUAIRT. DB'FHAN I
SÉA OIDHCHE S'AN TIGH-ÒSDA SO THALL ; AGUS
'NA CAOMHALACHD, DHEÒNAICH I G'UM BIODH
A' CHLACH SO 'NA CÙIMHNEACHAN AIR AN
TLACHD A FHUAIR I 'NA TEACHD DO 'N CHEÀRN
SO DE ROS.

And the literal translation thus :

> On the 12th day of the middle month of autumn 1877 Queen Victoria came to visit Loch Maree and the country around it. She remained six nights in the opposite hotel and in her kindness agreed that this stone should be a memorial of the pleasure she experienced in coming to this quarter of Ross.

The hotel, purely one may say a fishing hotel where good attention and good food is the order of the day, is beautifully placed in a sheltered bay backed by a hill called Sron a Choit, 970 feet high whose rocky tops rise above most beautiful natural birch woods. A small jetty was built in 1884 as a landing-place for the steamer which in those days plied up and down the loch, from Loch Maree Hotel to its western end near Loch Ewe, Tollie pier.

This steamer ceased to operate many years ago, but at the time, afforded an easy comfortable way of viewing the beauties of this 'Queen of Highland Lochs'.

The waters of Loch Maree are exceptionally clear, owing to the rocky and gravel nature of the bed and shores. It never acquires the dark and peaty tinge which very often characterises Scotland's many other lochs. Loch Maree's greatest depth is 360 feet ; mean depth 125 feet, and the volume of water contained in the loch is some 38,000 millions of cubic feet.

The steamer, named *Mabel* (not a very suitable Highland name to be sure ?), used to berth at the north-western corner of the loch, at Tollie '(a place of holes') just near Tollie Farm, and you can see some of the jetty posts to this day, nestling under trees and rock, beneath the rugged grey cliffs of this wild, yet 'gentle' beauty spot. This pier was erected in 1883 ; and on leaving it, Fox Point is on the left ; a low small promontory terminating in grey-white rocks, deriving its name from some legend of a fox closely pursued by dogs, taking to the water here ; either that or of some fox of unusual size being killed there. Behind here, the river Ewe leaves Loch Maree, where Inveran House and farm are situated. There are stepping-stones across the narrow waters and legend calls them 'sweethearts stepping stones'. Giant Fingal himself is supposed to have planted them there. (Oh yes, there are dozens and dozens of legends up Wester Ross ways !)

About half-way up the loch, the woods of Letterewe appear ('the Slope to the Ewe'). Near here may be seen the mouth of

a canal and on the hillside above, the track of a tram line in connection with bringing limestone from a large quarry further up ;
now, of course, defunct. Thence we see Letterewe House, a
delightful setting, and used as a summer residence by one of
Britain's tycoons. Both in and out of season, charming Mac-
Pherson, head gamekeeper and general factotum, keeps the estate
with its red deer under complete control. Just beyond Letterewe,
the Furnace burn falls into the loch ; the hamlet takes its name
from the old iron-smelting furnace established there by Sir George
Hay about 1605.

There is a story—still told to this day—of the first Presbyterian
minister who came one summer across to Letterewe to 'convert'
the people there. The folk in the wee parish were so incensed,
they stripped him naked and tied him to a tree to be literally
eaten alive by midges. He suffered agonies and was half demented
when he was finally released at night by an old, but kindly
woman. He fled as best he could, laying a curse upon the hamlet
to the effect that no godly people would ever inhabit Letterewe.

We then pass by and under Slioch's dominating gaze. Slioch,
composed mainly of Torridon sandstone, resembles, from some
angles of its conical shape, a spear-head and that is its Gaelic
meaning ; an ancient spear or lance and also that of an ancient
flint arrow-head. As you sailed close by its shore and looking up
at it, it just has the appearance of a vast wall, a mighty Gibraltar
in Wester Ross in fact. Loch Maree is never frozen over. The
red deer mentioned previously are often seen to swim across
from their forest to the many islands on the loch, just for a few
months ; then back again. From Letterewe and near-by, the
steamer would cross over to Loch Maree Hotel, and as you tied
up you would get a good view looking up the glen down which
the Talladale flows emptying itself in the loch. From Loch
Maree Hotel, the steamer would wend its way along the south
shores of the loch, passing Slattadale, thence onwards till it came
to Tollie again ; its starting-point.

There are twenty-seven islands in Loch Maree, all beautifully
wooded ; the principal ones are Isle Maree (named after St.
Maelrubha, who came from Ireland in 671 to found a monastery
at Applecross (A.D. 673), below Torridon, and which has a ruined
chapel and burial-ground ; and of which I will have more to say
shortly) ; Eilean Suthainn ('isle of fairies' or 'the everlasting

island') the largest, nearly 1 mile long and within it there is a small loch with two tiny islands ; Garbh Eilean ('the rough isle') ; Eilean Dubh na Sroine ('the black isle of the promontory') ; and Eilean Ruaridh Mor ('the big island of Rory') and called after a celebrated chief of the MacLeods. On this island, as well as on some of the others, no doubt, the illicit distillation of whisky took place during the good old days of the 1800's.

I have already said there is much superstition up in the north-west country ; this generally seems to be the case in most mountainous countries. The supernatural comes to light and takes on form in many ways : mountains and the weird shapes they throw out in the dark and closing mists ; old gnarled and twisted trees ; lochs with inky-black, deep, still waters ; and the long-drawn-out stilly nights—all go to make up legends, yarns and superstitions.

There was the belief that a draught of Loch Maree water was a sure cure for many a disease ; in fact it is on record that many invalids had bottles of such water sent them in the certain belief of its curative powers. Nowadays I suppose it would be whisky from Loch Maree, should there ever be such a brand or blend !

Among older superstitions was the Druidical sacrifice of bulls on Isle Maree which continued as late as 1678. The aforementioned St. Maelrubha, who brought Christianity over to these parts in the 7th century, allowed this, giving it a Christian aspect ! In those later years the sacrifices seemed to have been connected with the resort to the island for the cure of insanity. This is recorded in the Presbyterian annals.

Yes, there are legends by the score : of a Wester Ross woman who had spent one year with the fairies ; that certain peculiar noises and moving lights foreshadowed a death ; that plants bedded when the moon was on the wane would never survive ; that a stick cut from the bird-cherry tree prevents one being lost in the mist ; that whales attack boats newly tarred, and that breaking of the Sabbath brings swift retribution.

But it is of Isle Maree, or Eilean Maree ('the eye of Loch Maree') that I wish to particularly refer, for our 'foreign' friends.

Queen Victoria visited Isle Maree on 16th September 1877 whilst she was spending the six days at the hotel. It was the Sabbath day and Her Majesty graciously read a short sermon to her Gairloch gillies. She then fixed her offering in the wishing-tree, it being understood that a wish silently made when making such an offering would be realised ; and that should anyone remove or steal any such offering, a misfortune to the person would follow in its wake.

Near the celebrated wishing-well stands this oak tree studded with nails and hundreds of copper coins. To each of these was originally attached a piece of clothing belonging to some patient who had visited, or been brought to the spot. I must confess I have plugged more than one penny into that famous tree myself over the years.

In all probability coming to the island for the cure of insanity dates back to the time of the saint. The procedure was for the party to row several times round the island and those next to the afflicted forcing the lunatic three times into the water covering his or her head. They then stepped on the island, the patient knelt before the altar, then went to the wishing-well, drank some of the water, and finally attached some offering to the tree. They all then rowed back again to the mainland.

This well, so legend has it, lost much of its power later on, because a shepherd who had a mad dog took it to the well and pushed it headlong in. The following day the dog died, and a few days later the shepherd also died !

After St. Maelrubha's death, he became the patron saint of this district. His name is variously known as Malrubius, Murie, Mourie and latterly the corruption Maree. There can be no question but that this island and this loch bears the name of this saint.

In respect of St. Maelrubha's death, four parishes lay claim to the honour of being that in which his remains lie : Applecross, Ferintosh, Gairloch and Farr. There is no doubt he was the greatest of Celtic saints, and by whom throughout Scotland some twenty-two churches were founded around the north-west coast, Skye, Harris, Argyll, Islay, Loch Fyne and up at Lairg in Sutherlandshire.

There is yet another and sweet love-story attached to Isle Maree that I must relate. It was told me nearly twenty-five years ago by 'Willie the gillie' of Badachro, whom I mention later on ; and as Willie is—or was then—a Justice of the Peace, I feel sure readers will not query its authenticity ! This story is also told in that old book, written seventy-five years ago (and now out of print), *Dixon's Gairloch*, to which I am indebted for certain historical and factual data *en passant* ; and it would seem the two stories are substantially the same.

After St. Maelrubha's death at Applecross, 21st April A.D. 722, the holy College of Iona appointed a successor to his hermitage on Isle Maree. He was an aged religious man reputed to have great sagacity and piety, one whom the local folk, as well as the Norse Vikings, could call on frequently for ministrations of religion, as well as to obtain his wise counsel. The Vikings held this district in subjugation, but to all alike, Celt or Norwegian, he gave his blessings.

There was a young Norwegian prince, Prince Olaf of royal blood, who was the chief of the Vikings in this part of the north-west coast. Not only did this parentage warrant him being their chief, but his personal bravery and daring also enamoured him to his fellow clansmen to be their leader.

They all lived in the prince's war-galley, but during the winter months they would seek shelter and comfort in some of the islands of Loch Ewe. The prince would oftimes come to Isle Maree to see the venerable saint and solicit his advice and blessing.

In due time our noble prince fell in love with a Norwegian princess, but he hesitated to bring his lady-love away with him to live on board a rough war-galley, as a life of that nature and in such surroundings was not befitting such a lady of rank. He accordingly sought the advice of his friend of Isle Maree. This blessed saint suggested the building of a high tower and enclosure near the west side of the isle, so that the prince could bring his bride there, surrounded in peace and quiet by her maid-servants and still be close to his royal highness' galley on Loch Ewe.

This was done and Olaf brought his beautiful fair bride to Isle Maree where they were married by the aged hermit. The princess and her servants were enraptured with such a romantic secluded setting. Everyone was happy and life for the young lovers was one round of passionate delight.

His comrades, however, were planning another expedition and begged their leader to join them on board and sail away to plunder. His young wife was distressed beyond all measure when he told her he had to go and join his comrades and that he must leave forthwith. Shedding copious tears was of no avail to our warrior, who was impetuous and highly strung, and so after hours of sorrow she allowed him to go off on this exploit.

But what if something dreadful should happen to him ; or for that matter, if something should happen to her during his absence ?

In talking over such grievous ideas they both thought of a plan to let each know how the other had fared in advance.

When the prince was returning up the loch, he should hoist a white flag from his barge on Loch Maree should he still love her and all was well ; if not, then a black flag would be flown.

This was arranged ; and the princess too, when she saw her master's boat approaching was to leave her retreat in her barge and to fly a white or black ensign accordingly. Both then would know in advance each other's thoughts.

The years went by, as they do in all fairy-tale books, and in due course being victorious, the prince and his party returned safely and anchored at Poolewe. With feverish haste he got into his barge all ready for Isle Maree, raised his white flag of success and love, and urged his oarsmen to row fast to his beloved.

But all through these years, the princess had been filled with anxiety and foreboding. Did her lover, she wondered, prefer his exploits of war and plunder to that of the quiet and stillness of Isle Maree—their home where they could raise a family—or in fact was he really faithful to her when out of her sight ? Was this exploit, and others too, a mere pretence for him to court the love of another woman ? Under this spell of jealousy and distrust she thought of a plan to test her darling's affection.

When the prince's barge was sighted the princess and her maidens set off in her barge with a black flag amast ; not only that but a bier was placed in the middle of the barge on to which the princess stepped, and reclining with the apparent sleep of death on her, a white shroud was spread over her still body. Then her attendants feigned utter grief in all this play-acting.

As Olaf's boat drew nearer he could see a black flag was waving from his beloved's barge—the flag of death ; and he was beside himself with anguish and despair, being quite unable to control his agony of mind. When the barges drew alongside the prince leapt aboard, raised the shroud, and seeing that his dear wife was dead, flung up his hands to heaven, drew out his dirk and plunged it straightaway into his heart, dying instantly.

Now this was certainly not what the princess had expected, albeit she had assumed a posture so deathly real ; full of grief and stricken beyond all measure, she drew the dirk out of Olaf's heart and plunged it into her own bosom.

She did not die until her barge turned back to Isle Maree, where the holy man was waiting at the slipway, and was able to administer the last prayers of comfort ; then she silently passed away to join her beloved Olaf.

The two bodies lie buried in the grounds of the tower of the island, now in ruins ; and a stone and two crosses mark the grave to this day.

Truly a sad, sad story, but one that many old locals seem to have heard of in their byegone youth. We will treat the legend as true, for it will then lend a special air of romance to that lovely saintly island ('the eye of Loch Maree') set amidst the loch bearing its name—a gem within a gem.

As in J. M. Barrie's play, *Mary Rose*, there is one island in particular that 'likes to be visited, and where one never grows old'—Isle Maree.

Loch Maree was probably once a sea-loch ; the river Ewe which links it with the salt water of Loch Ewe is only $3\frac{1}{2}$ miles long—doubtless the shortest river in Britain.

Anent Loch Maree, a story is handed down from generation to generation that one day after Culloden's disaster to Prince Charlie, a stranger with fair hair and clad in tartan, came to a wee farmstead near the present Loch Maree Hotel, asking for food and shelter. On the morn's morn he left and gave the wifey a gold piece. News that a stranger with gold was in the neighbourhood spread as fast as news *does* spread in the Highlands ! The next night, a shot rang out in the stillness, and later on the dead body of the young man was found, robbed of everything. It was subsequently learnt that the young laddie was Prince Charlie's valet, who was carrying French gold pieces. A day or so before this event, two vessels had been sighted in Poolewe bay, and it was assumed they had come to pick up this man and his gold.

We must now proceed on the final 10 miles of our journey to Gairloch. It has taken a long time to reach, but 'it is better to travel than to arrive' the proverb says, used metaphorically here of course. Life is like climbing a mountain ; the climb is what matters, and we have climbed our way so far through a wonderful region of the British Isles and will soon arrive at our haven of 'self-completeness'. Everything we have left behind us is not only far away in terms of miles, but far away in terms of spirit.

So we wind our way, passing Slattadale (which we had seen from our dream-boat a short while ago) thence we leave the shore of Loch Maree which we have followed for more than half its length, and cross inland—'westward to the sea', through narrow Kerrysdale. Rising a little to catch the last glimpse of Loch Maree through a little forest clearance, kindly thought of and made for the tourist's benefit by the Forestry Department exclusively, we drop down into Kerrysdale where, at Kerry Falls, there is a small yet prettily built hydro-electric power station.

From there, skirting the Kerry river (said to be the Norse for 'the copse river'), passing the small stone Kerry bridge (the turn-off for Badachro and Red Point), passing the factor's house and down the brae to see the 'Gairloch' village sign close to the post office and bridge with Flowerdale House through the avenue of trees on the right, and the harbour of our dreams on the left.

We are in Gairloch, Wester Ross ; and at the post office I end this chapter, only to start a new one for Gairloch itself. It surely deserves that honour.

CHAPTER 4

GAIRLOCH

WE have now arrived at Gairloch, at the 'post orfice'—but unlike Wullie's at Badachro (whom you will shortly meet), it has no shop. 'Chust a "post orfice".'

Gairloch, on the sea-loch of that name, overlooks the islands of Eileann Horisdale (sometimes spelt Isle Horistle) and Longa. Away to the south-west across the Inner Sound of the Minch you have the distant views of the Cuillin hills on the southern part of the island of Skye. Southwards, the view ranges over the Flower-dale forest peaks in which Baeshoen, 2869 feet, is the highest, while still further south rises Beinn Alligin, 3232 feet, one of the splendid wild Torridon peaks, overlooking lonely Torridon, of which I shall have something to say later.

Now, from the post office, which is the hub of the postal service here for Strath, Melvaig, Badachro and beyond to Opinan, we cross the old bridge (near the Old Inn—now modernised) viewing the harbour on the left, and on the right up the avenue of trees, Flowerdale House which, for long, long years has been the west coast residence of the Baronets of Gairloch—the Mackenzies.

Flowerdale house is built in two sections; the old part erected in 1732 by the ninth Laird and second baronet of Gairloch (and so called because of the profusion of wild flowers), was the very first slated house in the district. In the First World War it was used by Prime Minister Lloyd George and his Cabinet, who several times met here, particularly when the Irish question was uppermost. In those days Winston Churchill was only a junior secretary and was given a tiny attic room, whilst David Lloyd George, of course, had the biggest room of all, together with a luxurious adjoining flat. The house has a large vegetable garden and luscious strawberries are grown and sold locally.

The whole house and 'policies' are very well sheltered from the south-west storms so prevalent here in the winter. There is a saw-mill on the estate ; for during the years many forest trees are cut down and sawn up for general marketing.

Passing this avenue and rising up the brae, we pass the one and only bank. It may come as a surprise that this small bank opens at 9.30 a.m. and 9 a.m. on Saturdays ; against the common custom of English banks, which open at 10 a.m. This early opening is certainly not due to the tremendous banking business that goes on up here, for most of the ordinary folk have no bank account (I refer to this 'peculiarity' in the chapter 'Across the Bay'). It must, I feel, be due to their being so ultra-particular in counting and recounting the notes, so as not to err on the wrong side in giving you an extra £1 over and above! The cashier studiously checks and rechecks, and this takes time ; and so this, maybe, accounts for their office hours being longer than their English counterparts? One never knows! for once you pass Garve nobody hurries—not even the bank cashier!

After the bank the 9-hole, 1975-yard golf course appears on the left, and then we round the corner where the Church of Scotland stands, almost opposite to which is the beautiful 300-year-old Gairloch cemetery (studded with many trees) now closed, and which I heard one local wit call the 'dead centre of Gairloch'.

There once stood in this churchyard the Church of St. Mael-rubha. Many are buried in this old cemetery who were known far beyond the bounds of the parish. Then up the steep incline (with the new cemetery on the right) stopping at a 'lay-by' vantage spot near the War Memorial and look down upon the famous golden sands of Gairloch—'Gairloch Sands'—almost a mile of perfectly level sand, and where one can wade out in this secluded bay, say 100 yards or more, and still only be waist deep in the clear, blue water washed by the Gulf Stream.

The stretch of the bay is so wide that you feel alone with the world, even during the busy tourist season ; for never are these sandy beaches here over-crowded ; they are so extensive that a hundred people or more would hardly be noticed.

The War Memorial commemorating the First World War stands silently overlooking the bay, and has sixty-three names inscribed round its sides ; men from Gairloch, Strath, Badachro,

Red Point, Poolewe, Mellon Charles, Melvaig, Inverasdale, and Kinlochewe. As you mount the twenty steps up from the road-side, you read the inscription facing you :

Erected by
Sir Kenneth and Lady Marjory Mackenzie in memory
of their son Roderick I. Mackenzie, Lieut., Black Watch
and the men of Gairloch
who gave their lives 1914–1919

And on the base is the quotation :

'Be thou faithful unto death, and I will give thee a crown of Life'.

Passing on, we drop down with the Free Church of Scotland on our left, the manse on the right (advertising bed and breakfast!) to Gairloch Hotel, a 3-star 55-room hotel erected in 1872, and enlarged over the years and now equipped with all modern con-veniences. I have patronised this hotel for nigh on fifty years ; it has a most attractive frontage, commanding a beautiful situation 80 feet above and close to the edge of the large horseshoe-shaped bay of Gairloch. Wonderful views are obtained from all the front windows of lounges and bedrooms—the Isle of Skye, the Cuillins and on clear days and nights Stornoway in Lewis and the south end of Harris.

During the Second World War it was taken over by the Royal Navy as a hospital ; for Aultbea, 15 miles further on was a very important base in those perilous Atlantic convoy-days. It is very popular during the season, and well-nigh impossible to get a room 'on spec'.

In connection with the last war, my mind goes back to 1938 midsummer, when I was staying in the hotel. Packed to capacity though it was, I was told (as I 'phoned my dear old manager friend from Skye that I was coming over that evening) there was 'no room in the Inn', even for Bee Jay! I nevertheless came through, knowing there was nothing like the 'personal touch' with the receptionist—besides, how was I to know that someone else booked in might have died on the way coming !—and got tucked in to a room on the top floor of the servants' quarters facing the back ; and tucked in it was, almost like the Arran days ; a skylight just over your head was the only means of daylight, with a chimney-pot that looked as though any minute a slight breeze would bring it toppling down, crashing through the

window right on to your head. And, of course, I was paying
'seasonal rates'! But the company was good both downstairs
and upstairs 'in my servants' quarters'; in fact I must confess
that there was far more conviviality and camaraderie those days
than now. Today there is far more of a clique, or coterie going
around; or should I say not 'going around'.

But to hark back to this fateful midsummer day. We all
listened in to a crackling old-fashioned wireless in the front hall
(there were no loud-speaker extensions those days, not up at
Gairloch) about 7 p.m., to Hitler's tirade over 'one more piece of
Europe' theme. It was a very vehement speech that almost burst
the valves in the small radio machine, for I am sure you could
have heard the dictator's voice over at Badachro; and it left us
all aghast.

There was an Italian head waiter named Louis those days, and
Italy then was on the fence but leaning towards Hitler. Rushing
upstairs after the speech to get some money to drown my upset
nerves and sorrows in the bar, I found Louis careering around
the narrow wooden corridors 'up my way', excited beyond all
manner of means, popping in and out of the various maids' rooms
saying what was, or what was not going to happen and clad—
yes, this is perfectly true, and if Louis is alive today and should
read this he will surely remember—in his stiff evening dress shirt
and tails, black socks and suspenders, but *no* trousers on! And
his shirt *was* stiff right down to the hems I remember. Worried
and anxious though I was, momentarily I laughed as I think I had
never laughed before; such comedy! and so did the girls as they
kept popping their heads outside their bedroom doors. And
Louis 'barging' along, throwing his hands and arms around as
only these foreigners can, fully dressed without his pants! What
had happened I don't think anyone knew. He must have been
partially dressed when 'Heil, Hitler' came through and he rushed
to keek his ear round the corner to listen and then—well, forgot
the rest!

I said the hotel was packed to overflowing. The next day it
was empty; we all thought it wiser to go home and 'wait and
see'. 'Here today, gone tomorrow.' That is what a great number of car-cum-caravans are doing now; moving on all the
time; mostly in search of weather, I fear!

On entering the hotel (we are now back to our first seeing the

hotel—a page or so earlier) and booking in we see from the corner
of our eye, a rack of coloured postcards for sale, 'Gairloch Hotel ;
Fàilte do Ghearrloch'—welcome to Gairloch Hotel.   Quite
appropriate.   As a real means of welcome, I would have liked
the architect for the reception office to have had those Gaelic
words emblazoned in some special Highland manner on the wall
behind the counter, so you could be at once impressed by its
meaning as soon as you had blotted your signature on arrival.
This would lend further 'Highland atmosphere' until such time
as you got around to the cocktail bar and asked for a Glayva
liqueur.   *Slàinte.*

Yes, it is a wonderfully situated hotel, unrivalled in its outlook
really ;   superbly decorated, efficiently managed and first-class
food.   Quite a number of the old and faithful servants of this
grand hotel are now living in the village, enjoying their well-
earned retirement.   It is pleasing to see them—links and memories
of those good old days—and to talk to them of those byegone
times ;   Matty, Alick, Willie and Morag particularly—and in
a 'big way', Marion, of the old public bar days.   We will have
our afternoon tea here (tea with home-baked fresh scones, butter
and jam I hope !) and then look around Gairloch and the parish
more fully.

Gairloch is a very large Highland parish, for it covers an area
of over 200,000 acres and ranks as the fifth biggest parish in
Scotland.

It is larger than the county of Rutland in England, and bigger
than Clackmannanshire in Scotland.

In 1880 the population was over 5000.

In 1911 it decreased to 3300.

In 1951 the population again dropped to 1990.

In 1961 the census puts the figure as 1763, nearly 50 per cent
decrease in fifty years.

The parish has a tremendous coast-line, very indented and
possesses innumerable and lovely sandy beaches—all unrestricted.
No charge for hire of beach deck-chairs in Wester Ross, as per
all English seaside places.   There are no deck-chairs !   No Council
attendants 'pouncing' on you demanding 6d. or 1s. for a chair
à la England.

There are more than twenty-three peaks of over 2000 feet in
height ;   five of them reach over 3000 feet.

Taken as a whole the people's livelihood may be aptly put as 'one foot in the sea, and one foot on the shore'; in other words, fishing and/or cultivating their bit of land.

In early days it was nothing for the young men to tramp on foot over to the east coast, Fraserburgh and such-like towns, to earn twelve weeks' money for the herring fishing; then tramp all the miles back again in time to fish at this side of the coast. What a journey! And what stamina was required in those days in order to survive.

Formerly this countryside was held by the Macbeths, and to this day one may see small islands on Loch Tollie—between Gairloch and Poolewe—that were supposed to be fortressed by the Macbeths. They were 'thrown out' by the MacLeods (though I believe one family of Macbeth is still living in the parish) away into the forests of Applecross; but the MacLeods in turn gave way to the present Mackenzie clan.

The northern-most boundary of Gairloch parish is at the river, Little Gruinard, thence it follows down the centre of that river to Fionn Loch (white loch) and Dubh Loch (black loch) and the mountains to the north-west of Loch Maree, including Letterewe, Loch Maree, Kinlochewe and as far as the western end of Loch a' Chroisg, the other side of Glen Docherty, namely almost adjoining Achnasheen. The boundary then follows in a south-westerly direction going across the ridge of Beinn Eighe and Beinn Dearg and coming out at the sea at Diabaig. From there, we have the whole coast-line, Red Point, Longa Island, Melvaig, Cove, Inverasdale, Poolewe, Aultbea, Isle of Ewe, Mellon Charles, Mellon Udrigle, Laide and back to Gruinard— our starting-point.

In short, from Gruinard to near Achnasheen, across to Diabaig (near Torridon) up all the coast-line, Red Point round to Gruinard.

The parish is governed by the 'District Council of Gairloch', the District Clerk's office being at Poolewe (he is also the Welfare Officer); and comprises six elected Councillors and two (*ex officio*) County Council members. All serve for a term of three years, whereupon an election to the whole Council takes place.

This triennial bloc-election saves the parish much expense; for it should be realised an extra £30 or £40 spent can easily affect the rates by a penny or so in the £.

The name Gairloch is composed of two Gaelic words, gearr

meaning 'short' and loch. This sea-loch, which gives its name
to the parish, is appropriately called 'short' as compared with
Loch Broom, Loch Ewe and other more deeply indented arms
of the sea.

The Lairds of Gairloch are the Mackenzie family. The first
Laird was Hector Roy Mackenzie, born 1440, succeeded to the
title in 1494 and died in 1528. It was he who received a grant of
Gairloch from King James IV in 1494.

Earlier on in part 1 of 'The Journey' I referred to the prophecies of the Brahan Seer. This remarkable man makes several
references to Gairloch which form interesting reading. The
first is anent Gairloch House, wherein he records (early in the
1600's be it noted) 'A dun, hornless, cow (supposed to mean a
steamer) will appear in the Minch off Carr Point, in Gairloch and
make a "geum" or bellow, which will knock the six chimneys
off Gairloch House'. Gairloch House, or the Tigh Dige of the
seer Coinneach's day, was the old house which stood in the park
on the right as you went from the bridge in the direction of the
present mansion. The walls were of wattled twigs, wicker work
or plaited twig hurdles, thatched with turf or divots and surrounded with a deep ditch, which could, in time of approaching
danger, be filled with water from the river, hence the name
'Tigh Dige', 'house of the ditch'. It has been suggested the
seer's prediction referred to this stronghold, although the ancient
citadel had no chimneys to fall off. The present mansion, however, is called the 'Tigh Dige' and strangely enough it *has* the
exact number of chimneys—six!

Then again he predicted that 'a bald black girl will be born
at the back of the church of Gairloch', which has been fulfilled.
During one of the usual large gatherings at the sacramental communion a well-known young woman was taken in labour, and
before she could be removed she gave birth to the dark baby,
whose descendants are well known I believe, and pointed
out in the district to this day as the fulfilment of Coinneach's
prophecy.

Another prediction that duly 'came to pass' was that 'a white
cow will give birth to a calf in the garden behind Gairloch House'
also that in 'Flowerdale, a black hornless cow will give birth to a
calf with two heads'; it, too, came to pass. And he prophesied
that 'the buck-toothed laird will leave the estate of Gairloch

without the rightful heir'. Sir Hector Mackenzie of Gairloch *was* buck-toothed.

As regards postal affairs for this region in the olden days, it is impossible to fix the exact date when a system was established.

Originally a 'post runner'—a man on foot—came from Dingwall by Strath Bran and Glen Docherty to the head of Loch Maree, the same way as we travelled. Thence along the east side of the Loch to Letterewe and on to Poolewe. If necessary he would come on to Flowerdale when the Laird of Gairloch was in residence, which would be the summer and autumn.

Sometimes he might have gone by the west side of the loch to Slattadale, then over the pass by the Kerry Falls to Flowerdale.

There was no post at all during the winter months. Even in summer the runner only came to Gairloch once a week, but when a second runner was employed, the post bags were brought twice a week.

After construction of roads the mail came by horse and trap three times a week, and in 1883 the post office authorities granted a daily mail, except, of course, on Sundays.

There were no roads in Gairloch until the military roads were made, which took nearly the same course as the present county roads and can still be traced in places. It was all part of the system of military roads constructed under the supervision of General Wade (mentioned in the preceding chapter) in the first half of the 18th century, *i.e.* around 1745. By the following century these old roads had become virtually impassable by wheeled vehicles.

The potato disease commenced in August 1846, bringing havoc and untold hardships to the crofters of Wester Ross. The road at the upper end of Loch Maree and Slattadale was begun the following spring. Government steamers used to call in at Gairloch enquiring as to the poverty and distress caused by this widespread calamity. A Destitution Committee was set up in Edinburgh with the primary object of 'road making' as a means of helping the out-of-work crofters. Nearly £3500 was spent on the Loch Maree road ; and the Committee also assisted in the making of other roads on the north and south sides of Gairloch.

I have already drawn attention to the superstitious characteristics abounding in this part of the country. The Brahan Seer had (as a 'gimmick' we would call it nowadays) a perforated blue divining stone given him in a most exceptional manner whereby he became gifted with second-sight. When he first looked through the stone however, he was deprived of the sight of that particular eye, and he continued ever afterwards to be 'blind of an eye'.

Such a stone, charm or spell is called the *sian* and not only can such a charm help predict the future, but it could by means of a certain incantation render any object that it was wished to conceal, invisible either for the time being or for all time, subject then to brief periods of visibility recurring either at the end of every year, or as was more usual, at the end of each succeeding seven years. I may say there are quite a few people around Gairloch who still believe in the *sian*.

There is on record the case of one Alastair of Charleston Gairloch (a wee house situate near the pier, and to this day the name still appears, although the building is not that of centuries ago) who was a dealer in illicit whisky and was frequently engaged in shipping cargoes of it between Gairloch, Skye and Longa Island. At this time a certain Captain Oliver was commissioned by the government to put an end to this smuggling business, and he cruised up and down the Minch keeping a constant and vigilant watch on any strange craft. Apart from his main vessel he had a smaller one which was utilised mainly for the sea-loch observations, so that Gairloch and any other loch Captain Oliver might be watching, was veritably blockaded. When our smuggling friend Alastair was afloat and he was approaching a government vessel, he would pronounce the magic words and with the aid of the *sian* his ship would become invisible to anyone else ; and so it would seem our Captain Oliver was always thwarted !

Another time, he brought casks of whisky down Loch Maree and when he reached the narrows where the Tollie burn discharges into the river Ewe he landed and hid the casks in the moorland near Tollie Farm ; and making certain signs with his hands made the casks in their hiding place invisible. Later on when requiring the whisky he sent his men over from Gairloch—those who had been with him when he buried the casks—to collect them and

bring them to him. But his men searched high and low, unable
to discover their whereabouts and it was not until our charming
charmer Alastair went along himself that the casks made themselves seen to him and his men!

During the rule of the Pictish kings (the Picts was a name
given to a race that settled in the Highlands of Scotland, so named
because they tattooed themselves) the Norwegian Vikings made
continual raids upon the Highlands, at first as lone pirates and later
on as followers of Harald Haarfagar, the first king of Norway.
These Vikings with their unique and gaily decorated boats used
to put in during the wintry months to small islands off the western
seaboard, laying up their craft for that stormy period. The
Island of Longa, in Gairloch bay, exhibits the Norwegian suffix
a, meaning an island.

It has been thought that the Danes scarcely ever came across
to the west coast, but those Danish invaders who were here were
driven out in 1040. There can be little doubt from records made
at the time, that both Norwegian and Danes intermarried with
the women of Gairloch. One can discern certain Norwegian,
Danish characteristics in some faces of the Gairloch people even
to this day.

The Celtic inhabitants of the north-west Highlands have
always been enthusiastic over *poetry* and *music*.

One, William Ross, was a very celebrated poet—or bard—
and was universally known as 'The Gairloch Bard'.

He was born at Broadford in Skye in 1762. His mother was
a native of Gairloch and daughter of the renowned blind piper
and poet Iain Dall, also known as John Mackay. His father built
a small house on Aird the site of which, Leas-a-Rosaich, surrounded by rowan trees, can still be pointed out. It was the
headquarters of the Ross family from which they came and
went; and here it was that Ross died. He was educated in
Forres and later joined his parents who had moved to Gairloch.
His father was a pedlar and young William went along with his
father in his journeyings through Lewis and the Western Isles,
and so became acquainted with the Gaelic language in all its
different dialects. At the age of 24 he was put in charge of the
Gairloch parish school and was most successful in his work there
and his reputation grew. He studied Latin and Greek and became
quite a master of those difficult languages. He acted as precentor

in the Gairloch church. From his youth upwards he was never a robust lad and he died in 1790 in Badachro near Aird farm at the early age of 28.

He was buried in the churchyard at Gairloch and it is recorded the whole population of the district were present to pay their last respects to a very clever man. He was of their race, their blood and bone. They knew and loved him well.

Many years later, in 1850, a handsome monument was erected over his grave through the efforts of Mr. George Ross, a clansman of his, who for many years was head keeper at Flowerdale House, Gairloch.

The monument bears inscriptions in both Gaelic and English and reads :

> In memory of *William Ross*, sometime schoolmaster of Gairloch, better known as the Gairloch bard, who died in 1790, aged 28 years, this monument is erected over his grave by a few of his countrymen and others headed by the amiable and accomplished proprietor of Gairloch, in testimony of their respect and admiration of his extraordinary genius and great native talent 1850.
> His name to future ages shall descend,
> While Gaelic poetry can claim a friend.

He truly was acknowledged as the foremost Gaelic scholar of his day, and his poetry, it is said, came from the heart.

It should be remembered that a song is composed under two conditions—the air or sound (Gaelic fonn) and the metre or measure. The air is the melody holding the words in a smoothly-flowing order ; the metre is the number of syllables in the line. Both these elements occur, and must occur, in the same song.

In a tour Ross made to Stornoway he met one Marion Ross —mayhap a kinswoman of his own—and fell in love with her. His passion or infatuation was only on his part, not on hers. It is believed there was, however, a secret engagement and Marion invoked fire from heaven to consume her if ever she proved unfaithful.

Not long afterwards she married a sailor, a Captain Clough and went to Liverpool, his port, residing there. But her thoughts constantly turned to her real lover, Ross ; and it is thought that when her husband was away on long voyages she wrote to Gairloch suggesting that Ross should meet her. He journeyed as far as Stirling on this secret mission but there his better sense prevailed and he retraced his steps to Gairloch. He spent many nights in the open before reaching his father's cottage and, broken in mind and body, took to his bed for the last time. When the unhappy Bard was breathing his last, his thoughts and soul went to far off Liverpool to make claims on Marion, the fulfilment of her promise to wed or the end which she had invoked heaven to send upon her. She was at that moment with the help of her maid dressing in white preparing to attend a ball. A knock was heard at the door and she turned white with fear. The maid answered and told her that a tall young man in Highland dress was waiting without. She heard her mistress whisper 'William Ross'. Marion went to the door but there was no one to be seen. She was holding a lighted candle in her hand, and that very instant the flame was blown inward setting light to her flimsy garments and she was burnt to death. The fate of the hapless Marion had been fulfilled.

The monument—over 100 years old and exceedingly well preserved—is in the form of a stone urn (with a flame at the top), standing on a 15-inch square pillar, the whole being nearly 6 feet high ; and is situate a little distance up on the right hand of the old graveyard after entering the iron gate.

Another great poet, author and piper was one John Mackenzie who collected and edited the work entitled, *Beauties of Gaelic Poetry*, which contained many of the Gairloch bards' Gaelic love songs, unequalled for noble sentiments and tender passion to the fair maid who had jilted him. Early in life Mackenzie was apprenticed to a travelling carpenter, and during his travels he carefully noted down all the Gaelic songs and stories he heard and of their origin. At Gairloch he spent much time copying William Ross's poems and then occupied himself to the completion of *The Beauties of Gaelic Poetry* which took him some twelve years. It has all down the years been looked upon as a standard masterpiece of work on Gaelic poetry. He also wrote *The History of Prince Charlie* in Gaelic ; and was the author of the English-Gaelic part of MacAlpine's Dictionary.

He translated into Gaelic many religious works.

He died at Poolewe in 1848 whilst he was preparing a new edition of the Gaelic Bible.

On a projecting rock outside the Gairloch churchyard there stands a handsome monument, with the inscription :

In memory of John Mackenzie, who composed and edited 'The Beauties of Gaelic Poetry' and also compiled, wrote, translated, or edited, under surpassing difficulties, about thirty other works.

In grateful recognition of his valuable services to Celtic literature, this monument is erected by a number of his fellow countrymen, 1878.

Gairloch and district in its days has seen many worthy men connected with poetry and music; for where there is poetry, there is generally music to be found; and where there is poetry and music, there is generally piety to be found. Gairloch parish has been a religious parish since the days of St. Maelrubha came to Loch Maree and built his first cell there on Isle Maree.

Prayer meetings are held in the little hall twice a week. Communions are held twice a year; the fourth Sunday in June and the second Sunday in October, and these Sacramental gatherings last from the Thursday forenoon till the following Monday afternoon. And the schools have a holiday also during communion 'week'.

It will no doubt come as a surprise to many that amongst Highland glens and landscape and so far away from 'civilisation' such an industry as ironworks could have existed. But such is the case. Iron ore was worked from very early times (there is evidence as far back as 1500) and the remains of blast furnaces—slag and dross—can still be traced, as well as charcoal deposits. This iron-smelting was known as 'Iron Bloomeries'!

The ancient ironworks of Gairloch were all near burns so that the water could be used to drive the machinery.

Early in the 17th century, about 1605, Sir George Hay worked ironstone on the northern shore of Loch Maree near Letterewe. The furnaces consumed over 100 acres of forest annually and a group of ruined houses marks the village of Furnace near and below Slioch (this was mentioned on our steamer trip). There were also other iron-furnaces at Talladale near Loch Maree Hotel, and near Poolewe.

Many of the workers came from Fife and remained in Gairloch and district for several generations. Deposits of bog iron ore as well as charcoal deposits have been found in many places around the Gairloch parish, notably between Aultbea and Laide, Cove, Inverasdale, Strath, Lonemore, Little Sand and North and South Erradale.

Let us hope in these years of ours that charcoal burnings and iron furnaces may never again raise their ugly heads and be set going to mar the beauties of Loch Maree with smoke and refuse. We have no wish to be earmarked, like some English areas as 'The Black Country'.

Reverting to 'charm' or the *sian* again, there is another Gairloch belief which is worth recording if only to be read in lighter vein. It concerned one Duncan MacRae who lived near Poolewe and was 'gifted'.

He was a faithful follower of Bonnie Prince Charlie, and after Culloden, assisted in the Prince's escape, always keeping close to his master using his 'charm' to dumbfound the government pursuers. Funds were often coming over from France to this man Duncan, to be handed over to his Prince at convenient times and places. A small chest of golden sovereigns was given over to him for concealment until there was an opportune moment to deliver it to the Prince in person.

Duncan and his men brought the chest of gold across from near Aultbea to Cove, and from there carried it up the hill to near Loch an Draing, not far from the lighthouse near Melvaig, and there they laid it on the ground. Duncan made use of the *sian* and the magic formula to make the chest invisible.

It is still universally believed in Gairloch that the gold is yet there, visible though, only (as in the previously reported 'Alastair of Charleston' case) once every seven years ; and then only for a very brief moment of time. True ? Well it makes for pleasant reading and thoughts !

Leaving the hotel and going further along we pass the house of the Registrar of births, deaths and marriages. One of the oldest and most respected citizens of the district is Hecky, and a friend to countless during all his days. We have known each other for many moons and it was through him I had the chance in 1923 (as mentioned 'In the beginning') to buy what is now the youth hostel away beyond Strath at the point overlooking the Minch, Skye, Harris, Lewis and even Labrador on a clear day ! An unrivalled situation ; *magnifique !*

He has been a busy man all his days ; a commanding figure in Gairloch and Strath ; a key man if ever there was one. In his official capacity he has married many a young couple at his home, and I am thinking this should appeal far more as a romantic place and setting for elopers than uninteresting Gretna Green.

Of course it is further to travel from over the border, but what is distance—or time—to elopers, so long as they have a few pounds in their pockets ?

He performs the ceremony under the 1939 Marriage (Scotland) Act at a fee of 7s. 6d. All that is needed is fifteen days' residence in Gairloch parish plus seven days ; for Hecky must put up the respective names on a sheet of paper and 'stick it' on a side window at the General Stores in Strath for one week 'for all the world to see'. Then zero-hour is at hand, two witnesses, and the 'affaire' is all over in a matter of minutes.

Of course, should the contracting parties give wrong information as to ages, nationality and such-like they would be liable to a fine.

The same period procedure applies to Gretna Green ; so, 'all things being equal', why not plump for Gairloch you love-sick lovers ? It would be more difficult for mother to find you up here amongst the Highland glens and bracken !

Venturing on, we come to the telephone exchange, a *very* busy centre with underwater cables to the islands, and the latest extension has been to Iceland from a point entering the sea at the shore near the Free Presbyterian Kirk ; thereafter, a newly opened beautifully arranged cafeteria 'The Wild Cat'—not a very Highland name, and let us hope its proprietors have not embarked on any wild-cat scheme ! I am sure they have not, but the name calls for a pun !

Here at the road junction, where there is a convenient 'convenience' (where it is recorded a cow calmly walked out of the ladies' side as a visitor was entering. What comment *that* caused I can hardly imagine ! At any rate the cow seemed to know which was ladies' and which was gents' !), one can go straight on up the hill and over the moors to Poolewe, or turn left, as we do, passing the police station, complete with one cell, wind our way along the far-too-narrow road, pass the village school Achtercairn (which has turned out many excellent scholars who have travelled afar and made their mark) then the Free Presbyterian Kirk, and over the bridge, passing the Kirk Hand Weave Store which deals in the usual Highland knitwear one sees at so many places in the north. (The name has nothing to do with the Church ; 'Kirk' merely happens to be the name of the owner). I think these Highland Home Industries and weaving shops should advertise more than they do and beyond their own village ; for their produce is excellent and fascinating—far more so than the trashy-flashy trinket shops you come across in High-land towns.

If they want a slogan for their woollen goods, I suggest—'FROM EWE TO YOU!'

Most of the knitwear in these shops is the work of local women and some of it is very beautifully done. They make a profitable income to their meagre fare during the winter months and the beginning and continued rise of this 'home industry' can be ascribed to the saying 'sweet are the uses of adversity'. During the years of the potato famine 1846–48, the people were in dire need ; large sums were raised to help them and those in charge of Gairloch parish undertook to support all of them in February 1848 until the following harvest—the able-bodied men working on the roads ; the women by knitting. An expert was obtained who supervised the women's work and it was not long before 'Gairloch stockings' obtained a ready market by reason of their superior quality. Other small Highland parishes followed suit ; the Scottish Home Industries Association was formed to look after everything concerned and to bring the trade under a more business-like footing. And so it has continued to this very day. All the crofters those days owned sheep and these yielded wool which was teased, carded, spun and dyed at home from dyes gathered in nearby dykes, ditches and streams. One can see this art of wool being teased, spinning wheels being worked by foot and tartan rugs and scarfs being made by hand today in many parts, particularly in Skye, and notably at Portnalong, not far from Talisker distillery on Loch Harport, west of Sligachan.

We are now in Strath ; for where Gairloch finishes, Strath begins. Onwards past the Swedish-type wooden houses, we pass the one and only bakery. And *what* a bakery to be sure ! worth coming all our way even to get the freshly-made rolls each day. The chief baker himself is a veritable master-man ; and why not ? for his name is Wallace ! Whether his Christian name is William, and is related to the famous Scotch hero who defeated the English at Stirling Bridge in 1297, I cannot say. Perhaps not, for he looks upon his 'dough' with far greater affection than the mountains and scenery surrounding his artistry. Perhaps he kneads the mountains of dough in the early hours of the mornings with a claymore ; who knows !

Continuing, we pass Kowloon Stores, with the name Mac-kenzie lettered as owner—not 'Hoo Flung High' which you think would be more appropriate—for 'Kowloon' is across on the mainland of China from Hong-Kong, which I know so well —but it appears the original store belonged to one who spent some years in Hong-Kong and Kowloon, and hence the name. We now come into the village of Strath proper, to its small square with petrol pump, ironmonger's shop, post office, and the general stores—groceries, papers, milk, electrical appliances, face powder, lipsticks and all the cosmetics, shoes, baby's outfits, bikinis, Andrew's Liver Salts—the lot! And just a few yards further along, the butcher's. That comprises everything; and truly that 'everything' is a hive of industry and activity all during some twelve weeks of the 'season'; the wee boot-repairer included!

You can get almost everything in the eating and haberdashery line; for so far afield it is amazing what goodly stores you find here; far superior to any within miles. The nearest place that has any good shopping facilities is at Dingwall, 60 miles to the east; to the north-west, nothing; to the south Kyle (a long journey indeed and across Strome Ferry too); to the north, nothing until you go far across the country to Thurso. We are very fortunately served for our means of existence; very. One thing missing is a hairdresser's (and am sure the ladies miss one too!). I have to journey to Dingwall (or Strathpeffer) once every two months for a hair-cut; and 'look you' what an expense that involves? At times, and during the dark wintry months I call on my neighbour who is really an adept in his way, for he learnt the art from a German when he was a prisoner of war for five years in Germany.

The post office is an extraordinarily busy place even out of the 'season'; the amount of business Kenny, assisted by his cheerful, courteous wife Cathey, puts through during the year would stagger any equivalent in an English village. And you need all your wits about you to run a post office: to know all about licences, pen-sions, money-orders, transfers, savings books and 101 other minor matters—to say nothing of the large amount of clerical work entailed in sending to head office at Dingwall weekly accounts of all transactions (even stamps!). This, as well as in the season, trying to soothe agitated, neurotic women visitors by finding accommodation for them; those who arrive with no place booked, and certainly none in mind. Yes, Kenny will have to go in for stocking large supplies of handkerchiefs, to help mop up the tears of distress shed by so many wandering beauties, sadly needing a man around them to organise their in-comings and out-goings! Then we must not forget Tommy, the cheery 'postie', who goes merrily on his rounds in a nippy little postal-van. Day in and day out, icy roads or pouring rain, Tommy carries on, tramping miles sometimes to out-of-the-way crofts, delivering even one receipted bill! 'The Post must get through' is the motto. I am pleased to record the chief postmaster at Dingwall presented him on 10th March 1962, at the Gairloch P.O., with an Imperial long-service-medal—close on fifty years' service I be-lieve ; or was it more ? Truly deserved indeed.

Verily the postmaster is one of the most important figures in a Highland village. He knows to put your letters and parcels aside if you make it a habit to collect them yourself ; and should he look out of his scratched piece of painted window and see your car in the square 'jalousing' you are in the near-by stores getting your milk and 'messages', you will find your mail on your driving seat, all ready for you. Service with a capital S ; and miles away from 'nowhere' too! Tell me of another place in all Britain where you get the same privileges, the same attention, the same individualism as here ? I am afraid you cannot ; for this is Strath, Gairloch, a place in a million, but by no means a million in the place, unless it be a million *fàiltes*—a million wel-comes—and that I will grant you.

Up through the village, crossing over another small bridge, with the ever-pleasing, spotlessly clean butcher's shop on the left, with the part-time 'butcheress' in charge thumbing over her ready-reckoner (the leaves crumbling to pieces with so much over-work) for you need remember in her day there was no such thing as the 11-plus, and therefore so many pounds and ounces at so much a pound confuses one's brain after 'sixty glorious years'! And then onwards we see the well-built attractive-looking Gair-loch Old Folk's Home (mentioned in a later chapter), and con-tinuing with the bay close by on one's left, there is nothing but a few crofts, small houses or bungalows, until the Youth Hostel at the point. Thence, still hugging the bay, comes Little Sands— a glorious clean, fine, sandy beach stretching unreservedly as far as the eye can see, with desolate Longa Island in the foreground.

C

Proceeding, comes North Erradale (just a hamlet) and, finally, Melvaig—the end of the road, nine miles from the Wild Cat.

It is of little historic interest this journey to Melvaig, but the somewhat twisty road is brightened in places by the views one gets in the distance. There is one deep cave *en route*, into which, legend has it, a piper is said to have led a band of men in search of gold ; and never returned. The sound of his pipes was heard in the neighbourhood for many a year after his disappearance. This kind of story is common in many parts of Europe— so similar to the 'Pied Piper of Hamelin'.

Melvaig : just a post office and a few houses. From here one can carry on, along a minor roadway, over the hill three miles to lonely Rudha Reidh with its lighthouse. This landmark is pronounced 'Rue Ray'.

As we have reached the end of the road, we must retrace our wheel marks back to Strath, and then take the other road, near the Wild Cat, to Poolewe and Ullapool.

This is a new journey and new country, and therefore demands a separate chapter ; but before concluding I must relate a true story connected with the Second World War.

In those days Gairloch, starting from Flowerdale onwards, was a restricted area, as, from Gairloch all along the north-western coast-line, much secret naval and military activity was always going on, and everybody, young or old, no matter whether they had lived here all their lives or not, needed a permit to pass the barrier set up ; even if it were only to do some shopping in Strath or going to church.

One good old lady lived near the pier head, and one Sabbath, walking along to the Free Presbyterian Kirk, and reaching the barrier, found she had forgotten her pass. The sentry on guard stopped her going through, albeit she looked innocent enough. He was adamant ; much altercation took place, and finally the old dear, waving her Bible in the corporal's face, shouted, 'This is the Lord's Book that is taking me to Heaven, and this is the Book that is going to take me past your barrier to the kirk right now'. And with that she brushed him aside and stamped along the road to worship, leaving him—to say the least—taken aback ! For he, poor fellow, had little ideas about religion and the religious feelings of these great people here.

CHAPTER 5

THE GREAT SILENCE

IN the dawn of Sunday 5th June 1960, tragedy struck Gairloch of such a magnitude that no one in living memory can recall its equal. Four Wester Ross men were drowned when their boat capsized in Gairloch bay, off Longa Island near the village of Strath. Two others of the party of six managed, with super-human effort, to swim ashore, exhausted and almost lifeless after clinging to their upturned craft for over three hours and watching their companions collapse, lose their holds on the boat and dis-appear, one by one, into the darkness of the cruel sea.

The Saturday night they set off, around 8 o'clock, for a spot of fishing, was a beautiful, breathless June night in the quiet bay, and the sea as calm as a millpond.

The tragedy was all the greater because the four men who were lost were the four key-men of this little Wester Ross village : the doctor, the veterinary surgeon, the leading grocer and the one and only garage proprietor ; Hugh, Robin, Roddie and Angus, all married, and between them seven young children were bereft of their fathers. But for the hand of Fate the two others, one the Gairloch butcher, the other a brother of the grocer's, might well never have come back.

Four key-men in a small, very small, rural community. The village, and indeed the whole countryside, was stunned and shocked, sad and silent over this devastating blow. All fine men doing fine jobs in the service of the people. In a village such as this everyone more or less depends on everyone else—on each other both professionally and socially. And they were all young men, 40 years of age down to 32 years.

I knew Angus and Roddie well ; in fact I was speaking to the latter a few hours before he went off to fish, and Angus did a small job for me on my car that Saturday afternoon. Everyone and everybody was happy, and contentment was uppermost amongst us as we joked and passed the usual pleasantries.

I happened to be living, at the time, across the bay at Badachro, when about 11 o'clock on the Sunday morning word came through of the tragedy. At first I thought there must be some mistake for such a mortal blow to have happened ; but no, it was all too real. My Sunday's joint was left untouched. Everybody around was so dazed we just sat, staring blankly, saying inwardly, it can't be true, and thinking also of the stricken widows. Later on we went into Gairloch to hear fuller details, and then quietly and silently motored back.

There was a Great Silence over the bay ; a silence conscious to one's very touch ; even the waves lapping the shores of Gairloch and Badachro seemed to be lapping them with a gentle reverence. Silence, a Great Silence.

The week opened with the news claiming headlines in all the Scottish and English national papers, with such captions as 'a village mourns'. It became known from north to south, from John o' Groats to Devon and Cornwall, and from east to west. In the village itself little groups of people gathered outside their homes to talk of the tragedy ; but all were too shocked to say much. One just took on a sort of blank, hypnotic look.

The week was wet, but somehow or other the heavens brightened on the Tuesday 7th June, the day of the funeral. Not only the whole village, but folk from far and wide—from the Highlands and the Lowlands—came to say farewell at a service held in the open air, and at least 500 people crowded round the 150-year-old sycamore tree at the golf course opposite the Church of Scotland. (This old tree is a landmark for men returning from the sea. There is a natural hollow near by where the Free Church communion services were held up to 15–20 years ago, at which I had often attended, and where, in the olden days, folk came by bridle-path and boat to attend. It is said to have been scooped out by the giant Fingal for a bed where his white cow might calve, and it is still called *Leabaidh na bà Baine*, or the 'Bed of the White Cow'.)

There was no tolling of a church bell—just silence. In the

village the shops had never opened since the disaster occurred. It seemed as though the whole countryside had died too. I have been at many funerals, at home and abroad, but never have I attended such a simple but impressive service, and one which brought so many tears. The service was conducted by the three ministers of the three churches of Gairloch : the Church of Scotland, the Free Church and the Free Presbyterian Church. They shared in the Gaelic and English service. Tourists on the sandy beach below listened in silence as we all sang the haunting psalm 'Coleshill'. Across at the little churchyard we all gazed sadly at the masses of brightly coloured wreaths and flowers.

This was the end of a chapter in the life of the village of Gairloch. But in this quarter everyone is everyone's friend, a closely knit community, and Time, the great healer, will give new and leading figures to take over where others left off.

I took a Colonial friend across to the funeral, who was staying with me at Badachro, a friend who had travelled greatly but who always appeared to me to be a man that little or nothing could stir. His philosophy of life could be summed up by saying he had yet to meet anyone, or anything, or see any sight to which he would, so to speak, 'take off his hat'. After the funeral we went down to the hollow, lolling reminiscently under the shade of the sycamore. Everything was quiet and peaceful, as the mourners and the cars had all gone. The sky was blue, flecked now and then with white clouds ; around us the greens of the tiny golf course, and beyond, the cruel sea—which had struck so harshly three days before in wiping out the community's leading men. We sat on and on, and suddenly a more than deep hush seemed to descend upon us. The very atmosphere seemed to be charged, to stand still, waiting, as it were, for something to happen. And then, without any warning, a small brown bird rose above us, and as it rose it sang, and up and up it soared till it vanished as a little speck in the sky ; but the sweetness and fittingness of its song seemed to be a symbol. A perfect song, sung perfectly, the same notes as when the world first began ; a song that makes the hearts of men of all creeds, colour, speech, or nationality, look up with thanks despite their many sorrows.

We sat motionless, and looked, listened and thought ; and turning to my friend I saw him slowly rise, and taking off his hat he stood in reverence and bowed. What a fitting climax to an ever memorable afternoon. We both stood for a while, not speaking. There was no need to speak ; there was no need to pass comment on what we had thought or witnessed both then and at the funeral service previously. *We just took off our hats ;* and that was all. And it seemed to be enough.

So ended a never-to-be-forgotten day. In the simplicity of our surroundings, the effect on one was tender and solemnising. It seemed to take us 'within the veil'.

The new graveyard, and the 300-year-old one (both restful in their simplicity) are not far from the water's edge, surrounded by trees and wild flowers, where the lap of the waves on the golden shore can be heard. We may well describe these sacred plots as 'where the sound of living waters never ceaseth, God's quiet garden by the sea'.

As we wended our way back over the bay, my mind recalled the verse :

> Shadow and sun, so too our lives are made ;
> Yet see how great the Sun, how small the shade.

and two stanzas of the *Rubáiyát* of Omar Khayyám :

> Would but some wingéd Angel ere too late
> Arrest the yet unfolded Roll of Fate,
>   And make the stern Recorder otherwise
> Enregister, or quite obliterate !

> Ah Love ! Could you and I with Him conspire
> To grasp this sorry Scheme of Things entire,
>   Would not we shatter it to bits — and then
> Re-mould it nearer to the Heart's Desire !

Things 'come to pass' it is true ; and those who remain have a duty in life to carry on, although in thoughts one may never forget ; 'The Silence that is in the starry sky ; the Sleep that is among the lonely hills'.

Those hearts that were lost were woven of human joys and cares. The years had given them kindness, and at such an early age, Dawn was theirs—and Sunset. But all was to be ended, and we who are left will look on them with fond remembrances—

> Not just today, but every day
> In sorrow we remember.

There is generally a calm for those that weep ; verily :

> The storm that wrecks the wintry sky,
> No more disturbs their deep repose,
> Than summer evening's latest sigh,
> That shuts the rose.

CHAPTER 6

THE GAIRLOCH NIGHTINGALE

FLORENCE NIGHTINGALE (1820–1910), an English nurse who did yeoman service in the Crimean War—a heroine in fact—and whose system, in principle has since been universally adopted, and who received the Order of Merit in 1907, is surely a name that conjures up the best of our ideals.

In 1853 when England, France and Turkey fought Russia, and British troops landed in the Crimea and won the battle of the Alma river, the cry went out from the sick and wounded 'why have we no sisters of mercy ?' In short, Florence Nightingale assembled nurses and equipment and went out there into a veritable Hell of chaos ; this soft-voiced woman with only the love of humanity as her reason and purpose. Not only was she an organiser, purveyor and schoolmistress, she was a nurse dressing wounds and comforting soldiers, and assisting at operations for hours at a stretch with an utter disregard of contagion.

She was known as the soldiers' angel, and when the war was over, and she returned to England a weakened woman, a fund was started for a school for nurses, and in one year a sum of £40,000 was raised; and it was then, in 1859, Florence Nightingale began, at St. Thomas's Hospital in London, the very first training school for nurses.

That school reformed the so-called hospitals of England, and indeed, of the whole world. Her life of 90 years was full of action, despite the fact that for some fifty years she was a sick person.

What has all this to do with Gairloch ? I will tell you.

There is a similar soft-voiced, dedicated woman born and

bred in Strath, Gairloch, and presently, after a life-time of nursing
service, living in a small cottage that veritably touches the edge of
the sea, devoting the closing years of her super-active life to looking after and caring for her two invalid sisters, one of whom has
been bed-ridden for many years.

I call her 'My Lady Alice', and in this instance also, I reverently bow and 'take off my hat'.

She was born, as I have said, in Strath, Gairloch, in her aunt's
house, a small cottage bearing the beautiful lilting sound of *Beul-
na-Mara*, Gaelic for 'mouth of the sea'. When in her teens, her
mind turned to nursing ; in fact even to this day, many or most
of the young girls in Wester Ross take up nursing as a career—
far more, I believe, than in any other part of Scotland. Nursing
and the sea appear to be the call of the women and menfolk. In
due course, towards the close of the 19th century she left home
and went to train at St. Marylebone and St. Thomas's Hospitals
in London, closely following in the steps of Florence herself. In
those years every girl that went into training there received a
grant of £5 from the Nightingale Fund, but my lady Alice
apparently just missed getting such a grant for some obscure
reason ; probably a time limit had been placed thereon. Whilst
there, she was not long in showing her outstanding capabilities,
not only as a nurse but as an organiser. Another Florence
Nightingale 'came to pass'.

Time marched on, and soon the First World War loomed
ahead and, in 1914, having come into personal contact with
many Harley Street doctors, she headed a team of workers and
was drafted abroad ; Italy—who was then our ally (in which
country Dr. Castellani's name comes to my mind, as he was many
years previously in Colombo and the doctor to my Company
there, and who became world-famous in respect of his discoveries
of new serums to combat diseases caused by the ravages of war)—
Salonica, Greece and up to the Austrian border : and in many
instances she and her team actually were in some of the districts in advance of our troops, preparing, ordering ; for ever
watchful.

When the war finished in 1918, she returned to England and
was fittingly honoured and decorated by King George V himself
(and Queen Mary) with the Royal Red Cross medal, the military
counterpart of the British Red Cross—a beautifully designed

C 2

medallion and ribbon. This, apart from a scroll she prized previously, personally signed by Queen Alexandra.

But this was only the beginning of 'my fair lady', as her attention began to focus on the Far East, and for over fifteen years, from 1923, she was in Colombo, Ceylon, where I first came to know her. We were close friends, relaxing in our odd hours by golfing, dancing, dining and so forth. Of course, we were both much younger then. However, though young we had a modicum of reason and a sense of proportion ; she in her sphere and myself in mine. During those years she was the propelling figure of the Kandy hospital—Kandy, the old capital of Ceylon, 2000 feet above sea level, a real jewel, set amidst a semitropical background, and which in the Second World War was to become Louis Mountbatten's Eastern headquarters—then on to the hospital at Nuwara Eliya (pronounced *new-railia*), a fascinating health resort 6000 feet up, with mountainous scenery and a climate very like Scotland. Later she was sought after to become the matron of the extensive General Hospital in Colombo itself, and finally the supreme head of the De Soysa hospital, also in Colombo ; a hospital devoted to sick native children and women—Ceylonese, Tamils and Indians. Here she worked wonders and was looked upon as the 'Great White Chieftainess', literally transforming the whole institution. Strange to relate, one of the leading doctors who formed her team in Italy eventually found his way to and set up practice in Colombo, and we three became very drawn to each other.

Eventually she retired early in 1939 (two years after I had shaken the tropical dust off my feet) to live in peace and enjoyment at the old wee cottage at Gairloch again, and where the sea still lapped the front door steps and the mountains of Torridon, in a sense, swept down to the sea, like the mountains of Mourne.

Did I say retired ? Only a few months later, the Second World War broke loose, and again, at her advanced age, she volunteered for active war work and was drafted to Devonport Military Hospital. But not for long there, for the Scottish Department of Health, St. Andrew's House, Edinburgh, which was virtually in charge of all nursing arrangements in Scotland, soon claimed her, and she was to be a dominating figure once more in Scottish nursing history.

She was appointed head of the hospital that was made available by the Ministry of Works in the huge mansion of 'Meller-stain' in Berwickshire—situated 6 miles north of Kelso and 10 miles south of Lauder—the stately home of the Earl and Countess of Haddington, where she was the king-pin for six years, 1943–1949. Whilst at Mellerstain she was sent off at times to deputise at various other war hospitals, where the matron might happen to be away ill and so forth. Such places included Stirling and Killin, where near-by at the Duke of Breadalbane's large and sumptuous Taymouth Castle which had been converted into a special hospital, patients came under her charge.

Then in 1949 she really *did* retire, four years after the war had ended, mark you, although the authorities were loth for her to do so ; and despite her countless activities, as well as fifteen years in the sweltering heat of the tropics—for Colombo is only 7 degrees off the equator, and with the constant humidity of a green-house, it certainly does take toll of one's stamina and par-ticularly so of a woman's—today she is still very active, though living on 'borrowed time', and daily caring for her two dear and near ones.

When she left Ceylon she visualised and planned quiet travels to Scandinavia, America, Canada, Australia, and so on and so forth, as she wished to see even more of the world as well as enjoy her well-earned leisure years. But though we may plan, we cannot foretell.

From all I have written, is it no small wonder that 'I take off my hat' to her ? And equally do I wonder if any of you who may read this chapter can touch even the fringe of such a life of devo-tion and self-denial ? I doubt it very much.

Today a figure of Florence Nightingale stands on a lofty pedestal in London. Surely it would not be out of place to sug-gest that alongside such an illustrious woman should be recorded the name of 'My Lady Alice of Strath' ?

Her truest monument, however, is not one modelled and set up by hand.

It is to be found in the realms of unrelentless energy and aid to the suffering which, in times of nation-wide trouble, the world opens its arms for ; and not in vain, namely the noble profession of Nursing—and written with a capital N.

Closely allied and linked to all this, is the care and attention given the old folk at the many homes for the aged dotted around the country ; but only sparsely dotted I am afraid. We could do with many, many more.

In Strath, Gairloch, there happens to be one such home, named 'Strathburn'. In the telephone directory you must look for it under the Ross and Cromarty County Council heads, where it is styled 'Gairloch Old People's Home'. This home was opened by Sir John Stirling, County Council convener, and related to the Mackenzies—the Lairds and owners of Gairloch—on 12th May 1960.

The opening was quite a signal occasion for Gairloch, and colour was added to it by a notable piper—Alex MacRae, a member of the Duke of Atholl's Highland Army, who was Gairloch born and bred—who came up from Blair Atholl, where he has a business, specially to 'play his pipes' at the luncheon and at the opening ceremony. The luncheon was given at the hotel to quite a large gathering of those who were closely connected with this new institution, and who had come a distance. When the luncheon was ready Alex piped the guests from the lounge into the dining-room playing 'The Mackenzie Highlanders', and whilst the main course was being served, marched round the tables playing a selection of marches ; and before finishing stood in a recess and played a Strathspey and Reel.

At the Home, 2 miles away in Strath, after Sir John had declared its opening, Alex played an appropriate slow march—a Gaelic melody called 'Mo Dhachaidh' (my home), the translation into English of the commencing Gaelic words of the song being 'sing cheerily, couthily, canty and free ; Oh this is the hour of sweet solace to me . . .'

A word, in passing, of the Atholl Highlanders—the only private army in Britain—may not be out of place. The Duke of Atholl lives at Blair Castle, Blair Atholl, situated 7 miles from Pitlochry and before you start the climb to Dalnaspidal (1500 feet), to Dalwhinnie, Newtonmore, Kingussie and on to Inverness.

The Atholl Highlanders were first raised in 1839 as the personal bodyguard of the Duke. The army remained an illegal force until 1844 when Queen Victoria and Prince Albert visited Blair Castle. For three weeks a detachment of Highlanders kept guard over the Royal couple, and the Queen was so impressed with their efficiency that she presented them with a set of Colours the following year. The regiment does not appear in the Army

List ; it has no barracks, nobody gets paid and its last proper parade was in 1913. The army has never fired a single defensive shot in the line of duty. Its only purpose is as ceremonial guard to the Duke of Atholl at Blair Castle, which has been the fortress home of the earls and dukes of Atholl for 700 years.

Membership is strictly by personal invitation of the 29-year-old Duke. Officer rank is an honorary commission bestowed on family friends of the Murray clan ; lower ranks are usually drawn from employees on the Blair Atholl Estate. The private army boasts one V.C., a D.S.C. and a D.F.C. Our Alex in particular, was, during the last war, H.Q. Coy. piper in the 1st Battalion of the Black Watch. He has been a piper in the Atholl Highlanders since 1938, and is a corporal. He and the others play round the Duke's table, usually at Christmas and New Year or at other times when His Grace's friends are staying with him. Altogether, at the moment, there are seven pipers and a pipe-major and they play as His Grace's pipers on special occasions throughout the county of Perthshire. The pipe-major, the Duke's ex-head gamekeeper, is 73, and has been a member of the High-landers for forty years. Another has been in the regiment since 1911, fifty years ago.

The 'Strathburn' Home, built by Messrs. Logan's of Muir of Ord, has thirteen bedrooms and can accommodate twenty-one people in all, and is exceptionally well planned ; everything being thought of to ensure the maximum efficiency and the maximum of comfort with the minimum of trouble. The staff consists of a matron (a fully qualified trained nurse who left a Glasgow hospital as ward sister to come here), a nurse auxilliary, cook (and a very good baker too, for I can testify to her scones and pancakes the day I had tea at Strathburn), kitchen and bedroom (ward) maids and of course Duncan the 'man about the house'.

The staff quarters with their own dining- and lounge-rooms are beautifully fitted out, just as the Matron's private suite is so fitted. The general building comprising the big lounge (and radio), smoke-room for the men, dining-room, luggage-room—this latter particularly systematically arranged—and other minor rooms, is 'polished to the nines', and I felt I should have brought my slippers with me to change into as I stepped from the wet muddy pavement into the delightful warmth of this 'haven'. I talked with many of the residents, all of whom had a smile of contentment, and who went out of their way to say how happy they—and everyone—were. In the ironing-room, I spoke to an old lady who must have been nearer 90 than 80 years of age, who daily gives a hand operating the electric pressing/ironing machine (a great 'little' gadget), and she said she 'loved being here and giving a hand' ; in all this I felt I might have been Prince Philip himself paying an official visit. It was most touching.

The architects have certainly 'gone to town' on this job at 'Strathburn', and the one who designed the kitchen comes in for my loudest praise. The Home caters for those living in Wester Ross, and entry—when there happens to be a vacancy—is per agreement of the House Committee-members who meet at intervals under the chairmanship of Gairloch's Church of Scotland's minister.

There is no sick bay attached to this Home, or allowed for in any way ; the matron has certainly made use of a little chiropody room, turning it into a glorified first-aid room, but this is far from sufficient and I think when such Homes are built they should be designed to include a proper clinical bay and be staffed accordingly ; for it should be remembered we are 90 miles away from Inverness, the nearest hospital. I am sure our Welfare State could afford this essential, for it certainly cannot be classified as a 'luxury' addition.

As I remarked earlier, the country can do with hundreds more of these Old Folk's Homes. Modern medicine continues to increase the number of years old people can expect to live ; but when will we strike the solution of making those extra years happy ones ? Our population is getting older. Fifty years ago, elderly people represented only 7 per cent of the population ; today they represent 15 per cent—more than double. I am afraid we have little reason to be proud of our treatment of the elderly, seeing to it they are happy in the spending of their remaining days in peace and quiet comfort, but rather we should hang our heads in shame ! In other countries the elderly are venerated. Here the fate of many is to be shoved around from one son or daughter to the next, like a pawn in a game of chess. One case in the South, of an old widowed lady living in a Council house who was ordered to 'tidy up your garden or quit' ; she collapsed after trying to wield her spade, poor soul. We hear also of an old widowed Scottish woman being refused water at a 100-year-old spring well, at the edge of her croft, by a 'squire' who appears to treat his tenants as natives. Well, of course they are natives ; they have lived on their land and croft for generations ; yes, they are natives—but not unlettered savages. Those who, whether they be individuals or Councils, are engaged in this work and programme of looking after and catering for the old folk, are always spoken of in a glib manner as doing a 'great work'. Well, how about joining in the greatness ?

Then we must not forget the District Nurse and her little black bag. In Gairloch we have a fine character in 'our Annabel' —not Annabel Lee, to quote the American song ! She is constantly out and about looking after and ministering to the sick and needy (as well as having a gossip here and there!), and taking much work off the country doctor, who is held in great esteem. Her district extends from Gairloch to Melvaig in one direction ; and from Gairloch to Red Point in the other direction. Provided with a car, a house and a 'phone she is at anyone's beck and call ; and I am sure many an old body is thankful for our Bella— 'tinkle' I name her ! She also deputises for the Poolewe nurse (and vice versa) when occasions arise.

Not only does she carry her little black bag—and a weighscale to keep record of baby's weight—but if you chance to look in her car you will see the Bible well to the fore ; and it can be taken for granted that to some of her old and bed-ridden patients she will oft-times read them a chapter from the great Book ere she leaves them ; so offering comfort to them in more ways than one.

A great country, and great women-folk too. The trouble with the District Nurses up in these Highland villages is that they only hold the post—on average—three years. And why ? Well, they get married ! I won't say it is because of their pretty looks, for they may feel embarrassed ! So I'll let it go by saying 'It's the uniform that does it'.

So in Gairloch, far as we are from 'civilisation' and up-to-date hospitals and clinics, we have a Florence, a Home, and a Nurse. These, together with a resident doctor—and not forgetting the 'Vet'—constitute a praiseworthy team which I am certain is the envy of many a neighbouring parish.

So, to the Royal College of Nursing and all its allied services —'I take off my hat'.

CHAPTER 7

ACROSS THE BAY

FROM where I write, I face Isle Horrisdale, Dry Island, and behind them the quiet village of Badachro ; from there, the hamlets of Port Henderson, Opinan, South Erradale and Red Point are hidden from view by the land since the bay curls round. Over the bay the hills of Torridon, and further still, the table-topped Beinn Bhan range, 20-odd miles away, towering amidst the Applecross Forest.

It is of the immediate 'bay across'—Badachro—and Torridon that this chapter deals.

To reach the bay across—the peninsula as I term it, much to the inhabitants' displeasure !—you turn off the Gairloch main road at Kerrysdale bridge—signposted merely Port Henderson 5 miles, Red Point 8 miles.

It is a tortuous, narrow road, but pleasant enough unless you have to travel it three or four times a day, when it would become monotonous and an eye-strain to any driver.

There were, as I have said before, no roads in Gairloch and district until the military road was made. At the time of the potato disease and widespread famine, money was received from the Destitution Committee's Fund (set up in Edinburgh to make more roads) to carry on the road to Badachro ; and, of course, today the tarred roadway goes right to Red Point where, looking across the sea, the lighthouse at Rona's tip is clearly seen. It is but 6 miles from Red Point (along the high cliffs looking down on Loch Torridon) to Diabaig, the last hamlet reached by road from Torridon village. If ever there is a road made linking these two points it would indeed form a magnificent circular tour: Gairloch, Diabaig, Torridon, Kinlochewe, Loch Maree, and Gairloch. But then this would be a luxury road, serving no villages or crofts, and therefore does not seem feasible these days of 'squeezes'.

Turning off then, at the Kerry bridge, you wander on and on as though you were driving up and through a tree-lined approach avenue to an English country manor house. Everything is still, even quieter than usual, and you pass nothing that hurries. The former Shieldaig Lodge—now an hotel—comes suddenly to view, with its prepossessing lawn rolling lazily down to the water's edge ; another touch of English (Thames) countryside. From thence you carefully negotiate the many bends and come to the wee cluster of two bungalows and two houses at Leacnasaide, hemmed in by trees and bracken ; a very haven for midges ! All still, and very English in outlook, for the road gives no distant vistas of hills or mountains until you start to rise further on, passing such a beautifully named house as Innis Bheatha ('Valley of the Birch'), and then you catch a glimpse of Gairloch bay and the 'mainland' across.

Eventually 'swinging high, swinging low' you come to the top of the brae leading down to the village, signposted Badachro, and immediately you are 'in town tonight', within a stone's throw of the post office, inn, and school—the latter now closed until such time as more babies are born ! I always think a village without a school is not a village any more ; for the childish noise and laughter associated with a school is part of village life ; it is what you expect, and, without it all, you sense a feeling of emptiness.

In days of yore, Badachro had a large fishing station where curers purchased the herring, cod, ling, etc., from the fisherfolk, and exported their catches in their own boats. It was said the cod fishery of Gairloch was historical. It was carried on by two firms who had curing houses at Badachro, Dry Island and Eilean Horrisdale—isle of happiness. Alas, that is no longer ; but perhaps it is just as well, for I am sure such a curing factory would desecrate the quiet and peace of this 'sleepy village', approached through 4 miles of sleepy valley !

I have previously remarked that once you pass Garve nobody hurries. Certainly nobody hurries in good old Badachro : in fact it is a village where nobody moves, let alone hurries ; for you will count yourself lucky if you see any living soul about between October and April, excepting Daisy and Sarah, the two cows that make Badachro famous. For Badachro without either would not be Badachro at all !

In the season, of course, it is a different kettle of fish (for fishing is still the livelihood of the few able-bodied men around).

The few houses there are, put up their accommodation signs, clean their windows, and put a dab of paint on here and there and generally freshen things up. Then the rush begins, sleep is over; movement starts, the hedgehog comes out, the hive is full of feverish buzzing activity, mobility reigns, legs of lamb, shoulders of mutton, chickens, beef, even haggis—all being ordered or allowed for, ready for the 'foreign invasion'. Soon the car loads arrive, emptying their noisy cargoes; cooking carries on apace; the rustle of pound notes can be heard exchanging. Whilst others come and others go, the rush goes on around the clock:

> The pretty girls and buxom daughters
> Married women in their forties,
> Who out of season look so trig,
> Full of bounce and health and 'vig',
> Now have no time for paint or powder,
> Just one mad rush, as noise grows louder;
> Until the end, when all are beaming,
> Tax is dodged, and pound notes teeming,
> In this village quiet yet scheming.
> And Grannies too, three score and ten,
> Are in it; strange, the lack of men!

Well over 5,000,000 people stayed at Scottish hotels and boarding houses in 1961, apart from 470,000 'bed-nights' in Scottish Youth Hostels. Added to all this are some 250,000 who stayed in camps and hostels in national forest parks; and tens of thousands of other holiday-makers who took camping/caravan holidays. European visitors totalled nearly 600,000. These are truly astronomical figures and speak volumes for Scottish scenery and hospitality.

Yes, one mad rush, and women ruling the day, washing plates, cutlery and linen, peeling potatoes by the hundredweight, clearing and setting of tables, cutting peat, milking cows, collecting eggs, feeding hens and geese, and getting in the hay, feeding the cats, watching 'Ginger' does not steal anything set aside for the visitors; coffees, teas and then to bed, just for five or six hours. Comes the dawn, when this catering cycle starts up all over again. Feeding becomes the password, for they tell you, and rightly so, that part of a Highland holiday is Food with a capital F. The way to a man's heart is through his stomach it is said, and the way also applies to a woman's heart, I am sure, up here. I have never seen so much, put on so small a plate, so often, anywhere else in Britain. My! my! this is the life, you say to yourself if you're a visitor. And behind scenes washing up, you would hear the same comment: 'Aye, this is the life!' Hundreds of pounds are quietly banked away. Did I say 'banked'? Well, hardly. It is put in drawers, or under the mattress, or in the oatmeal chest, for if you banked it and the Income Tax smart Alecs got to know, well—I mean to say! It's not done in Ross-shire; and what pleasant dreams you can have sleeping upon 500 crisp £1 English notes or 1000 crisp ten-shilling notes, that you know literally lie between you and starvation in your old age, when you can relax, sit back and tell your children 'those were the days'. The English came, and saw, and no, not conquered, but paid! In the season you live off the victims; in the winter you live off one another. Fishing and feeding; and in the winter there's no fishing!

But on the Sabbath, all nicely dressed and composed, the locals wend their way to the Kirk, and at Badachro one needs to go by car for the nearest Church is at Gairloch: the Church of Scotland, the Free Presbyterian and the Free Church; and more than likely most of those 'across the bay' attend the latter house of prayer; where you stand at the prayers and sit at the singing, giving thanks to Providence—and England!

I cannot take you past Badachro and on to Red Point without mentioning the promontory known as Aird. It looks down over Isle Horrisdale and Dry Island. Singular that an island should be called 'Dry', with nothing whatever connected with alcohol; but it seemingly takes its name from the fact that when the tide goes out one can walk across the stones, or causeway, to the little island and not always have to take a boat.

Aird is a lovely open spot with a farm-house facing the setting sun; all so peaceful in the evenings despite the daytime ordeal of coping with so many hungry mouths.

In previous chapters, 'I took off my hat'. In this chapter I take off my hat again. Many years ago the houses in Badachro and Aird were in a ruinous state; but a new and vigorous generation arose with the spirit of the grand independence of their Highland forefathers. They had passed through lean—very lean —times. I have known one family who have lived in this district for six generations; that when times were bad and some of this later generation lived for a while at the back of a wee shop in the 'big city', the young members (kids really) used to sell their left-off shoes and clothes, and sometimes the clothes they were wearing (which, though threadbare, were not considered 'left-offs' by *their* standards), to get a shilling or so to help their widowed mother eke out an existence so they might all have at least *one* meal a day ; or to give her a little 'extra', an orange or apple—some added comfort—when ill in hospital (long before our National Health Service of course). Truly a hand-to-mouth existence (that some of us more fortunate ones may never have known), but bringing out the family's grit and dour determination to pull through—'smeddum', or 'guts' to put it tersely. Later on in years, coming back to the ruined remains at Badachro, the family (still young) and mother—living on borrowed time, widowed let it be said from the First World War at the early age of 35—kept the ancient land and farmstead going, even without the help of her only son who was killed in the Second World War eighteen years ago. Carrying on a farm of 300-hill and 12-arable acres and turning the house into a summer boarding house to help pay the way ; and 'pay the way' just about summed it up. This is typical of Scottish Highland tenacity and vigour. Ponder over it : vigour at close on 73 years of age ; vigour notwithstanding all the trials and worries of life ; vigour with all the trimmings, as we town folk know it, stripped and removed. All this, and far from enjoying good health.

In the parlour, set in a small black-edged *passe-partout* frame, is a letter signed by King George himself relating to the death of her son. It is couched in simple homely words, and I offer no excuse in reproducing the text here :

> The Queen and I offer you our heartfelt sympathy in your great sorrow. We pray that your country's gratitude for a life so nobly given in its service may bring you some measure of consolation . . .

So hangs a fitting tribute from the King of England on the wall of a farm cottage in the lonely fastness of Wester Ross.

Close to this Royal touch of reassurance I would like to see these soothing words, also simply framed (written over half a century ago—in 1908—by Miss Louise M. Haskins of Clifton, Bristol), which were quoted by the same King George VI in his Christmas Day broadcast to the Empire in 1939, shortly after the outbreak of the Second World War :

And I said to the man who stood at the gate of the year :
'Give me a Light that I may tread safely into the unknown'.

And he replied :
'Go out into the darkness and put your hand into the hand of God ;
That shall be to you better than a light, and safer than a known way.'

Is it then no small wonder that 'I take off my hat' and bow in admiration to such a family, to such a woman, to such a life-history, to such a masterpiece of endurance and the 'Keeping of the Faith', that enabled those so stricken down to rise above such odds, such misfortunes (mishealbh) and—what is so significant these days—to keep afloat on an even keel ?

To this woman, her plucky family (and to many others similarly placed) I take off my hat and raise my glass : *Slàinte Mhath ;* and may Allah bless them, all Lairds of Aird.

I have termed this village 'sleepy' ; one that out of season you would say Time passed by. But not so the post office ; it is always busy on watch, always getting first-hand news, as indeed one can say that of all the post offices in the Highlands. In England if you want to know anything, you ask a policeman ; up here, it's the post office where you get all the information you want— and more ! Whether it is that the village policeman is rarely seen, or happens to be 'off' at Inverness for the day should he be needed, I wouldn't know ! But the fact remains ; every post office, be it staffed by one lone male or female, knows everything ; and what it doesn't know it makes up. The P.O. and the local exchange are the two 'musts' to keep in with. Or else—. 'No, I am sorry there's no reply from Mr. Mackenzie's line ; I think I overheard him say last week, when he was 'phoning his cousin in Dingwall, that he meant to go over there today to see his married daughter for the day, as she had just had a bonny 9 lb. baby boy,' says the telephone girl to you, should you be ringing the said Mr. Mackenzie.

Yes, these post office people know all, particularly 'Whiley Wullie' at Badachro—canny Wullie. And then 'Willie the Gillie' is another who knows all ; another character, *alias* Nelson because of his blind eye (First World War), *alias* His Excellency the Justice of the Peace, a connoisseur of good whisky ; an acknowledged believer that there is no such thing as bad whisky !

his only real complaint in life being the littleness of small bottles! and I am sure his favourite ballad is :

> If whisky was a river
> And I were a duck,
> I'd dive to the bottom
> And never come up!

Willie was, in his 'palmy days', a tailor ; and a very good tailor too. In 1938 I gave him a commission to make me a plus-four suit—the first I ever had and incidentally the last—in Lovat shade. He got the material from Harris, a really good piece of tweed, and made it for me whilst I was staying at the hotel that summer. I used to go 'across the bay' to be fitted now and then, and, of course, it became part of the ritual to put something flat in my hip pocket before I went! I think it took 'Nelson' five months to complete that order, for truth to tell, there were periods of 'cessation' when his eye was giving him trouble! However, it was duly finished *à la* Savile Row : a perfect fit, a perfect colour, leather-covered buttons—the lot! and I was very happy with it, especially so as it only cost me about £5, plus, naturally, the 'extras' (say another £5, for whisky was cheaper those days), to which my T.T. and religious friends would say eternal damnation would fall upon tailor, suit and me!

However, it suited me A 1 ; in fact I wore it constantly during the war whilst working for a particular War Ministry in Edinburgh, and simply could not wear it out. It was the real Mackay —sorry, I mean Lovat! Just as Willie had finished my 3-piece, there came to the Gairloch hotel a firm displaying woollens and tweeds, and with their permission I paraded round the present dining-room—then a recreation-room—with a card printed bearing the words 'made locally by the one and only tailor in Gairloch, William Macrae of Badachro'. I believe 'Nelson' secured several orders from English and American visitors, and was making quite a nice living out of tailoring when the war came along and he could get neither tweeds nor orders. And his eye became more troublesome!

I may therefore claim to be the first—and possibly the last— male model in Wester Ross! A real *man*equin to be sure !

But to hark back to W. T. W.—'Wullie the Whiley'. I must try and get even with him, for he seems to get the news even before it's out. One day I will tell him a story or bit of gossip, and, when getting halfway through with Wullie interrupting by saying 'Yes, I ken', I'll stop and wait for him to finish off the yarn—if he can ! (There is another dear old soul on the mainland of over 80 years, Ann, wife of a wonderful old Highland 'Gentleman', his nickname 'Willie Lauder', a veritable landmark of Gairloch. This good wife never goes out of her home from one year's end to another, yet always (and I repeat, always) knows what is going on ; how many guests there are in the hotel, what they had for dinner that night, what staff troubles are going on, and a 1001 other tit-bits.) Amazing ! London's M.I.5 has nothing on Gairloch—or Badachro—believe me ! The 'Bush Telegraph' in the Highlands is definitely a sure and reliable source of information !

But 'oor Wullie' is a kind, obliging soul, always on the watch to see who is going past; his 'keek-hole', scratched out of the white painted glass in his window, lets him see from 'within' what's going on 'without' ; not the other way round ! Canny manny ! Though he may be out of a stamp or particular postal order you want, you may have to take two to make up the amount you need—so paying out two poundages instead of one ; crafty, eh ? But to continue from the Wullie and no stamp or postal order episode ; he will always nip round from behind his iron curtain (grille) and hand you over a steak-and-kidney pud. from the deep freeze, wrapped up in a few telegraph forms that had strayed from one side of the 'Emporium' to the other. Of course, as Selfridge once said, in his early days, 'A shop without a "post orfice" is no worth a damn !' Many a time I have been in and shouted out 'Wullie', and heard his voice answering but no sign of him anywhere, until suddenly, away over at the shop end I would see his head rising up from behind a tower of biscuit tins, and his eyes looking up at you like those imploring, love-sick eyes of a spaniel, and saying, 'Yes, Bee Jay, and how are you this morning ?' Yes, oor Wullie is a grand chap, full of dry Scottish humour, who lives for his post office, his 'Addwell' calculating machine, his shop, his sister (Crafty Clara) and his widowed mother. 'Crafty', a fine, bonny lassie, helps in taking the mail round, getting 'late-night' news also by her winsome ways ; and mother (the sweetest Highland character you will find anywhere), what of her ? She keeps the home fire burning, cooking

and baking (and what baking!) and also 'taking in' visitors. By
that I do not imply 'rooking' them ; on the contrary, they treat
them like royalty, like the prodigal son of old, by continuously
killing the fatted calf; and when seated if you took a quick, quiet
look at her round the corner carving up each meal in the back
scullery you would spot her in her characteristic attitude of having
her mouth slightly open and her tongue out as she wielded the
knife, cutting the joint, chicken or whatever it might be, slice by
slice. Many of us have peculiarities in doing certain things ;
mother's was her tongue! though she would never admit it.
And what soup! both mamma and Clara are monarchs of the
stock-pot. Soup is really soup in Scotland ; none of your 3-star
English or Scotch hotel watery *consommé* concoction. I have
seen a whole side of brisket in the stock-pot, lying snug and
bubbling amongst different vegetables by the score, cut up
'intil't' ; and my! the smell of it all, 'very tasty, very sweet', with
say, a dessertspoonful of sugar put in—an old and favourite item.
Yes, here you get soup made, watched over and nursed, like a
young mother gloats over her first-born child ; soup unknown
anywhere else in this country—perhaps in the world. Soup, the
whole(some) soup, and nothing but the soup!

Here, then, we must take our leave of Wullie (not before he
shouts out from behind that tower of tins, 'Here it is'. 'What?'
says I. 'Why, that 3d stamp you wanted yesterday ; underneath
Carr's of Carlisle ; well, well ; hush be quiet, it's myself that
found it!'), Clara and mamma, the latter 'waddling' around—
and that seems to be the most fitting adjective—in her own sweet
way and time, makes haggis her shining speciality ; should you
get her closely guarded recipe, then I am sure you would be in
the running for filching the recipe for Glayva from the monks of
Skye. And as though mamma has not enough on her plate, she,
or Clara, or both, must always see to letting Daisy, the cow, in
by the front gate marked 'Keep Shut', and manœuvring the beast
into the byre for milking every night ; and if it's wet she takes
down the old red blanket hanging close by and rubs poor Daisy's
backside down first to make her cosy for the night ; and as she
carries on with the milking generally talks to the beast in Gaelic
as though she were a baby and a member of the inner household. Daisy in turn would snort a bit as she was munching a
turnip given her to keep her active mind occupied and away from

the milking process. And the hens too ; they know her and Clara as well as they know their own cockerel! Fed well on Indian corn, and luscious scraps from an old stone-jar receptacle kept handy in the kitchen and filled from the visitors' tables, they respond in a regular and prolific manner ; the eggs dropping here and there like the sound of pennies when you press Button B in Wullie's kiosk! Yes, dear mamma is a real Highland-born character, with many old wives' tales to tell. Once, when we were talking in the kitchen and helping to do the potatoes, and 'Smokey' was sitting up on a chair washing herself, mamma looked up and said 'there's Smokey washing her face, and her paw's going round her ears ; that means we're having fish for supper!' And so it was. And then when getting a leg of pork from the butcher at the door, tells him she'd like 'a *right*-hind leg of pork, Alec'. 'Why, mamma,' he says, 'how can I tell which is which?' 'Oh,' says she, 'don't you know ; a pig usually scratches itself with its left hind leg and so the right leg has not so much work to do and therefore is more tender!' To Wullie, mamma and Clara I unreservedly 'take off my hat'—a wonderful household.

We must now say adieu, adios amigos, to Badachro, as we follow the road a couple of miles on to Port Henderson ; but not perhaps before mentioning another of Wullie's activities and side-line (though as partially an honorary one it is devoid of much 'crispy' glamour), namely, of his being the area's meteorologist. Oh yes, you need brains to be a meteorologist, for it's as difficult a job as it is difficult to pronounce or spell. Daily, and with strict routine, does he record on a charted sheet the rainfall of Badachro—the rain-gauge (measuring-glass) apparatus being established in the middle of the potato crop at his home. This must be taken at 9 a.m. each morning (and I quote 'the rain gauge should be read at 9 a.m. and entered as rainfall for the PREVIOUS DAY') together with—in column 4—'remarks, *e.g.* snow, frost, continuous drizzle, sharp rain, storm, wind, etc.' (quoting). 'Och, aye! they're particular down Badachro-ways.' And then each month such records are sent, over his signature as 'Observer', to the North of Scotland Hydro-Electric Board's office in Edinburgh. What they do with such cards is anybody's guess, of course! Nobody, but nobody, will know!

The story goes that one day Wullie was away, Clara sent the

maid out to get Wullie's gauge-glass so she could mark down the rainfall. The maid, newly engaged from down south, appeared back at the front door with the measuring-glass, and, catching sight of Clara going upstairs to make the beds, shouted out—with visitors around picking up their packed lunches—'Here's Wullie's water ; what shall I do with it ?'

So we pass on, giving a glance in at the main store to see if the key-man of the village has finished reading the day's chapter of his book (if not, he should have done so, for it's past 9.30 in the morning), and along open moorland, passing the pretty loch abutting the roadside—Loch Badnahachlish—reach Port Henderson, where there is a farm and stores serving the few houses and crofts there ; and a telephone kiosk, emptied once a week by 'oor Wullie of Badachro'—a truly versatile man, oor Wullie !

Talking of post offices, the villagers seldom buy more than one or two stamps at a time. Should they have to write a letter and have no stamps, and the P.O. is closed, they merely push their correspondence in the box and three pennies—or more as needs be—so that in the morning when the postmaster is making up the outgoing mails, he has to put stamps on those unstamped letters, to the extent of the money found in the bottom of the box, and he says to himself, I'm sure many a time, 'och chrupelan', a sort of 'oh dear' or 'fancy that' meaning, in English ! Or maybe he'll mutter, 'that's that old de'il "Sewerage Ali" or "Black Jimmy" out of stamps again !'

As to Port Henderson, there is no 'port' now, but seemingly long years ago there was one Roderick Mackenzie, an elderly and much respected boat-builder. When young he went one day to a rocky part of the shore, and, whilst gathering bait, he suddenly saw a mermaid asleep among the rocks. He got near her and managed to seize her by the hair. She, in great embarrassment, cried out that if he would let her go she would grant him whatever wish he might ask. 'Rorie' requested a pledge that no one should ever be drowned from any boat he might build. On his releasing her, the mermaid promised this should be so. I am told by an old lady now living in the district that this is a true story—or at any rate the essence of it is true, for there is much superstition around these parts—that the promise was kept throughout Roderick's long life and his boats continued to defy the storms and seas ;

in fact I believe one or two of his boats are still afloat this very day ; eighty years or so old.

From here, another mile or so brings us to Opinan ('little bays') where the sandy beach and sand dunes stretch for miles, and you always find yourself alone, or nearly so, looking right across to Skye with the tip of Rona Island and lighthouse showing. A post office and telephone completes the last link with the outside world ; from Gairloch to Red Point there are just three 'phone kiosks and two post offices. At Opinan post office you ring the door-bell which connects with the postman's house 50 or 60 yards away ; and the postman's wife (her husband being away at the salmon fishing at Red Point) takes the kettle off the hob, looks out of her front door to see who might be pressing the bell, and then comes trundling along to see what you want ; and if it's only a stamp you need—well, 'twill be hardly a smile you'll be getting ! Not so business-like as Badachro you say, but then Opinan is but a wee bit place which the stage-coach seldom visits ! On now to another hamlet, South Erradale, and thence to Red Point, where you look down on Loch Torridon.

And it is of Torridon now that I would tell you ; of the Torridon Hills I look upon and see every day I waken at Strath ; and every day they seem to look different by reason of the angle the morning light and cloud falls on them, a veritable peacock-parade of colours. There they are, every day of every week of every year ; and yet no two days the same. And this has been the case for millions of years, for they are considered to be the oldest hills in creation.

Torridon lies at the western end of Glen Torridon, perhaps the finest and wildest of the Wester Ross glens. The road to Torridon is overshadowed by the might and majesty of Liathach ('the Gray one') 3456 feet above sea-level, a terraced mass of Torridonian sandstone topped with white quartzite (frequently mistaken for snow). Beinn Eighe ('The File Mountain', 3300 feet) and Beinn Alligin (3021 feet) also tower upwards, keeping the monarch of these hills, Liathach, company. Liathach is composed of more than three miles of steep terraces of red sandstone, most difficult to climb.

These mountains are of immense interest to geologists, who come from all quarters of the world to study them, for this Torridonian sandstone is some of the oldest rock in the world, so old in fact that no fossils have been found in it, an indication that the rock was laid down before life first appeared on this earth. This red-coloured sandstone is about 4000 feet in thickness. Above this, the Torridon Red, lies a thick-bedded whitish rock referred to above, composed of quartz-grains plus a highly meta-morphosed fine sandstone.

The Torridon mountains are known as 'sedimentary' rocks, as opposed to 'metamorphic' rocks, the product of alteration by various geological processes of rocks of diverse origin.

The phenomena of the glacial period are truly shown in this Loch Maree-Torridon area. The strata in general run parallel to the loch's axis, proving the existence of an immense glacier that moved to the sea down the deep hollow now filled with water. Further evidence of glaciation is the number of terraced thrust-planes which must have been borne by the ice sheet dropped from the parent rock in the line of the ice movement.

These hills of Torridon make a striking picture in the varying glows of sunset ; in short, as I have said, this precipitous range, as well as many other mountains in the north-west Highlands provide a wealth of attraction to everyone, especially to geologists in studying so many of the geological problems which still remain unsolved. Torridon for them has a unique interest.

Torridon and Annat villages practically adjoin one another at the head of Upper Loch Torridon, which is part of Loch Torridon itself—a big arm of the sea—which also has Loch Shieldaig in its fold. The loch is broad, deep and lonely-looking, crowned with these mountains of sandstone that glow like liquid gold in summer sunsets ; and in winter present an eerie wildness. The loch also embraces the great Ben Damph forest.

To reach Torridon you turn off at Kinlochewe and travel some 12 miles of good roadway, comparatively wide and straight, through Glen Torridon, to the head of the loch. The area between Kinlochewe, Loch Maree and Glen Torridon is partly a national forest park, though a fair area of old forest has been cut away some years ago.

This journey of 12 miles takes you through wild scenery unsurpassed in grandeur (and again I stress) of loneliness. This utter wildness surely gives us a lesson in humility ? No sea-loch in Wester Ross is encircled by such terrifying 'massiveness'.

About 4 miles along the road Loch Clair is passed on the

left ; near-by one can see the seat used by St. Maelrubha when he journeyed between his two cells at Applecross and Loch Maree (Isle Maree). Further along this roadside heaps of stones can be seen at times, made by passing funeral parties in the olden days ; for here one is in the midst of—

> A land of wayside cairns—the place
> Of resting for the biers of death,
> And tokens of a fading race
> And relics of forgotten faith.

When you are about halfway to Torridon you will not fail to see on the left side of the glen an extraordinary array of hillocks close together and rounded off ; and this little fascinating area is called the 'Corrie of 100 Hillocks', or sometimes as the 'Valley of 100 Fairies'. These singular mounds are due to the natural action of ice and water in prehistoric times ; the streamlets depositing a series of hummocks of debris, which gradually covered the ground as the ice retreated, leaving these corries behind.

Coming to the head of the loch, the road forks ; left to Annat, a quaint-like village (or hamlet I should rightly call it) where a big scheme is now under way, constructing a new wide road over the hills to Shieldaig, and thence down to Loch Carron. When completed this will cut out going through Achnasheen and the 25 miles from there to Loch Carron village. It will be a magnificent run through to Strome Ferry ; and more direct. Taking the road straight on from the Annat fork brings you in a few minutes to Torridon village. It is *but* a village, and whenever I have been there it has seemed to be siesta-time ! either that or fast week and communion, for no one seems to be out of doors ! I am told regarding the Second World War, the local people hardly knew of its happening ; and that today the only thing they believe true in the reading of the daily newspaper, is the date ! Strange then, they spend money on buying a paper ?

Mr. Duncan Darroch was the original proprietor of Torridon Estate since 1872. An elegant mansion house was built on the shore, 2 miles beyond the village, and near the road turn-off to Diabaig. Torridon House it is called. This estate, and the estate on the opposite side of the loch, Beinn Damph estate, now belong to the Earl of Lovelace.

Passing by the half-dozen houses in Torridon village, not forgetting our friend the village postmaster, we come to the

8-mile run to Diabaig over a fine macadamised road, but with many hairpin bends, such as you encounter in the Alps and which no one but an expert driver should attempt. I rate this 8-mile journey, passing Alligin village 1 mile away down on the shore, as one of the most—if not *the* most—spectacular in Scotland, with superb views going and coming back. Perhaps you could call it the most fascinating, and one that many a driver mayhap would offer up thanks upon arriving back in little Torridon village again, safe and sound!

The last time I travelled the road was with the county's road engineer—a skilful driver if ever there was one—which was fortunate, for high up in the mountain pass (and sometimes you come to the crest of a rise where you cannot see—until you are *on* the crest—whether the road goes straight on, turns right, or veers left) we suddenly came upon a funeral party (the road foreman's mother) complete with several cars, the coffin being on a lorry ; looking neither to the right nor left we managed to steer clear of each other by inches ; but to anyone but an expert handler of cars, I felt we would have joined that funeral party! Either that, or suffered nothing short of a nervous breakdown for years to come!

So ended a memorable ride to Diabaig ; and believe me I would not have missed it for all the corn in Egypt, let alone the tea in China, or all the oatmeal eaten west of Garve! There is a sweet old-world jetty when you get down to the village nestling on the seashore ; shades of the past when 'puffers', of the Para Handy age, called in with supplies of coal—and whisky. You can easily turn round there for the journey back—after taking a large neat brandy of course!

A marvellous journey and experience of but 8 miles ; that's all, just 8 miles of wonderment you have never known before in this country. I beg readers not to miss it, for once seen it will remain in your memory for all time. And should you do the 8 miles in a smallish car, 'Och aye, there's nothing tae it ; there's nae bother at a', at a'.'

If only there were a connecting road between Diabaig and Red Point, 7 miles, what a tour! What a journey! What a thrill! 'Mon, mon it would be sensational.' Heroism at its best! And when you left Torridon, offering up a prayer, you would say 'Gairloch, here I come!'

CHAPTER 8

GAIRLOCH—ULLAPOOL

W E are now back in the 'Wild Cat' country ! or, in other words, just near the junction where, taking the main road up over the hill and across the moors, brings us to Poolewe, 6 miles distant. *En route* we pass Loch Tollie (Tollie meaning 'a place of holes') and then get a charming view of this —the western—end of Loch Maree, with Beinn Airidh Charr in the background, and which, on a bright sunny day, almost rivals the other view of Loch Maree from the top of Glen Docharty and before dropping down to Kinlochewe, you will remember. It was from somewhere near Loch Tollie that Horatio Mac-Culloch's great painting of Loch Maree was made.

There is a very nice, sheltered, secluded spot down the side road leading to Tollie Farm and, a little beyond, which brings you right down to the water's edge of the loch, pebbly, but very lovely and restful, little known to the ordinary visitor.

On the side of the main road to Poolewe, barely a mile from 'Wild Cat' junction, there is a big boulder on the right called 'The Shoestone' (Clach nam Bròg) which derives its name from the fact that in olden days the women walking over the hills barefooted on their way to church at Gairloch, carrying their shoes and stockings, rested at this boulder for a while and put on their footwear here so as to present a proper, neat and dignified appearance upon arriving at the Kirk ; and on the return journey, off came their shoes and stockings again at this spot.

Pity such a custom were not in vogue today ; at any rate it would be better than the pile of empty tin-cans and rubbish lying alongside the boulder today, thrown by our lovers (?) of nature ! I often wonder whether the same people throw their empty cans and cartons of milk under their chairs and tables in their own homes ?

There are many other legends *en route* at almost every tarn and rock. One tarn, into which the defeated warriors in local

feuds were compelled to throw away their arms ; a rock where
two lads were killed and buried by their ruffian uncles, who
brought the blood-stained shirts, to show they had done this foul
deed, to the one who had enlisted their services in the murder ;
but a friend of the two youths stole the shirts, used them in
evidence before the Crown and obtained just retribution ; a
cairn where coffins were laid down when the bearers needed
refreshment ; and the 'Field of Blood' where cattle used to be
herded together and bled, as blood and oatmeal were the ingredients of 'black puddings' then, even as we know them today.

From Tollie Farm (side road) we drop down the steep Croft
Brae to the short river Ewe, to Poolewe lying at the head of
Loch Ewe—a big sea loch. Poolewe is just another small village
with the usual post office and store. The District Welfare Officer
—who lives in Strath—has his office here. He is assuredly one of
the key-men of Gairloch parish. As mentioned earlier, since he
is clerk to the District Council as well, he is a very, very busy
man ; for with his dual duties, his work takes him throughout
the length and breadth of this extensive, 200,000 acres, parish. A
District Nurse is also stationed here. There are two hotels of
fishing renown, excellently managed and where one can relax in
the full enjoyment of peace, good food and, above all, moderate
charges.

Just beyond Poolewe is Inverewe House and Gardens (the
subject of a special chapter later). The estate was purchased by
the late Osgood Mackenzie in 1862, which he transformed from
a bare rocky peninsula—as barren as the barren rocks of Aden—
into the now world-famous gardens, gifted to the National Trust
in 1952.

Proceeding northwards, the road rises high, very high, and precipitous in some parts above Loch Ewe, to Aultbea ('Awltbay').
This is a really beautiful run and a magnificent drop down to
sea-level into the village, with Isle of Ewe in the middle of the
loch, literally beaming at you. Here again, there is in Aultbea
a fine medium-size hotel situated at the water's edge, perfectly
managed and well renowned for fishing, good food and very
reasonable charges.

Isle Ewe, legend has it, is believed to be a haunt of fairies ; and
the folk of Aultbea often said, long ago they saw strange moving
lights on the little island and even heard soft fairy music wafting

across the bay. The tale is told of a whale, smelling the tar of a new boat lying at anchor off the island, came in from the Minch, struck and broke the boat, resulting in the drowning of three men ; and so the belief sprang up from this that whales attack newly-tarred craft.

The pier and tracks of the 'boom' across the mouth of the sea-loch (for Aultbea was a naval base in the Second World War) are about all there is of note here—except perhaps the large community hall (built out of a Nissen hut by the navy) which is complete in every detail ; it has a large stage, tea-room, cloak-rooms and is capable of seating many hundreds of people. The weekly dances there are widely known and patronised, and often a B.B.C. small orchestra comes through to officiate. Conviviality is greatly in evidence ; the very pretty local girls, the Isobels, the Bellas, the Cathies and others lending the necessary glamour ; and for repairs and improvements this small village can easily raise several hundreds of pounds. Yes, much joviality and *slàinte mhaths* prevail each week here ; and very nice too !

Shortly, Aultbea will be extremely busy with the building of new oil-tanks, piers, and so forth ; and this, it is thought, will bring into the village at least 500 men (and their families) involved in this work of construction. So Aultbea will look to being a 'boom-town' in more senses than one !

From here we carry on across another peninsula—or shall we say, neck of land—to Laide, a very tiny hamlet at the southern end of Gruinard Bay, with Gruinard Island facing us and the Summer Isles afar off. There are eight small isles which make up what is known as the Summer Isles ; and the whole provides an enchanting panorama. These Summer Isles were the scenes of much smuggling in the 'good old days'.

There is a lovely little sandy beach and bay a little over two miles north of Laide named Mellon Udrigle ; a nice cooling name too ! On the way you pass Loch na Beiste which long years ago was haunted and inhabited by a monster (the devil) and no walker would ever venture past this evil loch. In order to allay the fears which this legendary beast had upon the local folk, and which the local Free Presbyterian minister failed to exorcise, it was decided to drain the loch. This, however, was found to be too formidable a task, so they resorted to killing the water Kelpie by emptying barrels of lime into the loch ; and nothing further

D

was heard of this 'beastie', only the name of the loch reminds us now of this legend.

Still another piece of legend which is recorded as taking place as late as 1826, and connected with Mellon Udrigle.

It was communion week, miles distant at Clachan church, Loch Broom. All the men-folk of Mellon Udrigle were there, but it was too much of a journey for their women-folk to undertake. These latter witnessed a remarkable sight. The whole sea near Priest Island, situated almost in the middle of Loch Broom, appeared to be filled with warships, and everyone was greatly excited.

They saw the galleys being filled with soldiers and arms and were rowing to the shore as fast as their oars could bring them. One of the women left the crowd and made for her house to bury her jewels and money in the sand out of harm's way. The young girls were told by their elders to take to the hills, to Green-stone Point—which is the tip of the peninsula—as the Redcoats' reputation was very questionable regarding women.

For a long time everyone watched the galleys pulling shore-wards, but strange to relate no boat reached the shore and no soldier landed. It was undoubtedly a vision corroborated by hundreds of witnesses; possibly it was a mirage that accounted for this phenomenon.

In 1914, eighty-eight years later, the Grand Fleet under Lord Jellicoe at the outbreak of the First World War, used this and other nearby bays and lochs for his bases. Possibly what the inhabitants of Mellon Udrigle saw in 1826 was the forerunner of things to come?

Priest Island, one of the Summer Isles aforementioned, is reported to have got its name in a peculiar manner. An Excise officer had been sent to investigate smuggling which was believed to be taking place near Laide. To avoid and throw off detection, he disguised himself as a priest and asked to be ferried across Loch Broom to Achiltibuie; but the boatman, being suspicious, left him on Eilean a' Churich (this island under review) instead, and thereafter returned to the mainland to market the brew. When the illicit spirit had been safely disposed of, the boatman returned to the island to collect the angry 'priest', and that is how this island was called Priest Island, or Cleric Island, to this day.

From Laide and winding our way with the sea close by, we reach Gruinard Hill (Cabeg Hill), which has now been widened and affords easy passage, and we view the wonderful beach of white sand and blue water which on a warm sunny day resembles a tropical lagoon. Further along via Little Loch Broom we arrive at Dundonnell with An Teallach ('The Forge') (3483 feet) towering in the distance. Now we leave the sea and the road we are on is one of the several destitution roads in the Highlands which were built to provide relief during the famine of 1851 ; the Gairloch-Loch Maree road as previously stated was one of the first schemes to be really effective as a measure to provide work, food and money for the practically starving Highlanders. The Dundonnell section to Braemore (at which junction we meet the road from Garve-Ullapool) was achieved through the efforts of Mr. Hugh Mackenzie of Dundonnell, but great difficulty was experienced going through peat-bogs, deep gorges and the like and the track is today still known as Destitution Road. Dundonnell is a popular climbing centre to which climbers come from all parts of Britain.

At Braemore junction, where there was a prisoner of war camp in the First World War, turning left we commence the road up by Loch Broom itself, to Ullapool. A footpath near Braemore Lodge leads to a wooded gorge (now belonging to the National Trust) where you look down 300 feet to the Falls of Measach, also known as the Corrieshalloch Falls ('the dirty corry or hollow') ; a most remarkable defile, the water tumbling over like the 'graceful drapery of a Shetland shawl'. The differing colours of the rocky walls, combining with the silver of the cascade and being themselves in the wooded canyon and chasm below is a spectacle you cannot afford to miss. The extensive Lael deer forest that one passes *en route* here adds a softer note to this wild country. From 1865–1916 the whole of this valley was thickly wooded with larch and spruce, but much was cut during the 1914–18 war ; and has now been reafforested.

A little over 10 miles further along Loch Broom ('Loch of Showers') we are in Ullapool standing at the entrance to Greater Loch Broom with, let us hope, the striking view of the fishing fleet anchored in the bay.

The beauty and splendour of Wester Ross is still to be seen in this village of white-washed cottages and countryside. It is the largest village north of Gairloch, and out to sea like a fleet at anchor (if you will pardon my repeating these words but they are so apt) lie the Summer Isles, already named, and a sunset over these islands can be impressed on your mind for many a long year.

Ullapool, once entirely a fishing village, is first mentioned in the Fishing Acts of 1587, but fishing did not really flourish until the late 1700's. In 1788 the British Fishery Society proceeded to lay out and build Ullapool village as one of their chief stations. They erected a pier and large stores and the village those days was presided over by a Provost, John Mackenzie. In 1847 it was all sold to James Matheson of Lewis for just over £5000; and the fishing flourished for many years bringing many benefits to the inhabitants. Ice was an unknown quantity in this area in those days, so boiler houses were built and the fish partially cooked to preserve it for transport. They were called 'boil houses'.

Herring fishing during the winter months then brought prosperity to Ullapool for many years. In its train came gutters, packers and curers, all requiring accommodation taxing the resources of the village to the utmost.

An interesting yet sad affair took place in January 1905 and I quote from a local paper of that date :

. . . The worst storm within living memory fell upon the village. During the previous six weeks a very intensive fishing had been in progress and never in the history of Loch Broom were such high hopes entertained for a prosperous season. The fishing fleet dropped anchor in the harbour and the crews settled down to enjoy a well-earned Sunday's rest. On Sunday morning a south-east wind sprang up and the crews could be seen putting on extra anchors and chains. By midnight the boats seemed to be riding the storm and the inhabitants of the village went to bed. At 5 a.m. the wind increased to hurricane force—one boat furthest windward dragged her anchor, she came down on her neighbour—and so on shorewards until every boat in the fleet was mixed hopelessly with each other. All with one exception, the 'Isabella' which sank, came ashore on the beach. When daylight broke such a sight met the eye as one never desires to see again ; wrecks everywhere, boats nets, men, buoys, masts in confusion. At the end of Point Street, 'Lizzie' and 'Dragon' of Ardrossan and Glasgow could be seen lying broadside on the sea, waves dashing over them 100 feet high. Next came four fishing boats, then the Pier intervened ; again ten fishing boats, curing smacks, small craft—twenty-five in all, breaking up rapidly. A sorry sight miraculously attended by no loss of life. Towards afternoon five crews signalled they were in danger and must get ashore. Mr Mackenzie, fishery office, assisted by John Maclean, mason ; R. Mackenzie, merchant ; Macdonald, carpenter ; and

A. Macdonald, who constituted the rocket crew, rose nobly to the occasion. The boats' bush rope floated ashore on a hawser while the sea anchor supplied a breeches buoy and two men were taken off in this manner. The coastguard boat was the only one safe and suitable to use in such a sea, but some regulations bound with red tape prevented it being used. Messrs Mackenzie and Macdonald undaunted jumped into the boat and were preparing to effect a rescue when the coastguards, risking a breach of regulations, gallantly took over the boat and proceeded to the scene of disaster. Toole, Scott, and Saunders worked hard and, with spray and sea dashing over their boat, succeeded in saving thirty-six souls ; a very plucky piece of work.

The hardest part of the work now fell on the inhabitants—to house and feed 150 men within a few hours is no easy task even in a village. Mr Kenneth Cameron was equal to the occasion and within a very short time, had board and lodgings and food ready to supply to these men who, tossed all night in a terrific sea, were worn out and soaked to the skin. From Rhidorrach came two hinds, from Inverbroom two sheep and half a cart-load of rabbits, and these helped materially to supply a good meal for the destitute seamen. The damage to boats and nets was estimated at £5000. The Royal Lifeboat Society awarded 30 shillings each and a vellum of thanks to coastguardmen Scott and Saunders . . .

Today the pleasant little white-washed-cottaged-village of Ullapool is no longer historic as it was fifty years ago ; indeed none of these Wester Ross fishing villages are ; the fish seem to be lessening.

So we leave Ullapool down Loch Broom again to Braemore junction, taking, this time, the main road straight on to Garve, 19 miles away. But before finally saying adieu to Ullapool, I would recount the story of an Ullapool worthy who was trudging one wintry day to Laide. In order to remove a lump of snow from the sole of his boot, he kicked his foot against a boulder which became dislodged and started to roll down the steep hillside near Dundonnell. As it gathered speed it collected snow to such an extent that an exceedingly large snowball—an outsize one really ! —landed on the shore of Little Loch Broom. Some weeks later, when the snow melted, two fine stags and a hare were found lying dead beside the stone ! caught in the boulder's rapid descent. Strange the Highlanders with their legendary flair and taste have not called that boulder by some fairy name, but just left it lying by the lochside, unnamed and unsung ?

A few miles south of Braemore which we are leaving and off the wayside is Loch-a-Bhraoin, a fresh-water loch 4 miles long. Here are the graves of Lochaber men who had been cattle-raiding in the strath ; yes, these Highlanders were aggressors, even as there are aggressors today. They were followed by an Ullapool man in the guise of a beggar. When the raiders had supped well and were sound asleep, he snatched a sword which he had hidden under his rags and slew them all but one, the sentry, whom he spared so that he might tell the tale when he got back home to Lochaber.

To Garve again then, along a fine wide macadamised roadway made for travelling at 70 or 80 miles an hour ; across open country passing hydro-electric power stations. Across this wide expanse may be seen, over Direadh Mor, the remains of the old fir forest of Caledonia ; gnarled, bleached and twisted tree trunks, roots and branches showing white in the peat dykes where they have been bleached by wind and rain. Another legendary story is that the dense fir forest which in effect covered the whole North of Scotland years ago, and was a shelter and habitation for wolves and all manner of wild beast, was destroyed by fire, for many of the tree roots and trunks which have worked themselves through the peat show signs of charring by fire. The tale goes that the forest was destroyed by a Danish princess, named Donan, who was sent by the King of Denmark to destroy all these pine forests so that he, the King, would have the sole, and of course bigger, market for himself and his own grown timber.

We stop for a while at Aultguish Hotel for a nice homely tea ; past the great Strathvaich deer forests, into Garve.

At this point we have made a 'grand circular tour' as the coaching firms would advertise ; Garve, Achnasheen, Loch Maree, Gairloch, Poolewe, Aultbea, Laide, Gruinard, Dundonnell, Ullapool—and Garve. There is no more to travel in this vicinity hinging on beloved Gairloch ; no more to be said, unless it be 'will ye no' come back again' to this majestic country, which, though solid in character, alters it shape and scenery so frequently every day in consort with the weather's mood ; and to those who venture the long journey here, above latitude 57° and between longitude 5° and 6° I would say we have plenty of weather ! However, wet or fine, there is no harm in saying *Slàinte Mhath* ?

CHAPTER 9

SKYE AND PRINCE CHARLIE

IT may be asked what has Skye and Bonnie Prince Charlie to do with the main theme of this book, which is pivoted around Gairloch, on the mainland ?

The reason is simple, for I look out on to Skye as I write ; to the Cuillins and the 'Old Man of Storr'—a conspicuous obelisk of black trap-rock rising sheer 160 feet high ; the Storr rock itself rising to a height of 2400 feet above sea-level. It seems only a stone's distance away ; and appropriately enough my house is called 'Skye View'.

'*Eilean A'cheo fo Sgail Nam Beann Mor*—or 'The Isle of Mist under the shadow of great mountains'—that is the Isle of Skye described in the native Gaelic language of its people. The late King George VI called Skye 'the isle of kind and loyal hearts'.

Almost the whole of the north-west of Scotland (and the many islands) is charged with history ; but with Skye, not only history, but highly romantic history too ; that and the Cuillins with their practically world-renowned jagged knife-like peaks climbing upwards to the clouds, never dropping below 2500 feet. There are some 15-odd peaks in the Skye Cuillins over 3000 feet in height ; and surrounded by a bodyguard of lesser peaks they form a unique panorama unparalleled anywhere in the British Isles. Corries and wild mountain passes abound. The highest is Sgurr Alasdair (3250 feet) ascended from the wild but beautiful Glen Brittle. Not far distant, at the head of Loch Scavaig is the most weird and awesome loch that any country can boast of— Loch Coruisk. Sir Walter Scott immortalised it in *The Lord of the Isles* ; and on a rock nearby, chiselled out his initials. Loch Coruisk has been extolled by artists and poets alike. Its waters are dark and deep. All around are the grim Cuillin mountains ; and here desolation reigns supreme ; desolation upon desolation.

You cannot reach Skye by either rail or air. You *must* travel 'over the sea' to Skye ; a beautiful island about 50 miles long and about half that across, and it forms part of Inverness-shire.

It was first mentioned by Ptolemy in the 2nd century. St. Columba arrived in Skye in A.D. 565. Danes and Norsemen ravaged most of the Western Isles in their time. In 1098 the

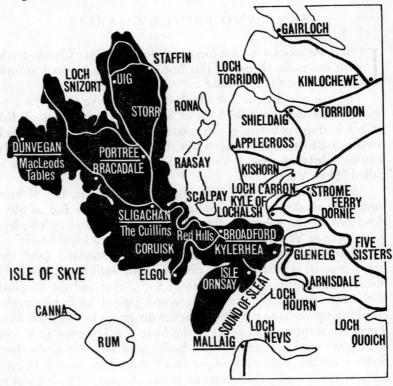

Norsemen occupied Skye for a considerable period ; but in the 12th century the son of Gillebride, Celtic Lord of Argyll, turned them out and became First Lord of the Isles. His grandson, Donald, was the first of the Clan Donald, and thereafter the MacDonalds, MacLeods and MacKinnons ruled Skye, being independent of the Scottish Crown. After King James V's visit to Skye in 1536, the Skye chiefs gave their support to the House of Stuart. They fought for King Charles II in 1651, and for King James VIII in 1715. When Prince Charlie raised his standard at Glenfinnan on 19th August 1745, he counted on the support of the Skye chiefs. But only the aged chief of MacKinnon was loyal. Later on he paid the penalty, for his lands were forfeited and his Clan scattered to the ends of the earth.

Except in the south of the island, Skye is really treeless. It enjoys, like Mull, very mild winters ; the islanders are mostly crofters, some enaged in weaving beautiful cloth, sweaters and the like, at Portnalong on the west side even to this day.

The usual gateway to Skye is across the ferry from Kyle of Lochalsh—the railway terminus completed in 1898—to Kyleakin, a matter of minutes only. From London one travels from Euston via Perth and Inverness to Kyle ; from King's Cross, via Edinburgh (or Glasgow), Fort William to Mallaig.

This latter town, a fishing and curing port mainly, is on the mainland, and by arranging with MacBrayne's steamer service there, one can take one's car across to the south end of Skye, to Armadale, where there is a really fine substantial large pier.

Mallaig is approached by a lovely run of some 50 miles, shortly after leaving Fort William. The road follows the railway closely all the way, and is almost unmatched for its combination of mountains, moor, loch, glen and coast scenery. You also pass Glenfinnan (aforementioned) ; the monument—now vested in the National Trust—was erected in 1815, where Prince Charles raised his father's (James VIII's) standard that fateful day of 19th August 1745, at a rally of the Cameron and MacDonald Clans, under Lochiel and Tullibardine. He had come to remove George II from the throne and place his father there—as had his father tried thirty years before.

Armadale, just mentioned, has a fine castle, the modern Gothic seat of Lord MacDonald, open to the public during the summer season. Armadale is called 'the Garden of Skye' ; its southern exposure and protection by the near mainland, and the lofty isles of Eigg, Rum and Canna save it somewhat from the ravages of the winter gales ; and there is a 'Riviera' feeling in the air on a soft summer's day.

The little village itself is clothed in tall trees, interspersed with the ubiquitous birch, giving it a very English look along the narrow roadway.

Journeying inland, up to Broadford, and making for Portree— 'the King's Port', the name being a corruption of 'Port-an-Righ', a title given when King James V with his fleet anchored there in

1540—capital and only town really of Skye, you pass Knock, where the remains of the old castle of the Lords of the Isles refuse to surrender to time or tempest. This whole area is known as Sleat ; 'brindled Sleat of the beautiful women'.

The quickest route of course is by Kyle of Lochalsh ferry ; in 1961 these spacious ferry-boats took over 192,000 passengers and 67,000 motor vehicles. Altogether, from all quarters, 218,000 people crossed 'over the sea to Skye' ; and 70,000 motor vehicles. Substantial figures surely.

Coming up from the south by the Caledonian Canal, one invariably takes the 'Road to the Isles', turning off at Invermoriston on the canal ; and to Lochalsh it is 56 miles. This road was originally constructed by General Wade. For myself, I consider a prettier way is to turn off the Canal lower down, 7 miles before Fort Augustus, at Invergarry, taking that road, meeting the one from Invermoriston at Cluanie Inn, and carrying on to Shiel Bridge at the head of Loch Duich—surrounded by the 'Five Sisters of Kintail', which form part of the Kintail estate, a National Trust Property, of 15,000 acres.

Near Shiel Bridge was fought the battle of Glenshiel on 11th June 1719 in which General Wightman's government troops defeated 2000 Highlanders—mostly MacRae's and Mackenzie's. The Highlanders were led by the Earl of Seaforth and assisted by a few hundred Spaniards who had landed from Loch Alsh from two frigates ; the remains of a storm-tossed fleet of thirty vessels sent from Cadiz by Cardinal Alberoni, to help the cause of the Old Pretender. The Spaniards surrendered, but the Scots escaped to the hills.

Travelling on to Dornie, a magnificent run, you then look down on the ancient Eilean Donan Castle—the Earls of Seaforth— which in 1932 was restored by the MacRae's. The Castle, on an island connected with the mainland by a stone bridge (but it can be reached by the shore at low tide) is a striking picture, set in magnificent surroundings. Once a stronghold of the Mackenzies, it was held by Spanish forces when British warships destroyed it in 1719.

Thence onwards passing Balmacara, where you can see the Cuillins rising grey in the distance—over the waters of Loch Alsh, you see the Sound of Sleat weaving a sea-quilt of green and purple, and you speed up and over the hill to Kyle of Lochalsh, where, if you stretch your arm out, you feel you can almost touch Skye.

As we are at Lochalsh and before taking the crossing over the ferry to Skye it is fitting to refer to this busy port as well as making mention of a very short, but pleasant run to Plockton.

The great Ptolemy appears to have recorded the existence of Lochalsh as far back as the 2nd century.

Lochalsh originally formed part of Argyll (not Ross-shire as today) along with the neighbouring parish of Kintail ; and early in the 18th century one half of that parish was split into the parish of Glenshiel and the 'Five Sisters'—those notable mountains above Loch Duich—were transferred by Parliament from Kintail to Glenshiel. Be that as it may, they are still known and spoken of as the 'Five Sisters of Kintail'.

In the 1200's Lochalsh was held by the Clan Matheson, whilst Kintail was inhabited by the Mackenzies. For many centuries, rivalry and intrigue existed, and in the early 1600's, Lochalsh was dominated by the Mackenzies of Kintail. Eventually Lochalsh came into the hands of Sir Alex. Matheson, Baronet of Lochalsh.

Early in the first quarter of 1800, Matheson went out as a young man to India, joining the firm of Jardine, Matheson & Co. —a firm which expanded and still functions as such, but more so in Hong Kong.

In 1801, the last Lord Seaforth sold Lochalsh to Sir Hugh Innes, whose descendant, Mrs. Lillingstone, became owner. She in turn sold out to Mr. Alex. Matheson.

Elsewhere I refer to the extraordinary prophecies of the Brahan Seer (born early in 1600, be it noted) and in connection with Lochalsh, I give the following prediction he made some 200 years before the event ; viz. : 'The day will come when the Mackenzies will lose all their possessions in Lochalsh, after which it will fall into the hands of an Englishman, who shall be distinguished by great liberality to his people, and lavish expenditure of money. He will have one son and two daughters ; and after his death, the property will revert to the Mathesons, its former possessors, who will build a Castle on Druim-a-Dubh, at Balmacara.'

So much so for the prediction.

Well, the late Mr. Lillingstone was an Englishman. He was truly distinguished for his kindness and liberality ; and he had a son and two daughters. After the death of his wife, the whole of Lochalsh came as noted above, into the hands of Alex. Matheson, so fulfilling the prediction. A castle was built, but at Duncraig, not so very far, really, from Balmacara.

I give yet another and astounding prediction by the Seer concerning Lochalsh, viz. : 'A Lochalsh woman shall weep over the grave of a Frenchman in the burying-place of Lochalsh'. Here again a native woman of Lochalsh did marry a French footman, who died and was interred in the burying-ground of Lochalsh, thus leaving the widow to mourn over his grave. Truly extraordinary. In those far-off days it should be remembered that a Frenchman in Lochalsh, and a Frenchman whom a Highland woman would marry and mourn over in the Brahan Seer's day, was a totally different set-up from the present day.

Reverting to Matheson and his voyage to India, he returned after about fifteen years to his native Highlands. He spent money in improvements of Lochalsh and other lands in Ross-shire, building Duncraig Castle, near Plockton. Since his death in 1886, the estate naturally changed ownership on several occasions. The present baronet is General Sir Torquhill Matheson who formerly resided at Duirinish Lodge, but now lives in Camberley, Surrey. The proprietors of Lochalsh are the National Trust.

The population of Lochalsh given at the last census in 1961 is 1800. Just over 150 years ago it was 1300. The population of the three parishes of Lochalsh, Glenshiel and Kintail in 1961 was 2264.

The railway was firstly laid only as far as Strome Ferry—on the south bank ; boats sailing up Loch Carron connected with the railway, taking and bringing passengers to and from Skye and Stornoway.

It was only in 1898 that the old Highland railway was extended to Kyle itself. Here again I record another remarkable prediction of the Brahan Seer's, viz. : 'The day will come when long strings of carriages without horses shall run between Dingwall and Inverness, and more wonderful still, between Dingwall and the Isle of Skye'. Over two centuries later, that prophecy was fulfilled. Truth is stranger than fiction, to be sure.

This train journey is equally as picturesque as motoring, for always there appear many and varied scenic vistas as the Iron

Horse rounds the several bends. One moment one may be
looking at the majestic Cuillins ; another, back at Loch Carron
and the mountains of Applecross ; and again at one moment
looking out to sea at the Isle of Raasay with its flat-topped,
volcano-type, Dun Caan.

There is one main street in Lochalsh, as in a number of these
Scottish towns and villages ; and it is a narrow street as visitors
will doubtless soon realise and walk with caution in these days of
such endless streams of motor-cars, lorries and buses.

As we pass out of the town (inland) approaching the next
small scattered crofting village of Badicaul, we look out to sea to
that imposing island, Crowlin. Then onwards following the
main roadway we come to the village of Erbusaig (a 7th-century
hamlet), another beauty spot of the west, where one can still see
peat stacked near each cottage and sense the smell from peat-
reeking chimneys. Shortly afterwards we take the minor road
off to Plockton, passing another old-world village, Drumbuie,
and then to Duirinish : situated on the river bank and overlooking
this village is Duirinish Lodge, mentioned before. In the 1400's
a serious dispute arose over Duirinish between the Chief of the
Clan Matheson and Lord Sutherland ; and in the resultant battle,
the latter was killed. Matheson was arrested, taken to Edinburgh,
found guilty and was beheaded.

Leaving Duirinish we soon reach Plockton, which long ago
was engaged in boat-building. It is a charming, picture-postcard
village, nestling on the sheltered inlet of Loch Carron. From the
War Memorial on a hill above the village, one obtains a wonderful
panoramic view of lochs and hills and of Duncraig Castle on the
far horizon.

Plockton has a fine old school, and above the Gothic doorway
the Arms of the Mathesons are carved.

We must needs return from Plockton by the same road back to
Duirinish ; then forking left we soon rejoin the main road to
Lochalsh and/or Balmacara and beyond.

This little 'circular tour', Kyle—Plockton—Kyle is but 12 miles
and should certainly not be missed ; for it is a 'must' for visitors
to Kyle and Skye. Lochs, moors, heather and hills unaltered in
their pristine glory.

The strait at Kyle is only half a mile wide. We cross at last to Skye and land at Kyleakin on the old stone pier that has withstood the storms of centuries.

As we land at Kyleakin, we see, on the left, the ruins of Castle Moyle, said to have been built by a Norse princess who married a Mackinnon. Mary was her name, and it was built to exact tolls from passing ships. The princess constantly pined for her Norwegian home, and when she died she was laid to rest on the mountain top, so that the winds from her homeland might waft gently over her grave. The name of the hill has been given Beinn na Caillich—The Old Woman's Mountain.

Now having reached Skye, with a population of 7765 according to the 1961 census, what briefly are we to put down in our diary that we must see, within a matter of say three days—for our American friends cannot spend too much time, you know !

We go to Portree, the capital of the island, with a population of a little over 1000 ; its ancient name I have already given. It has a fishing fleet, woollen factory, large hospital and the mail steamer is domiciled there. It sails daily at 8 a.m., except Sundays, for Raasay, Kyle and Mallaig, returning each evening to the little port on which the village looks down from the surrounding heights ; and this proves to be a most interesting day's outing.

Portree occupies a good position in Skye, as coach services radiate from there to all parts of the island. It was at Portree in one of the rooms of the Royal Hotel, facing the harbour, that Prince Charlie said goodbye to his preserver, Flora MacDonald, on 30th June 1746. In St. Columba's Episcopal Church there is a beautiful stained-glass window, dedicated to the memory of Flora MacDonald.

Taking at first a small tour north of Portree one goes by the Old Man of Storr, Staffin—where there is a youth hostel, bathing beach and cliff scenery. Overlooking here is the famous Quiraing with the sharp needle-rock as well as other fantastic chaotic pinnacles. The Table of the Quiraing is a grass-covered platform several hundred yards long.

Then on, passing Flodigarry (where Flora MacDonald had her first home after her marriage) to the northerly township of Kilmaluag and the fragmentary ruins of Duntuilm Castle, the ancient seat of the MacDonalds of the Isles. This has a wonderful site on a cliff overlooking the sea and must certainly have been impregnable as a fort from all attacks by sea. It is a fortress proclaiming its proud history, the joy and sorrow of the great chiefs and clan activity, the brilliant scene of war and peace. Near by is the ancient burial ground of Kilmuir, the 'Relig Mor' of the MacDonalds, where Flora MacDonald, that owner of a proud name in Clan and Highland history is buried. A fierce wind generally blows over this old churchyard. Flora MacDonald's son erected a marble tombstone over her honoured grave. The slab of marble, conveyed by boat to Skye, was cracked in its journey but it was placed in position, but only after a few months the stone base alone remained. Pilgrims to the grave had taken away fragments of the stone—sacred relics from a dearly loved shrine. A large granite Celtic cross was then erected, but the Atlantic gales blew it down and shattered it. But the head of the broken Cross still lies on her grave ; and a restored Cross now exists as a landmark far out to sea.

The Cross bears the inscription

Flora MacDonald,
Preserver of Prince Charles Edward Stuart.
Her name will be mentioned in history ; and if courage and
fidelity be virtues, mentioned with Honour.

Across the grave is a granite slab bearing the following words :

Flora MacDonald
Born at Milton, South Uist, 1722
Died at Kingsburgh, Skye, March 1790.

Near by is Port Kilbride, where Flora landed from Benbecula with the Prince, disguised as her maid, 'Betty Burke' on 29th June 1746 ; further on, coming southwards on this peninsula known as Trotternish, back to Portree, there is Kingsburgh House, where Prince Charlie had refuge and where in later years Boswell and Johnson were entertained by Flora and her husband on 12th September 1773. It is said Dr. Johnson occupied the very bed in which Prince Charles had slept.

The morning following the Prince's arrival, Flora visited his bedroom and took a lock of his hair (which is still treasured at Dunvegan Castle as I mention later). After that she took the sheet in which the Royal guest had slept. The Skye heroine later on took it to America and brought it back to Skye ; and when she died—two years after the Prince's death—it was her shroud.

In the afternoon Flora and the Prince set out for Portree, where as I have said she bade him goodbye. It is said when she lay dying, a smile came over her face as she breathed her last, saying, '*Criosd's Ailean's Tearlach Og*'—Christ, Allan and young Charles. A sad, sad story.

From Kingsburgh we return on our tour to Portree ; a run of some 40 miles.

The next tour (about 50 miles) would be from Portree to Dunvegan and back by Bracadale and Sligachan. Though these mileages sound insignificant compared with distances on the main motorways of Britain, yet owing to the narrowness of the roads, to say nothing of the hundreds of blind corners and bends, it takes one many hours to travel it all in comfort ; besides there are so many stops to make ; so much scenery to drink in and admire.

In this northern area of Skye there are great stretches of purple moorland, queer mountains and rocky cliffs ; of hardy, kindly, quiet crofter folk and historical places of Clan and Scottish interest.

From Portree then, for Skeabost Bridge, and inner Loch Snizort ; onwards skirting Loch Greshornish, another loch flowing into the bay of Loch Snizort. Further on, one comes to the Fairy Bridge, where one road going north serves the peninsula of Vaternish, via the village of Stein. This is a Norse name. Such characteristics are to be found in plenty in Skye (Skeabost and Carbost, to mention but two). King Haco and his fleet must have visited here as well as Kyleakin.

Carrying on northwards (it is well to see this Vaternish or Waternish area and then return to Fairy Bridge) the land grows fierce and wild. At Trumpan can be seen the ruins of the church that saw the massacre of the MacLeods by the MacDonalds of Uist, who in their turn suffered heavily when their boats could not escape because of the ebb-tide. It was in this parish that the MacLeods, sorely pressed in clan-battle, waved their fairy flag and saved the day. And as I soon record, the flag is to be seen this very day in Dunvegan Castle. It was originally captured from the Saracens and is supposed to be possessed of special virtues.

Retracing the 10 miles to the junction, the Fairy Bridge, we continue for a few miles when we reach Dunvegan, and its world-renowned castle lying at the top of the loch bearing its name. All roads lead to Dunvegan ; the castle standing on a rock, where it stood a thousand years ago, is the lure.

This castle and Glamis Castle in Angus are the two oldest inhabited Scottish castles. Dunvegan is the home of MacLeod of MacLeod ; and Dame Flora MacLeod of MacLeod, D.B.E., is the present chief of the Clan MacLeod. She has travelled the world over in the interests of her clan, never sparing herself, constantly speaking for and upholding her great big 'family'— strengthening the bonds of kinship which unite MacLeods everywhere. No Scottish clan has a more romantic or exciting history than Clan MacLeod ; and today no clan is more active—as a clan—than the MacLeods.

The story is told hundreds of years ago of one of the first ever MacLeods who had a hump and a long beard, as though he had swallowed a horse and stuck on the tail ! This ugly MacLeod, in his endeavour to perpetuate his race, tried to woo the three daughters of Lochiel ; the eldest flatly refused him, so did her next sister ; but the youngest and prettiest said, 'there never was a mound or a hump but had a sheltered side to it' ; and she married him and so the MacLeods today are as plentiful as midges !

Dunvegan Castle is so pre-eminent, that in Gaelic it is spoken of always as 'An Dun'—the fortress ; similarly the loch is always referred to as Loch an Duin. It is supposed to have been built in the 9th century by a Viking named Began. During the latter part of that century Norse colonies were founded in different parts of the Hebrides, and like many other Highland families the MacLeods are of Norse descent ; the founder of the clan being Leod, son of a Norse ruler. Of all the heroic figures of the Clan MacLeod, perhaps none remain so persistent in memory as the 25th chief, Norman, who ruined himself financially in saving his people during the potato famine of 1846-48.

The keep—the 11th-century sea-gate—and the lower part of the tower are all that is left of the original castle. The fairy tower dates from 1490.

It is a venerable building of various periods, looking, as Dr. Johnson commented when he spent a week there, 'as if it had been let down from Heaven by the four corners, to be the residence of a Chief'.

Although today the Castle has been greatly reconditioned and is in first-class modern order inside, it still presents a proud defensive front to the beautiful bay. It has come to be regarded as the Buckingham Palace of Skye.

Originally it was a traditionally Highland keep, surrounded by ramparts ; water on three sides ; ghosts on all four sides ! The great chief Rory Mor is still associated with its character, and his two-handed sword is there, a mighty weapon on the corridor wall. The fairy flag (already alluded to) is safely and religiously preserved in its glass case. It is a small square piece of very rich creamy-coloured silk—one time of course much larger—and on it are crosses wrought in gold thread, and several elf spots stitched with utmost care. This flag is supposed to have the power, on being waved, of saving the clan from three great dangers. It has already been waved twice ; at the battles of Glendale and the Stony Dyke.

The past of Dunvegan dominates the west of Skye ; it is the Iliad of Skye—a saga in stone.

There are many treasures to be seen in Dunvegan Castle ; Jacobite and St. Kilda relics. There is a very rare 'Amen' toasting-glass bearing the inscription, 'Donald MacLeod of Gualtergil in the Isle of Skye. The faithful Palinurus. Anno 1747.'

Palinurus was Aeneas' steersman in that Latin epic and the inference must be to Donald's aid in ferrying Prince Charlie from place to place in the islands and in assisting in Flora MacDonald's passage.

There is also a lock of Prince Charlie's hair. I may say I have come across so many alleged 'locks of Prince Charlie' in so many different parts of Scotland, even down to the border country, that I should imagine by the time the lovable Prince left these shores he must have been on the bald side !

There are many beautiful large-sized family portraits by Ramsay and Raeburn hanging carefully on the walls, and in these days of destruction of big family houses, Dunvegan stands unique in its hopeful, helpful future as a real home for the Clan Chief. For nearly seven centuries now, the MacLeod family have held unbroken occupation of this Castle. The appointed successor to the Chieftainship is Dame Flora's twin grandson, John MacLeod, who, in the summer of 1961, had been filling a principal role in a film of the Misty Isle. He portrayed a romantic young hiker who is keen to learn all there is to know about 'timeless' Skye— the isle that is a mixture of the modern and the old. The local 'lass' who paints a picture for him of Skye, is Fiona, the pretty young wife of the proprietor of one of Skye's hotels. The film is a documentary, in colour, and is mainly for showing abroad to boost still further the attractions of the Isle. Crofters, weavers and fishers all play a part in the film.

Trust Dame Flora, that indomitable charming 84-year-old Scotswoman, Skye's greatest emissary, to always be 'upsides' in the advertising of Skye! :

> Dame Flora with so many world-wide relations
> Would do well as a member of United Nations! . . .

Looking down from the towers, one sees a panoramic stretch of moors and mountains. The green MacLeod's Tables are the Norse-named hills of Healival Mhor and Healival Bheag and high from the ramparts can be seen the hills of Harris. Further on, the famous township of Glendale, the home of owner-occupier crofters—the scene in the past of Land League revolt with crofters' security of tenure as the prize. In this area is Boreraig near the northern tip of the peninsula known as Duirinish, the home of the famous MacCrimmon pipers, hereditary pipers of the MacLeods, where there is a memorial cairn erected in 1933 to this famous school of piping maintained here in the 16th, 17th and 18th centuries. They held their land of MacLeod by tenure of their piping. The course lasted seven years and the student had to learn by heart nearly 300 tunes.

Returning now from Dunvegan (visitors are admitted to the castle every afternoon except Saturdays and Sundays from 1st May to end of October) one makes for Sligachan via Loch Bracadale and its two arms, Loch Harport and Loch Beag, embracing another peninsula, named Ullinish. Passing along the north shore of the loch one sees the little crofting township of Struan. Then the majestic Talisker Head stands out on the coast-line. The far western isles of Barra and South Uist again seen from the head of the moor road joining in from Portree to Struan. The main road continues inland until it reaches the head of Loch Harport, a branch road leads down to Carbost (another Carbost is near Skeabost aforementioned) on the south side to the famous Talisker distillery. This name Talisker surely hangs 'peaty' on the tongue and lingers on the ear. The distillery is set in a lovely part of the country, miles away, it would seem, from anyhere ; everything there is so perfectly quiet, peaceful and restful. I paid a visit there three years ago and looked with great enjoyment to being shown round by the manager and sampling a little of the distillery's product and when he met me getting out of my car, I felt sure I was in for a pleasant and 'absorbing' morning. All was going well, when suddenly, looking out of his office window, he espied a car drawing up with his directors in it and already disembarking! He exclaimed to me that 'we'd had it' or words to that effect; and that he would not be able to show me round or even offer me the hospitality of a 'Talisker'. Shaking hands, however, I said, with a knowing wink, 'I'll be back'—and back will I go one day! Before coming into Carbost is a road leading to Glen Brittle, the road that winds through rolling machair till it reaches the foot of the Cuillins, giving another view of these famous hills. This area is now being gradually afforested, and the traveller has new relief to the eye in the stretches of plantation surrounding Eynort, where new hope in the reopened school has been given to an area that was before a depopulated hinterland.

Arriving at Sligachan we turn northwards the 9 miles to Portree; the same road we came along when we first put foot in Skye at Kyleakin ferry.

Sligachan is, to all intents and purposes, the hub of Skye. Roads and paths branch from it in all directions. On the south of the river a path leads up Glen Sligachan. Here Prince Charlie came one day in July over 200 years ago, his companion being Malcolm MacLeod. He tramped along this desolate glen on his way to Elgol and the sea. From Sligachan one has a wonderful view of Glamaig (2537 feet high)—a Vesuvian-type of conical mountain; and with the sun rising behind this monumental mass of nature, the effect is terrific.

These quick journeys just enumerated have—in essence— 'done' Skye. Skye remains an unspoiled island to be sure, and as I have said—and it bears repeating—its people are quiet and kind, and the Cuillins majestically awesome. 'When day wears to the gloamin'' one likes to relax and be cushioned in comfort and care, no matter how romantic or beautiful the surroundings. I feel sure Skye has these attributes—comfort and care—and more.

Yet let it not be forgotten Skye has had its full share of poverty and famine just as the mainland had. The potato famine of 1846-48 was more severe on the islands than on the mainland. When the Laird of Gairloch planned the road-makings around

Gairloch, Loch Maree, etc., hundreds of Skye men came over to Wester Ross to find work ; for the MacLeod's fortune then was at a low ebb.

Skye has in the past given much to the British army. It is said during the early years of Queen Victoria, 666 officers, 10,000 private soldiers and 120 pipers enlisted during a space of forty years. There are hardly that number living in Skye today ; but if and when the call comes, the active men of Skye will be there.

The crofters—the backbone of Skye—are now receiving direct help and encouragement from the Crofters Commission, as well as from Skye's own social council. The subsidies that agriculture in general is obtaining, have done great good to the small-holders, and now special loans and housing improvements of a capital nature are being administered by the Department of Agriculture. These, together with the wonderful work of the North of Scotland Hydro-Electric Board in bringing light to the majority of the crofting townships in Skye, have enabled the crofters to have and enjoy every modern convenience ; and it is only right they should, not only in Skye but all over the Highlands ; for the advent of electricity helps the housewife in her labours and it is well known for years and years she has had a hard, a very hard struggle and existence in having neither light nor water 'on tap'— that and living in primitive low dwellings, the rough thatch of which is weighted with stones, just to help keep the roof on !

This then, briefly, is 'Eilean a' Cheo' ; and to quote Alexander Nicholson :

> Jerusalem, Athens or Rome
> I would see them before I die ;
> But I'd rather not see any one of the three
> Than be banished for ever from Skye. . . .

And now, I would record the principal dates and journeyings relating to our Bonnie Prince Charlie who is so linked up with Skye romance and his Outer Hebrides exciting journeys, so that our visiting friends can—at a glance—trace these important details of history (and mind you they are important historical details) without having to search high and low, here and there, for 'where did he go from here ?'

Good judgement, or bad, the ''45' will always stir the heart

of man though many other well-planned and successful cam-
paigns are long forgotten. The 'cause' is now a thing of the
far-off past ; the 'ifs' and the 'buts' are buried long ago.

The inspiration of that romantic adventure, from the raising
of Prince Charlie's standard at Glenfinnan until after Culloden, is
found in poems, songs and ballads over the past 200 years. The
adventure will *never* die.

Prince Charles Edward Stewart or Stuart (Bonnie Prince
Charlie) first set foot on British (Scottish) soil on the Island of
Eriskay, south of South Uist, in the Outer Hebrides on the 23rd
July 1745, spending the night with his seven companions (known
as the 'Seven Men of Moidart') in a cottage. Before he came to
England he had consulted a soothsayer who had told him he
would win the English crown if he killed the first living creature
he met in Scotland. When he landed that fateful day on Eriskay
there chanced to be a beautiful shapely young maiden milking
her cow, and she came along with milk to the Prince. He took
it, thanked her and went on his way. One of his followers at
once said to him 'That was the first living creature you met and
you didn't kill her as commanded by the prophet'. 'No,' said
Prince Charlie, 'I did not. Not if I lost the crown and my head
with it would I have killed her.' Hence, according to the seers,
that was why he never became King ; and thus 'it came to pass.'
He was only 25 years old.

On 25th July 1745 he landed at Borrodale on the north shore
of the loch (south of Morar) from a French frigate, the *Du Teillay*.
(He was later, on 20th September 1746, after spending five months
since Culloden as a fugitive in the Highlands and the Hebrides
with a price of £30,000 on his head, to be taken off again at the
same spot by another French vessel, the *L'Heureux*, fourteen
months later in fact.)

He thus passed through Borrodale twice, sailing thence for
Benbecula (26th April 1746) and landing there from Skye on
10th July 1746.

From 25th July 1745 he gradually travelled the road to Glenfinnan where he raised his standard, 19th August 1745.

The monument there today—a wonderful monument in a
wonderful setting, too magnificent to describe in words—as I
have previously mentioned has inscriptions repeated on the walls
surrounding the pillar in Gaelic, English, Latin and French, to

commemorate the generous zeal, the undaunted bravery and the inviolable fidelity of the men who lived and died for Charlie.

> Let them tear our bleeding bosoms,
> Let them drain our latest veins,
> In our hearts is Charlie, Charlie,
> While a spark of life remains.

The fiery cross had summoned the clansmen to Glenfinnan. With the MacDonalds of Clanranald, the seven men of Moidart, Prince Charlie rowed up Loch Sheil to Glenfinnan to await the Camerons and others who joined to see the Marquess of Tullibardine raise the white, blue and red silk standard proclaiming James III of England and VIII of Scotland. And so it all commenced. Can you visualise a more inspiring, romantic setting ? For my part I cannot ; and once you see Glenfinnan for yourself, I am certain you will agree and more than agree. It is 'splendiferous' to coin a word.

From Glenfinnan he wended his way south towards Fort William on 28th August 1745. He carried onwards achieving a notable victory at Prestonpans over General Cope, 21st September. When he occupied Edinburgh the Prince made Holyrood his headquarters from 17th September to 31st October 1745. He reached Jedburgh, on the borders, on his way into England on 6th November 1745.

We all know his invasion was checked, and on his retreat from Derby, early December 1745, it is recorded he lodged at the County Hotel in Dumfries on 21st December 1745. Continuing his retreat he vainly besieged Stirling Castle early 1746. At Falkirk, 17th January 1746, he obtained a victory over General Hawley on his northward journey.

Then came Culloden ; Culloden Moor, 16th April 1746, where the fate of the House of Stuart was sealed. At 1 p.m. Prince Charles's 5000 to 7000 Highlanders, tired and hungry, were engaged by 9000 Government troops under the Duke of Cumberland, the third son of George II. The battle lasted less than half-an-hour, in which the Highlanders lost 1000 dead, and another 1000 or so in the subsequent flight. The English killed amounted to less than 100. Prince Charlie spent the day after Culloden at Invergarry Castle, later that year burnt down by the Duke of Cumberland.

Thence came, as I have said, five whole months of wandering trying to evade British capture—which of course he did.

From Culloden the Prince wore the clothes of his guide and travelling companion, Edmund Burke, and on 18th April this band of four, Burke, O'Sullivan, O'Neal and the Prince himself set out going southwards towards Loch Morar and reached Meoble the following day, rested awhile and then made for Lochailort, south of Morar and Arisaig, where, as always, Prince Charlie was expecting news of his followers ; and particularly from his friends in France. His party remained here four days, receiving sad reports from his scattered followers, news of further losses and little hope of any possible strong rally. There was no alternative but to leave Scotland, saddened and dejected, and as soon as it could be managed despite reports of continued patrols of the western coast by King George's ships and soldiers.

Charles thought of Skye as a safe haven until a French ship could pick him up and carry him back to France.

On the night of 24th April 1746, the Prince and party put off in an 8-oared boat from Loch nan Uamph, a sea-loch below Arisaig, and safely landed in Benbecula, at Rossinch at the south-east end of the island on 27th April. Owing to a heavy storm, they were unable to leave Benbecula till 29th April for Stornoway. They were blown far out off course, eventually landing on the shores of Loch Seaforth, some 20 miles south of Stornoway, which distance they had to walk.

They were not to be long in Stornoway, for the townsfolk were greatly alarmed and so, on 10th May 1746, the Prince, who needed no publicity—far from it—set sail again ; once again for Benbecula, still escaping the pursuers. (Scalpay, an island at the mouth of East Loch Tarbert—off Harris—was also a frequent refuge for Prince Charlie during his wanderings between 27th April, when he arrived at Benbecula from Borrodale, and 28th June, when he left with Flora MacDonald for Skye.)

From there to South Uist, Glencoridale 15th May—5th June. This hide-out at a forester's cottage was most acceptable, and although scores of the islanders knew of the Prince being in their midst, none would sell the secret, even for £30,000. (In those days this amount of money—in English gold—was truly 'worth a million'.) In South Uist, 2 miles north of Askernish on the west side of the island, and 5 miles west of Lochboisdale, the island's steamer port, is the village of Milton where are the ruins of Flora MacDonald's birthplace ; and it was in a hut near Ormaclett, 3 miles further north, that she first met Prince Charlie and agreed to take him over to Skye.

The Prince's party left Glencoridale on 14th June and made for the island of Wiay, off the south-east coast of Benbecula. Here they stayed four days, then back to Rossinch, Benbecula again for two days, only to be pursued by English men-of-war, but with luck they managed to get to Lochboisdale (South Uist) two days later. However, they were still living every hour in great danger, so decided to return to Benbecula once more. But with one companion only, O'Neal ; and this was on 24th June 1746 ; and it was here, in South Uist this time, that he first met his new preserver and companion (if only for a brief while) in his travels, Flora MacDonald, who was then visiting her brother and was due to return to Skye.

Should he now leave the Hebrides—where he was known to be—and risk adventure on the Isle of Skye ?

With government forces all around, Flora, who was an artful woman, landed herself in a guardroom until released by an officer known to her family, not before she had obtained a pass for herself, her maidservant, and an Irish woman helper by the name of 'Betty Burke' whom she said she was taking to her mother in Skye. The plan succeeded, and Prince Charlie became 'Betty Burke' disguised in clothes obtained for the purpose.

The party then left Benbecula and set course for Skye.

> Speed, bonnie boat, like a bird on the wing,
> Onward! the sailors cry.
> Carry the lad that's born to be king
> Over the sea to Skye.

As fate would have it, a French ship called in the South Uist area to pick up the Prince ; but he had just left.

That night, 28th June 1746 was, as usual, a stormy one when they set sail at 8 p.m. making towards Vaternish Point—the north-west tip of Skye. They arrived safely on the shores of Loch Snizort near Kilbride. 'Betty Burke' was left on the shore sitting on her baggage whilst faithful, artful Flora went to Monkstadt House to see her friend Lady Margaret MacDonald, through whose goodness she obtained a safe conduct for her Prince to

Kingsburgh House, some 14 miles south close to the shores of Loch Snizort Beag (the inner loch of Loch Snizort proper).

At Kingsburgh House he rested and was nursed by Flora, and was soon on his way again, disguised still, until they reached Portree. Here he discarded the 'Betty Burke' rig-out for the clothes of a Highland gentleman ; and it was on 30th June 1746, in a room at an Inn (now the Royal Hotel) that he bade a fond farewell to Flora MacDonald, with hopes of meeting again. He gave her his miniature and repaid a small sum of money he had borrowed from her, then cautiously left. But that reunion never took place. He set off with a small party in a small boat from Portree, crossing the waters of the Sound of Raasay to friendly, young MacLeod of Raasay, arriving there on 1st July 1746. Poor Flora, and I am sure all our hearts go out to her ; as I quote from the *Lament of Flora MacDonald* :

> She looked at the boat, which the breezes had swung,
> Away on the wave, like a bird on the main,
> And aye as it lessened she sighed and she sung,
> Farewell to the lad I shall ne'er see again.

It has been said in later history that the 'Prince' was not worthy of such devotion. He saved his own skin, but never remembered the woman who risked so much to aid his escape. Ah ! well ; such is life.

From Raasay, Prince Charlie roamed between Skye and the west mainland, always in hiding. August saw him at Glen Cannich the furthermost point reached in these 'wanderings'.

In September news reached him of the arrival of the French ship *L'Heureux* at Loch nan Uamh, near Borrodale again where he had landed just over a year before. That ship took him away to France, with a legend, on 20th September 1746.

He arrived in Scotland a man young in years, and young in outlook ; 6 foot tall, brown of eyes and with rich brown hair.

He left a bedraggled fugitive—with a price of £30,000 on his head ; but as we have read, none would sell their souls for 30 pieces of silver, let alone of gold. Had there been a real Quisling among any of the Highlanders, he would have been an easy prey. But even though a number of them refused to help in the campaign—and some even fought against him—*none* would ever think of handing him over to the Redcoats. Such was the Highland race. And one island in particular, whose population is predominately Catholic, cherishes his memory to this day—Benbecula ; where the army today has a rocket range established.

Thus ended the abortive, inglorious episode of the Jacobite rebellion of 1745 ; and of Bonnie Prince Charlie.

Charles Edward Louis Philip Casimir, to give him his full name ; 'Charles Edward, Prince of Wales, Regent of Scotland, England, Ireland, and the Dominions thereunto belonging' ; the Young Pretender (son of the Old Pretender James Francis Edward Stuart, son of James II of England, who in turn was the 2nd son of Charles I, 1633–1701, deposed in favour of William of Orange 1688 ; the Jacobites so-called being adherents of James II after he abdicated the throne) was born in 1720 and was only 25 years of age when he hoisted his colours at Glenfinnan in 1745 (19th August) ; and subsequently died a dissolute wreck in Rome in 1788 ; and was buried in the Cathedral Church of St. Frescati.

He was a Catholic, and when he landed in Scotland, all the Catholic priests of the Catholic glens became his most enthusiastic recruiting agents. Bishop Hugh MacDonald, Vicar-Apostolic to the Highlands, blessed his standard at Glenfinnan for the battles to come.

I suppose when he landed, so young, with good fresh looks, beaming and bounding with energy and enthusiasm, everyone—chiefs and womenfolk alike—fell for his 6-foot debonairness ; that, and the cause, cemented everything and everybody and one can well picture the shouting and uplifting of the claymores and swords, staffs and cromags, as his standard was unfurled that day of August 1745. But for Fate, would British history have been differently written.

Whenever thinking of the events of 1745 and the romance associated with the Prince, Flora and Skye, my mind turns to the sad farewell in that room on 30th June 1746—now well over 200 years ago, where one of the world's greatest romances tottered and came to grief.

I have been in that reputed room and can vividly picture the memorable scene ; a low room with a wealth of oak beams around. It was a wild stormy night, raining as rain can fall only in Skye ; it would be midnight or the very early hours of the morning. The Prince, 'my Prince' in Highland garb, 6 foot of immaculate Stuart tartan dress, with the ribbon and star of St.

Andrew across his breast (6 foot of chivalry that any lovable woman could fall for), fortifying himself with many drinks, whilst his men outside would be begging him to leave at once for the small boat lying at the jetty, with its bow pointing Raasay-ways. Not that any 'local' would touch a penny of the huge golden reward offered for his capture, but there was always the chance of a stray Englishman—a Hanoverian—coming in out of the drenching rain seeking room at the Inn. Nevertheless he tarries, for he cannot drag himself away from these precious moments with the woman he loves ; though all the while their keen ears are literally fastened to the heavily hinged oak doorway listening for any treads on the creaking stairway boards ; and in such a tense and historic atmosphere he pours out his love as few but Frenchmen can. Truly a heart-rending scene.

With much embracing and re-embracing he would beg of her to remain faithful to him and the 'Cause' and again and again praise her wonderful bravery, above all giving thanks to the Higher One who had brought them together.

The minute hand of the old clock would loudly tick on in the spluttering candle-light ; his men outside becoming more and more restless ; smilingly, yet tearfully and heavy in heart, Flora would beg of him to be ever watchful and that when he got safely back to France—as surely he would—to get in touch with her at once. She would come to him despite all difficulties ; nothing would stop her ; nothing ; for he was her soulmate and she worshipped and trusted him utterly and completely ; many waters or distances could never quench their love. He must know that, she says. He in turn would have said he would come back again, that he was still young in heart and in years, and one day he would welcome and escort her to St. James's Palace.

Giving her his engraved miniature, begging her to keep it always in her bosom next her heart and taking his small 'piece' as well as some brandy to nourish and warm him across the waters he finally bids her goodbye ; a long, lingering goodbye—a fare-well that lovers' lips, and only lovers' lips, can bestow so passion-ately on each other. She 'abandons' herself with desire and ecstasy as he holds her tenderly in his arms. It is touching and aching ; she on her part thinking all will and *must* be well, for are they not in love ; and that she will be journeying to France later. But he, on his part fearing the worst, feeling he will never return, never see her again ; that she was only a passing episode in his crowded historic path—just another stepping stone maybe.

He treads lightly and cautiously down the stairs never looking back, and she, Flora, holding the candle aloft, watches his every movement, and finally gently shutting the door of the Inn, he vanishes into the cold, unlovable night. She hears his footsteps tramp down to the sea and the boat drawing away.

What an emptiness ; what a void ; what an anti-climax to her super-human efforts in her aid to his escape ; but what an honour, and what a feeling of Regal pride and joy in knowing she, of all people it was who had come into Prince Charlie's life— her Prince ; her Charlie ; her lover—as indeed he truly was.

> Royal Charlie's now awa,
> Safely ower the friendly main ;
> Mony a heart will break in twa,
> Should he ne'er come back again,
> Will ye no' come back again ?
> Will ye no' come back again ?
> Better lo'ed ye canna be,
> Will ye no' come back again ?

There was no return ; no reunion ; not even a letter. She was forgotten, dismissed, 'rubbed out'. Romance had peeled off, so to speak ; Bonnie Prince Charlie was ripped of his glamour. It is really very sad.

If only that door were to burst open again with her Prince to reappear a few years (or even many years) later what an episode, what an historic event would have been written and recorded, as he rushed forward, clasping his Flora (still wearing his miniature around her neck) to his arms and murmuring, as he tenderly kisses her, '*ma chére, je t'adore*'.

Och, aye ; better lo'ed ye canna be ; will ye no' come back again ?

I would have liked it that way myself ; the typical fairy tale ending, despite what changes in history would have resulted ; but then I am of a romantic disposition.

Of Prince Charlie's many battles and wanderings, Culloden comes uppermost to one's thoughts. Culloden put an end to the '45 organised rising—it put 'finish' to the hope that the Stuarts would ever be Kings again. It was not, however, the end of

Highland bravery, loyalty or self-sacrifice ; nor was it the end either of slaughter, suffering and humiliation.

Culloden is a name of tragedy for countless Scots, a day— 16th April 1746—of futile sorrows echoing down the centuries ; the last war fought on the soil of Britain. The battle and its significance can only be matched by Waterloo, Dunkirk and El Alamein. It is the story of Scotland's saddest defeat.

'*Bliadna Thearlaich*', the Highlanders called it—Prince Charlie's Year 1745. It was indeed! After Culloden the wearing of Highland dress was forbidden by law ; the clan system in the old familiar sense—namely, a 'family', not a social hierarchy, was completely shattered by merciless measures. Glens were emptied by deportation or emigration. By the rigidly repressive Acts of 1746 and 1748 the old ties of clan kinship were cruelly broken. Henceforward until 1782, except by stealth, the tartan was unseen in the hills and glens, where before it had been the people's pride and joy.

It is fitting to record the chief of a Scottish clan is entitled to wear a crest badge surmounted by three feathers. It is the practice, however, for chiefs to allow their followers to wear the crest and motto in a silver strap-and-buckle badge. The plant badge of a clansman was a sprig fixed to his staff, spear or bonnet. It acted as a distinguishing emblem ; but there is ground for believing that it was used as a charm, like an amulet or talisman.

In 1782 the Duke of Montrose fought nobly for the repeal of the hated Disarming Act and was successful, but there was no immediate enthusiastic return to the tartan and the kilt. The old attachment to the Highland dress had died in a generation. The old patterns were forgotten ; so was the skill of making the dyes from the herbs on the hills. It was not until forty years later, towards the middle of the 1800's that a romantic interest in High-land dress was reborn. During this melancholy period the oppressed Highlanders dourly and silently endured their wrongs, brooding upon the loss of their ancient heritage ; but powerless. Gradually, and after the turn of the 19th century, Clan Societies grew up and multiplied in the New World and in Colonial Britain ; then slowly wherever Scotsmen dwelt, the sympathetic feeling of kinship was kindled and the tartan became symbolic, not of the Highlands alone, but of Scotland as a whole. And that is as we know it today.

It was savage legislation indeed, for, to the government, a Highlander was looked upon as a savage from the remote regions of Scotland. There were plunder and killings long after Culloden. Cumberland (the bloody butcher as he became known) started a reign of terror to subdue the Highlands for ever ; a veritable dictator, with one obsession 'suppression'. All this made way for the 'Clearances', in which hundreds of thousands of clansmen were banished, 'that a degenerate lord might boast his sheep'. Then the sheep went too.

Such was the aftermath of 'Charlie's Year'. Misery for the Highlands ; abject misery.

Today the site of the battle is marked by the cairn erected in 1881 by Mr. Duncan Forbes. The cairn is built of rough stones and stands 20 feet in height and 18 feet in diameter ; and on it is the following inscription :

THE BATTLE OF CULLODEN
was fought on this moor, 16th April 1746
The graves of the gallant highlanders
who fought for
Scotland and Prince Charlie
are marked by the names of their Clans.

The burial places of the various clans are denoted by the stones upon which the name is engraved, whilst those Highlanders who were interred irrespective of sept or clan, were buried in trenches, the inscribed stone stating whether the grave is that of any particular clan, or the resting place of members of several clans who fought under one standard.

There is a lot in a name, and Culloden carries a wealth of meaning. The legend of 'Bonnie Prince Charlie and a' that' can never really, in this age, hope to survive the misery and horror of this last battle in the north, still less the aftermath of sadistic infamy.

With the abortive night-march to surprise the Duke of Cumberland's camp, there was foot-slogging, misery and frustration and bickering between the chiefs. Prince Charlie's army was distraught, rations non-existent, and they were out-numbered and out-gunned. The slaughter of the wounded, the mutilation of both dead and living had a bloody-minded perpetuation. Stench-laden prison ships, river hulks, distant gallows and scaffolds, pestilence, survivors slave-shipped to the Carolinas—all this testified to the completeness (and let it be said, degradation) of the Hanoverian victory.

Yet legend tells of Jacobite triumph in defeat !

Whatever else, certainly no situation, political or otherwise, has been preserved in poetry and song as that of the Jacobite rebellion. One of the most beautiful is 'MacLean's Welcome', from which I extract a few lines :

> Come o'er the stream, Charlie, dear Charlie, brave Charlie,
> Come o'er the stream Charlie and dine with MacLean ;
> We'll bring down the track deer, and doe from the glen

> And the loveliest Mari in all Glen McQuarry
> Shall lie in your bosom till break of the day.

Nearly 220 years ago the Clan MacLean offered everything to Prince Charlie ; venison, drink and women. Such 'rewards' have been given the favoured ones in history since time began ; and so it will continue.

I have mentioned the 'bloody-ness' of the Duke of Cumberland ; and after the battle the butchery not only commenced but continued. More than half the Prince's army were slaughtered whilst lying wounded in the field.

There is the story told of a Highland officer who, wounded, still retained his proud bearing even in front of the victorious Duke. The Duke commanded a major of his—a Major Wolfe—to shoot the Highland scoundrel. The English officer, with all due respect to the Duke, refused to do so and said he would forfeit his commission rather. The Duke then got a common soldier to carry out his order and shoot the wounded Highland officer where he lay.

Thirteen years later, on 15th September 1759, that same Major Wolfe—then General Wolfe—stormed the Heights of Abraham and captured Quebec ; an outstanding victory in the annals of British history as we all know. He was, however, mortally wounded in the victory ; and strange though it may be—even stranger than fiction—Wolfe fell into the arms of the son of that self-same Highland officer whom the Duke caused to be 'murdered' in cold blood at Culloden.

Yes, the traditions of centuries lie buried at Culloden, but eventually this defeat *did* bring Highlands and Lowlands together to weld the Scottish nation as we know it once again. But the mention of Culloden makes for sad reading, and for sad thoughts.

And so I come to the end of Skye, of Bonnie Prince Charlie, of Culloden and of the Cuillins : the black Cuillins with their peaks pitted against peaks ; and in the early morning shafts of light, grape-blue in colour and still (always still) frightful, stupendously awesome ; so much so that with the dawn and the rising sunlight one feels a sense of 'gasp' at a sight which in certain aspects is 'out of this world'. The very names of some of the peaks—given them by the Vikings of old—speak of thunder and the God Thor—such as Sgurr nan Gillean, Sgurr Mhic Coinneach, Sgurr Ghreadaidh and Sgurr Alasdair (already named). Truly Skye stands alone, for Nature made it so.

We must not forget Skye is also THE land of the pipers of all Scotland, the MacCrimmons. This family is supposed to have been descended from the Druids, and to have been of Royal Irish line. One of the Irish Kings was Crimithan ; and there are some today who believe the MacCrimmons were descended from that King. There is popular tradition that the first of the MacCrimmons was brought from Italy to Skye by the Macleod of the day on his return from a crusade in the reign of King Alexander of Scotland ; and that the name MacCrimmon is derived from Cremona in Italy, the piper's birthplace.

The piping college of the MacCrimmons was known as the *Oil-Thigh*, and it was at Boreraig, about 6 miles north-west of Dunvegan in the Duirinish peninsula, that this college was situated, as I have remarked earlier. In the 18th century they gave diplomas to their successful students. On such diplomas were drawn a picture of Dunvegan Castle, the galley of the Macleod and various musical instruments.

When in 1745 the Chief of MacLeod decided to support the Hanoverian King, many of the clansmen refused to follow him, but Piper MacCrimmon put duty to his chief before anything else. He went into battle with a heavy heart knowing he was to be on the side of the butchers of Glencoe. He was to fight against kinsmen who were supporting Prince Charlie ; and he could never return to Skye with their blood on his hands. He knew he would never return ; his 'second sight' told him that. He plays farewell to Dunvegan for ever ; and his words to his piping go down in history as follows :

E

Farewell to each cliff on which breakers are foaming ;
Farewell, each dark glen, in which red deer are roaming ;
Farewell, lonely Skye, to loch, mountain and river ;
Macleod may return—but MacCrimmon shall never !

The MacCrimmons, hereditary pipers to the Macleods, have gone ;—their pipes remain.

At Dunvegan Castle is preserved the renowned *pìob ballbhreac* —or Speckled Pipe—said to have belonged to Padruig Mór MacCrimmon.

Yes, Skye is steeped in legends, romantic and otherwise. As remarked later on in this book, in the wintry months, when everything is at its loneliest, you can sense a Viking stepping out in front of you on the road or hillside with an uplifted sword, like the highwayman in far-off English days. The roads have tales of magic, of water Kelpies, of boys kidnapped by fairies, of boys killed by witches, of fairy bridges and of fairy cattle. You will see the small strongholds (or round duns) in which the inhabitants of those days took shelter from the Norse pirates, when they were seen coming in from the sea. Surely great days !

So we say, not farewell, but au revoir to the Isle of Skye—the Isle of Mist. For as likely as not we will return there again—and yet again.

Better lo'ed you canna be.

There is an ancient belief that if earth and sea were swept away, there would be seen written on the basic rocks of Skye the name of Macleod.

As a special note for visitors, the Skye Provincial Gaelic Mod (Festival of Song) is usually held in the month of June.

'Skye Week'—a programme of sports and entertainments throughout the island—is usually held the last week of May; and the Skye Highland Games held in Portree on the last Thursday of August; a wonderful spectacle and well worth coming a thousand miles or more to see.

CHAPTER 10

FISHING AND SHOOTING—WHISKY
AND HAGGIS

THESE four 'exports' have helped to make Scotland famous the world over ; the impulse at certain seasons of the year for the Englishman to come up to the Highlands to try and kill a salmon, shoot a stag and taste some real haggis, but probably above all, to drink the whisky which he says always tastes so much better when you sip it in its natural surroundings. If you take it with water I agree, but up here it is taken neat, and as soon as it is poured out you put your palm over the glass to keep the flavour in ! Whisky comes from the Gaelic '*uisge-beatha*' (water of life), and without good water there can be no good whisky ; and should you want to add water to your dram, then you want to add the water, the glen water, from which the whisky you are drinking is made ; you want the 'tang' so to speak, for what is the use of spoiling a fine whisky in alien waters ? And after a few rounds one is better able to talk about the monster that got away ! There is certainly an atmosphere in some of these *small* Highland hotels, and I lay emphasis particularly on the 'small', that seemingly cater for fishing and shooting. You are met at the front hall by masses of rods, lines, Wellington boots, and macs, all thrown anywhere, and further on, lying on the oak table, look upon the kitchen tin-plates with their glistening, speckled trout lying side by side—sardine fashion—the product of one of the visitors' proud catch that evening or early dawn. You all look at them to the sound of a babbling burn running round the hotel side, weaving up some story about them ; that that one must have taken some landing ; and that one, isn't it a beauty ; and you feel you need to know and talk to the lucky fisher in public. The other poor guests will then think that you must know a lot about fishing, talking to the distinguished angler of the day ! 'Well chaps, come along and let's have one'—and to the bar we go—and we may then overhear the facts that more would have been caught but the weather was too wet, or too dry, or too windy, or too calm. There are always plenty of excuses banded about. Not enough ripple on the loch, or too much ; or a Southern Belle motor coach passed at the time you were just about to land one, and the thirty-five or forty Lancashire loud-throated trippers let out one mad cry—and away went the fish.

Nowadays it seems the fashion to draw attention, in most of these hotel adverts or boards, to the fact of there being a 'cocktail bar'. To my mind I think this is quite out of place up in these Highland hotels set amidst and against the great wild tracts in Wester Ross. Why they have not kept to the old 'Dispense Bar'-sign days I cannot imagine. Who wants gaudy, flashy, cocktail bars with continental flavours, chromium fittings, etc., akin to the smartest slick ones in Piccadilly, and a smart Alec of a barman talking with a Cockney accent, dolled up in tartan trousers ? And with some futurist designs daubed on the walls that put the query to you—are you looking at them the right side up ? And even little aquarium fish tanks thrown in to add to the spectacular, with angel-fish floating around in bewildered circles ! Angel-fish, mark you, amongst the Bens and the Glens. And all set, as I have said, cheek by jowl as it were against grim but beautiful Loch Scotachinvar and Beinn Pibroch !

It is all out of place ; yet some managers and directors think it is all part of 'selling Scotland'. You can get all that at home (just like the iced cakes and swiss rolls for afternoon tea). No need to travel up 500 miles or more for that sort of atmosphere. No, George, you're overselling it all.

Then later in to dinner. We who do not fish, but are just spending a lazy healthful holiday there, will be eagerly expecting a real nice juicy trout coming along. Oh no ! they seem to have mysteriously disappeared behind the scenes somewhere. Once 'on view' the glory seems over, unless of course you—the angler responsible—particularly earmarked and labelled one of the catch for yourself and you alone, which I'm told is rare. Then as you come out of the dining-room you whisper to your girl friend, or wife or whoever might be with you, 'There they are ; that's the party who caught the fish ; bet they're enjoying them'. If you did but know !

Yes, these salmon and trout are wily fellows ; they have instincts just as we have. Such animal wisdom speaks volumes for some invisible Creator, who infused instinct into otherwise helpless little creatures ; and it all makes one think deep down at times that our Universe has been—and surely must have been—designed and executed by some profound Intelligence ; but how and when is so frighteningly unexplainable.

Examine this 'instinct'. The young salmon spends years at sea, then comes back to its own river, travelling up the very side of that river into which flows the tributary where he was born. What brings him back so precisely ? If you transfer him to another tributary he will know at once that he is 'off target' and will fight his way down and back to the main stream and then turn up against the current to finish his 'destination home' more accurately. There must be some hidden power ; truly the firmament sheweth His handiwork.

It is a fascinating story, full of intrigue, starting from the egg, a tiny red globe which lies buried in the gravel bed. From the egg he lives in the dark off the yolk-sac attached to him. The sac finished, he pushes his way out of the gravel, barely an inch long, and as he grows very slowly he may only be an ounce or so or a few inches long after two years there. One day the impulse seizes him, and all his compatriots, and they start down-stream to the sea, and when they taste the salt water they head out to sea and vanish, no one knows where. Yet he comes back, maybe in one or maybe in five years' time, but he comes back to the mouth of the river in which he was hatched. He will now be some 18 inches long and weigh 8 or 10 pounds ; should he have been away at sea longer he may be 40 to 50 pounds and strong, very strong. He carries on to his birthplace and never stops to feed, surmounting waterfall after waterfall. Before a salmon leaps over a weir and up a waterfall it judges its height by eye. The Freshwater Fisheries Laboratory at Pitlochry are studying the behaviour of the salmon very extensively. They pair off eventually, and when they reach the right bed the female swims close to the bottom, turns on her side and fans violently with her tail, digging a trench a foot or so deep, and expels her eggs, whereupon the male covers them with milt as they sink to the bottom of the trench. They are covered over, and then new trenches made and so the fertilising goes on, the female laying up to as many as 20,000 eggs. In due course the eggs come to life and the whole cycle commences again.

Recently government research into the spawning habits of salmon has provided a new and fairly accurate method of calculating the number of eggs the fish will lay, and it should now be possible for anyone who knows the lengths of female salmon going up-river to spawn to estimate, with a very good degree of accuracy, the number of eggs these fish will lay. The number of eggs in the ovaries of female salmon has been obtained and worked out on an average according to the size of the fish, and so the fertility of the salmon has been studied almost to a fine art.

On the journey up to Gairloch, and just passed Contin, a few miles before reaching Garve, one passes the Falls of Rogie (near the Quarry) a famous beauty spot. You can walk through the trees and in about ten minutes' time you come to a magnificent natural waterfall, and when it is in full flow you may watch, fascinated, the salmon hurtling out of the lower pools, up into the high torrent in this urge to reach the spawning grounds beyond. Some of the jumps the fish have to make from one pool to another above them may be as much as 10-foot sheer, and they make it in one mighty leap. These Falls are a veritable rockery of nature's own making, the waters tumbling down in a musical cascade.

The majority of the men of Gairloch and Badachro were, and are, fishermen. The two sea-lochs of the parish, the Gair Loch and Loch Ewe, abound with fish of some description. Very briefly the season and catches are as follows : February onwards, saith; March and April, cod; haddock in June and herring May to Christmas (now only to be found near the Outer Isles); crabs and lobster May to Christmas, and these are not so plentiful. If only six or eight are caught at a time, the boxes are sunk in the sea and filled up each day as more are caught, and then when a full box accumulates, packed up, loaded on to local carrier to Achnasheen and thence per passenger train to Billingsgate, London. Until near the end of the 19th century oysters were found about the heads of Gair Loch and Loch Ewe, but today they are, of course, unknown.

Fishermen are very superstitious, especially those from the east coast. Should any relative of the Captain's die, the boat is painted black the next time it goes in for an overhaul. There is never any whistling on board a fishing boat, or mention by name of salmon or rabbits—it is considered unlucky—and the crew would not go to sea if a minister should come down the pier and attempt to put a foot on board—it would be thought an omen of real bad luck and they would catch little fish. Should it be seen that a minister was coming along, they would send a wee boy, with a penny, to affront him and be cheeky or even swear at him, so delaying the head of the Kirk—as he admonished the boy—coming alongside.

Yes, these men have their own ways of thinking and believing; and you never see a fisherman without he is wearing some sort of a hat or cap or bonnet. You'll never catch any fish unless your head is covered!

As regards SHOOTING, well, we all know of the crowded trains going northwards on the eve of the 'glorious twelfth'—Grouse, 12th August—and of the fantastic efforts of someone or other (doubtless 'the other', a poacher) to rush the first grouse of the season down to London on the 11th, to be there on display 6 a.m. on the morning of the 12th; and at a fantastic price also.

Yes, there is much paraphernalia involved in the entourage connected with this 'glorious twelfth' business. There's the gamekeeper, the beaters, the loaders, the guns, the cartridges, the shooting-sticks, the dogs, the food, the drinks, the ice for champagne, the glasses, the flasks (not only of coffee but of brandy), the shooting-brake, the Mercedes-Benz and the party itself—particularly the womenfolk all dressed up for the part in tightly knitted sweaters—proclaiming without any doubt that they *are* women— mufflers and of course slacks. Some of these 'feminines' should look in the long mirror before setting out just to see if slacks really do suit them ; 'turn around' darling and see for yourself!

We're off, and by jove what a shoot! Everything laid on ; nothing left to chance, and you return to the 'big hoose' so proud at bringing down so many brace with so few shots. Ah well! that's that ; a glorious day and someone is paying for it—a glorious price no doubt. But who cares ? So long as it's not you who has to foot the bill!

And at night, during the house-dance supper interval, and you're sitting on the stairs with your host's attractive daughter, apologising for your poor dancing, saying, 'I'm a little stiff from Badminton, you know', to which she looks up at you with her blued eyelids and mascara lashes, her eyes full of 'you', and says, 'I don't care if you're a big stiff from Badachro' ! And you carry on telling her of the days you were out in Ceylon and ask 'where have you been all my life', then raise your unsteady hand and drink to her health in Pimms No. 1 ; and you spin the old yarn, sitting closer as you spin it ; then putting on more airs to impress, say, 'for years I've had a month amongst the Cairngorms in June, and a month in Wester Ross in September when the heather is at its best ; but this next year I'm having a change.' 'Yes,' says Mairi (for that's her Christian name of course), 'there's nothing like a change ; where are you going next year then ?' 'To Wester Ross in June and the Cairngorms in September,' you reply ! *Slàinte !* and you both ' *Slàinte* ' ; and then with the dance ended, the butler begins to switch off the lights, and the sheep commence to herald in the dawn, you mount the wide two-way staircase, holding on to the balustrade, and turning the handle of your appointed bedroom, hold her in your arms and kiss her goodnight in the one and only 'glorious twelfth' fashion. Ah, me ! you say, if only this glorious twelfth was every day— and every night ! It would then be worth fighting for, let alone shooting for !

Grouse exists naturally in certain parts of the Midlands and North of England, but his true home is Scotland. All attempts to rear and keep this little game-bird on the Continent have failed. The grouse pines away and dies outside of Scotland.

The golden eagle that has its home in many parts of the Highlands is a killer of grouse—the killer that the law protects in fact ; and recently some hard words have been given vent to in the Highlands as to the law concerning the protection of wild birds.

The golden eagle is a beautiful bird—but a beautiful bird of prey. It is thought there are close on 300 pairs of eagles in Scotland—protected—and it is calculated that each eagle accounts for one grouse a day ; and in the nesting season, far more. One case can be cited, and which was confirmed by camera, of nine grouse in an eagle's eyrie one day, and two days later, thirteen.

The grouse is esteemed as the best game for the superior flavour of its flesh ; there is more of a 'tang' in it than in partridge (1st September) or pheasant (1st October). This latter bird, of course, has got what the others have not—a glorious brilliant plumage. The cock pheasant is a perfectly lovely bird—too lovely to kill. There is one, with its mate, that often frequents my home in

a rural village of Yorkshire, and to see them strutting about the
lawn and under an 80-year-old yew hedge, in the very early hours
of a morning with their young—which on one occasion numbered eighteen, there must have been two families I am thinking!
(a 'Nye' of pheasants is, I believe, the group term)—is surely a
spectacular sight.

There is something 'out of this world' to go into a small hotel,
where the kitchens are so near the hall and dining-room that you
can smell what's-a-going-on, and to sniff the cooking of a dozen
grouse. You don't say 'Bisto' then ; you just come out with a
long 'ah'. Yes, I hark back to the small personally owned and
run hotel again as I consider *they* catch the Highland atmosphere
far more than the starry palatial hotels. At least mine host, or
mine hostess, will oblige you should you arrive late ; whereas if
you 'roll up' in an expensive Rolls car, or even a Mercedes-Benz,
obviously with money to spend, to a 'starry' hotel, and after
signing-in on separate forms that still seem to have a war-time
link, wanting to know your nationality (a wonder they don't ask
for your date of birth and if you're married!), and ask for something to eat with your long-awaited dram, you are told (though
it be only 10.5 p.m.) that 'sorry there is no one on duty ; the
still-room is shut and I haven't got the key', you feel as though
you will score out your signature, collect your bags—which are
still lying at your feet where you dragged them in from the wet
night (as there was no night porter)—and storm out to find another
and more homely spot. 'No night porter?' you say ; 'well
there is one according to the motoring book'. 'But you see,'
says the same couldn't-care-less clerkess with the peeky nose and
the shrug of the shoulders we all know so well, 'there's a shortage
of staff. Fellows and girls won't come up here ; it's too lonely ;
there's nothing to do at nights : no pictures, no dancing ; no
nothing' (as though *she* would want any night-life!), 'and the
local lads, oh! they're just a lot of houghmagandie Johnnies!'

And that all too familiar saying—it must be historic by now—
meets you sooner or later if you want anything. 'I'm sorry, I'm
busy and I've only one pair of hands and the hotel is booked full,
right up to the attics!' Yet you don't see many folk about! You
don't want to know about their worries. You've travelled 500
miles or more to get away from your own worries. No, these
starry hotels may be all right at times, but gradually you get to

know where the small really homely ones are—and you make for them, passing the big ones *en route* and as you do so, politely raising your hat and saying sarcastically, *Slàinthe Mhath !*

I have known a nice little guest house even, that kept a full-course dinner for two of their visitors until 11.30 p.m.—11.30 at night mark you—as they had gone over to Skye for the day and on getting back to Strome found there was a four-hour delay. This is true, for I was there. I know, when I had finished that full meal and coffee close on midnight, I would have called the landlady and her daughter in, bade them sit down near the warm peat fire, and toasted them and their good house with Glayva liqueurs all round (*Glé-Mhath* ; very good) ; and silently have told all those at that lustrous starry hotel to go and climb trees and branch off !

I am generally amused at some of the notices hanging in the Reception/Cashier offices at these star hotels. One in particular took my attention, reading, 'Have you left anything?' and when I paid the bill I looked at the notice, making the girl look round too, and said it should read, 'Have you anything left ?'

The DEER is an animal that cannot be left out in writing of the Scottish Highlands, for the red deer is indigenous to these northern parts. There are so few obstructions it is possible for these wild beasts to roam from the north of Caithness to the south of Argyll. The antiquity of the red deer in Gairloch itself is substantiated by their cast-off horns having been found deep in peat bogs, where they must have lain many centuries.

Deer stalking holds all the elements of eternity. Fishing is a brisk sport compared with this crawling, whispering vigil. Deer stalking is the crowning glory of the shooting season. I am told it is an arduous and absorbing sport.

There are a number of deer forests within easy radius of Gairloch : one across Loch Maree at Letterewe and another fine forest a friend of mine has between Garve and Ullapool, near Aultguish Inn—Strathvaich, in extent 25,000 acres.

From a recent survey it was estimated that Scotland has a deer population of about 150,000, occupying about six million acres. The marking of new-born calves with ear-tags is being tried out, and the coding of same can be read from about 100 yards, and at even greater distances, for their colour alone can give useful information in establishing the rate of growth of these animals, when they start to breed, and when they die of natural causes ; for up to now there is not sufficient known about the life of a deer, herd movements and how long they live.

To be a successful deer-stalker you must be a keen sportsman of athletic frame and hardy habits, with perfect eyesight, and be capable of covering 20 or more miles a day over the roughest of rough ground. Suitable clothes are important ; clothes that match up to the nature of the ground over which you are shooting. And of course you must sport a deer-stalker hat! now much in evidence at the various Highland weaving shops you come across in the Highlands. Known as a 'fore and aft'!

The greatest possible caution is required ; any false move in your approach may wreck your 'stalk'. Notwithstanding all your carefulness it may sometimes happen that the suspicious stag gets an alarm from a previously unseen sheep that has strayed into the forest, or from a crowing grouse, or a frightened mountain hare, or even from an eagle. You have to approach your quarry by such a route as not to be visible and that no breeze may convey your scent to the wary animal.

In fine weather the biggest stags are to be found on the highest hills ; in wet weather they are on the lower slopes. They move up wind when they feed. Your keeper must take due credit for any successful shoot. A good keeper has an unlimited and intimate knowledge of the habits and habitats of game. He has to be successful with dogs, and humane too, preventing any unnecessary suffering to the beasts that might arise in the course of the chase.

An interesting—and maybe in time, a serious—matter came to my notice in talking with the head keeper of Letterewe Estate, Loch Maree. They are subject there to a very heavy rainfall, between 80 and 100 inches a year, and, with strong winds coming across the Atlantic from the west, a certain amount of radioactive fall-out had been discovered in the livestock, in the thyroid glands of both sheep and deer. A very small lump, the size of a pea, seemed to form. A careful watch is being kept on this matter and investigations are now being carried out as to this 'activity' occurring, it is thought, from the large number of nuclear experiments being made by the Americans in the South Pacific.

In this Land of Venison, where, in some of the 'Deer' hotels innocent stags heads gaze down on you in the hall with such imploring eyes, you, who are not a stalker, feel acutely 'out of it'; afraid to talk of such sport for fear of using the wrong technical phrases (I do know you 'kill' a salmon, not 'catch' it ; as for a deer I think the term is that you are a 'slayer'!). You have venison for lunch, venison for dinner and venison sandwiches for your packed teas. Personally I am not partial to it, even with red-currant or rowan jelly ; it seems too lean a meat with little taste, but my Strathvaich friend and Member of Parliament tells me if it is cooked slowly and in a special way, it is *par excellence*. So far I have yet to find out what this special way is !

I am now back at the hotel dining-table and venison the main (and often the one and only) course is served me by the waitress as though she was offering me her complete dowry. Poor girl, if she did but know ! Then at the next table I hear the one-time Lieutenant-Colonel say to his wife (who, bearing a yellowish complexion through her make-up obviously denoting she and her hubby had spent the best years of their lives in India—Poona, no doubt) 'that was a beautiful beast my dear, a 12-pointer' (that's a 'Royal' you know ? No ? Well a stag which has twelve points to its antlers is called a royal, but a royal head is not necessarily first rate ; oh! no ; the best heads are distinguished by their wide spans, thickness and long points of the antlers and length of horn). But who am I to say all this. I should leave it to the officer-commanding at the next table to recall all that happened in the chase. 'Yes, a beauty, and we'll have his head stuffed when we get home, and hang him up in the porch of the Manor, my dear, for all to see and hang their hats on ! Stalked him for five hours you know ; then, blow me down, the wind changed ; he smelt us and we had to alter our line of approach. Another cherry-brandy dear ?' In the end, yes, there he is, hanging on the Manor wall ; poor old Charlie-boy, he's called. Truly 'The stag at eve had drunk its fill'.

A good stag is generally 8 to 10 years old at least ; and they are usually in condition for killing between mid-August and mid-October. Roaring begins towards the end of September, and a week or so later most of the older stags are out of condition. There is no close time fixed by law for killing stags.

Three mild winters increase the deer population ; but one bad winter after three mild ones may result in a 25 per cent loss in population. It is not generally recognised what a big factor a mild or severe winter can be to the deer population.

A stag casts its horns every spring and it is said the hinds eat the old horns. They—the hinds—have only one calf a year, about June. In the case of a stag with a very fine head, the sportsman may not wish to shoot it until its horns are quite free from velvet.

And this, I am afraid, is all I can tell you of deer-stalking. I wish I could not have told you so much, for, whatever their vices, I think the stag, its mate and the off-spring are too noble, and too lovely, to kill.

As a postscript to this, I would mention that in the churchyard of Clachan, Loch Broom-side, there is the unusual tombstone of the keeper who was killed by a tame stag. The tombstone bears a Latin inscription :

TOT CERVORUM VICTOR NON SENECTUTI
SED CERVO CESSIT

'This man having killed many stags, succumbed to a stag him-self—not to old age!'

Makes you think ?

WHISKY. I hardly think this subject needs any introduction or foreword ; as the secretary at a Board meeting generally starts off, *inter alia*, as 'we will take it as read', in this case we will take it as drunk.

Scotland has been famous for its whisky for centuries shall we say ; and the amounts made and sold have risen astronomically over the years. *Exports* have more than trebled since the end of the war and now stand at something like 23 million proof gallons. In 1960 the whisky industry sent 3 million proof gallons to the Commonwealth alone. Since 1745 whisky has earned a mam-moth £500 million in foreign currency. America drinks 'Scotch' to the tune of £36,000,000 a year. At home this rise is not so pronounced on account of the prohibitive tax. In 1849 the duty per proof gallon was 3s. 8d. ; by 1914 it had risen to £1 : 10s. ; in 1920 it was £3 : 12 : 6. Then during the war years it advanced by stages to £10 : 10 : 10. In 1961 the Chancellor of the Ex-chequer raised it to £11 : 11 : 11 per proof gallon, and a bottle of whisky costs 47s. 6d., the Chancellor taking 27s. on every bottle, so home consumption only runs out at a comparatively small total of 7 million proof gallons.

There are just over 100 distilleries in Scotland producing some 32 million gallons a year, of which nearly half are owned by one giant company, the D.C.L. As late as 1820 more than half Scotland's whisky came from unlicensed stills! In Glenlivet alone there were over 200, for in the valley of the Spey the burn-water there has some magic, indefinable quality, making its malt whisky so famous. Glenlivet is the heart and soul of Speyside whiskies.

There are well over 2000 brands of whisky on the market, practically all 'blended', and being so, they really have no geographical identity.

Malt whisky is made in pot-stills from malted barley; that is, barley that has been allowed to germinate for several days. There are about 90 pot-still distilleries in Scotland each producing their own characteristic brew, and this malt whisky goes off to the blenders.

It is this malt whisky that gives to blended whisky its flavour; for grain whisky—made from a mixture of barley and unmalted cereals in patent-still distilleries—has far less flavour and character.

Invariably wherever you travel, people prefer the blended whiskies; malts are more heavily flavoured and of course more expensive.

As you drive through the whisky country, Speyside in particular, there seem miracles at work and 'afloat' in the brown burns tumbling through the glens, and in the peat-reek. But a distillery is run on exact scientific lines just as you meet with in a laboratory. The whole quality of whisky revolves around the quality of its water. There is spring water, limestone water, peaty water, soft and hard waters and chlorinated water. Almost as many differing kinds of water as blends of whisky; they may be small, insignificant, minute differences, but differences all the same and that is what 'does it', a distiller told me.

To have a lovely whisky and add some indifferent water to it—if you really *want* to add water—is pure sacrilege. To the whisky of the place you *must* add the water of the place. I have said the differences in water may be minute, but are not the whiskies? Try for yourself; two glasses of the same whisky, adding to the one the water used by the distillery, and to the other, say, some of your own local water. You will be astonished at the difference in taste of each glass. In America today there is being offered for sale 'genuine Scottish water' to go with the brand of whisky you may buy. An export firm is planning to send 'cans' of Scotch water to suit all the blends exported all over the world ; a great effort, to be sure. So any hostess, at home or abroad, who wants to be 'up' with her neighbour should have cans of such water 'on tap'.

I noticed recently that Jimmy Logan, the Scotch comedian, is floating a company to send *bottles* of Scotch water to various parts of the world—suited to the particular whisky exported there—the water, being guaranteed to keep its flavour for six months ; and that last year the company, in its infancy, had sent nearly 150,000 bottles over to Belgium.

When tourists come to Scotland (to drink the whisky !) I think they should be asked which kind they prefer, not just given anything out of the bottle that chances to be opened at the time. Barmen (in cocktail bars especially) should be able to *explain* what the different whiskies are, *where* they come from and *what* makes or does not make for one whisky being better than another. It is a real art, and this art should be cultivated as a salesman would in his particular line of business. You would then get the tourist enthusiastic over a particular brand and he would go around praising it up ; our friends need guiding with the local knowledge of these whiskies : their origin and the why and the wherefore, etc.

It is said the only thing that will keep a Scot from drinking is illness ! and then someone is sure to prescribe a gargle of 'Scotchotis'—a special proprietary brand ! The lines of the song, 'When I get a couple of drinks on a Saturday, Glasgow belongs to me' needs revising, for in 1960 it is reported that for the first time there were more drunks arrested in Glasgow on *Fridays* than on Saturdays !

To be in at the making of illicit whisky must have its moments; its thrills. And I believe there are yet to be found such stills, and not so far distant from the Free Presbyterians of Gairloch ! Hush ! be quiet ! Thrills in procuring and making the apparatus ; and thrills in keeping a watchful eye on 'Mr.' Duncan the Excise man, travelling around at all times of the day and night on his specially 'silenced' silencer of his motor-bike.

The main difficulty was in getting copper for the worm (a long length of copper pipe wound spirally, through which the whisky is distilled). A local ironmonger appeared to be getting a far greater number of copper hot water cylinder tanks, for far more houses than were built, or ever likely to be built, in a certain village, and those cylinders contained the very thing, copper piping wound round and round. 'Chust the chob'; much of which found its way into other 'water' channels until such time as 'Mr.' Duncan's nose took on a more than reddish hue with inglowing suspicion and anger—'the whiles'.

Then it was Willie and Hector had to turn to other quarters to get piping, but get it they did. Next, how were they to bend it, for Angus, their 'ironmongering' partner, was now too nervous to oblige them in this direction.

After a few drinks from the old illicit brew, kept handy in a small cask in cases of dire emergency (and if ever there was one, there was one right now), they went out into the darkness and wound the piping round the garden post at the back of Sandra's house that Willie had just thought of; this was done perfectly as though Percy himself had plumbed the job from start to finish. Next, and the simplest job of all, to push the worm up off the post and then all would be ready, and away to the hide-out. But it seemed a long, a very long, way to the top of that post, far higher than their own 5 feet 9 inches height of manly growth. So they thought it would be better and quicker—as dawn was gaining on them—to saw off the post at the ground and carry the lot to their 'workshop'. But then again, it seemed thicker and tougher than they had bargained for, and their saw was not of the kind a lumberjack would use. Exhausted, another wee drink and another try, with no success at all. It was stuck good and hearty all ways and such a beautiful job, 'chust sublime'. Drunk with fatigue, excitement and 100° proof, they laid down near their handiwork, to take up the cudgels the 'morn's morn'.

But wakening at sunrise with the rain beating down on them, they found themselves looking up at the pipe coiled round an electric standard and a hydro-electric chappie on the spot looking angrily at his high voltage pole being so ultra-violated. And what was more, he 'himself it was', a friend of 'Mr.' Duncan, and knowing his telephone number also! Poor Willie; poor Hector; for 'Mr.' Duncan's motor-bike—this time without its special silencer so he could gather more speed—came purring round the bend; yes both the Exciseman and his machine were indeed purring. And the sequel could be read in that week's local journal under the caption, 'Sheriff Court at High Noon, Dingwall! Guilty!'

I think there is little more to be said about whisky. Grand medicine if taken in moderation. A classic example of the word moderation is what Willie, the Highland 'gentleman' (whom I mentioned in an earlier chapter), said to me one wet dreary night over a blazing peat fire in the public bar of the Gairloch hotel. Yes, the public, not the cocktail bar ; for the public bar in those days was cosier, warmer, more 'Highland' in its own local way, and the drinks were cheaper and maybe a little stronger ! He said : 'Moderation has aye been my rule Mr. Bee Jay. Five or six doubles is reasonable refreshment ; but after that—well, it's apt tae degenerate into drinking !'

Whilst this book was in the process of printing, I am grieved to record the passing away of my dear friend Willie, at the grand old age of 82 years. I knew Willie and the family for close on forty years. He was truly a great Highland 'gentleman' ; always respectful to the highest degree, and obliging ; lifting his cap whenever he met, or left you. I, and hosts of others will mourn him (as we did in singing the 23rd Psalm) for many a long year. He was with the Gairloch Hotel Company for 68 years. A faithful servant unto death.

Yes, taken in moderation, not to excess that you see pink elephants ; and that gives me a cue to this little ending. Two elephants were drinking when a pretty girl passed in a swirl of delicate strawberry hue. 'I'm giving this stuff up,' said the one elephant to the other, 'I'm beginning to see pink people now'.

HAGGIS : 'the' haggis as it is generally termed in Scotland.

If you look at your cookery book it's 10 to 1 you will never see the recipe for haggis, unless you look up the index and find the chapter 'Cooking for the Courageous'. And before I go any further perhaps I had better explain in some detail the makings of a haggis ; the dish that someone said contributed to the decline and fall of the Roman Empire ! And in this respect I do believe some English folk think haggis is a kind of rugged Highland animal, or else the particular name given to the strong, dour, bearded, 6-feet, hairy-kneed Highlanders found living in some far region of northern Scotland ; either that, or a boy's name ; Hamish, Haggis or such-like.

Well then ; here is a good real Highland recipe :

1 sheep's heart
½ lb. sheep's liver
½ lb. chopped suet
½ lb. oatmeal
2 chopped onions
½ pint soup stock
Teaspoonful of salt and pepper to season.

Briefly, you wash and boil the heart and liver for a while ; then mince it finely, put everything into a large bowl covered over with grease-proof paper. Put into a large enough pan and steam for two or three hours until the mixture is dryish and crumbly. Serve with swedes and mashed potatoes.

That is all there is to it !

And when you have had a second helping I am sure you will say with me, 'a Haggis for me ; a Gordon for you'.

The haggis generally comes into prominence on Burns Night or St. Andrew's Night (25th January and 30th November respectively). Whichever night, the haggis is the same ; its dress does not alter ; it just comes out wrapped up in its own lining of a sheep's stomach. 'Och, aye ; it's a fac' !'

It is served hot, steaming hot, and eaten with the usual knife and fork, not by brandishing a claymore or a skean-dhu at it, for a haggis is a temperamental exclusive morsel and quick to sense if you are acquaint with 'himself, himself' ; just as a horse can judge if it has a novice astride its saddle. And a tot of whisky (one of the 2000 brands will do) poured over it, and you then feel you can call the Duke of Argyll your uncle ! Take courage in your hands and make a hearty meal of it, for a haggis respects courage. Haggis, *the* haggis, ranks as a V.I.P.—Very Important Pudding. Did not Rabbie Burns term it 'Great Chieftan o' the puddin' race' ? And *that* turned its head and it became famous overnight.

I heard of a true case of a haggis being ordered from Scotland, by an Ontario Burns Club and being interned by the Canadian Agriculture Department ; the official reason given being that the haggis arrived without the government seal, which every parcel of imported meat must have. Too bad !

And yet another case, this time from Australia ; a present sent from Edinburgh to a Scotch lassie there never reached its destination. A letter from the Adelaide Customs said it was not allowed into Australia, and consequently it was in quarantine, would be

confiscated and destroyed. A similarly-worded letter was sent
her from the Health Department for Animals, 'Seized, and to be
destroyed!'

So English folk who thought, and think, a haggis is an animal,
are not alone, are they?

I can imagine that Ross-shire lassie bursting into verse:

> The Haggis is coming; hurrah, hurrah,
> We'll soon feel the tang from Gairloch afar;
> But alas, the Customs' declare it's awa',
> For the haggis, 'tis alien; ma, oh, ma.

The Medical Research Council, in all seriousness, have had
'the haggis' under test recently and pronounced judgement on it,
that it was 'no obscene bag of rubbish'. Just that. Except, they
add a corollary to the effect that it is 'only slightly inferior in food
value to fish and chips'. What cheek! What consternation *this*
will cause up in Wester Ross, to be sure. Of course, they are
silent about its taste; and after all does not taste—in life's mild
enjoyment—sometimes overrule 'vitamistic' values? If it's 'a
meal you want, then it's haggis you want' is a bright and snappy
slogan, despite its vitamin content or its basic formula.

Not only have you to take account of its 'constituency', but
you have to consider the method of approach to obtain its topmost
value, for as I have just said, the haggis is a temperamental subject,
a delicate bite, all on its own.

To the native Scot, the haggis is akin to porridge. He has
been happily brought into this world and subsequently reared
in this land on these two fundamental dishes, which many term
as succulent. Those who look askance on the dish, scorn the dish,
ridicule the dish may—for all we know—do so in envy? Whatever is said for or against it (Medical Council included), nothing
will shake the real Scotsman—or me, for that matter—in being a
staunch addict of this grand onion-flavoured oatmeal, with all
its chopped up what-you-may-call-it ingredients, steaming hot,
with its modicum of 100° proof Highland Malt Scotch Whisky
from Glenlivet distillery (8 years old, no less) poured over it,
with reverence, precision and great precaution against spilling
even one precious drop on this one precious dish. I would almost
go so far as to say, 'A haggis a day, keeps the doctor away!'

Och, aye; the snow is on the bens, the haggis is on the boil, and the hunter home from the hills. At times it rains ; but who cares, for a rainbow curves all over the village and over the bay, its colours reflected in the sky and on the snow-capped peaks— a wonderful background to the mountains of Torridon 'that sweep down to the sea' ; far more majestic than 'the mountains of Mourne that sweep down to the sea' ; for they are grandeur personified looking outward from Gairloch.

As the psalmist says, 'I to the hills will lift mine eyes' ; and so does one in Gairloch at such a time, with minds aglow, inspired and reverent.

Yes, the haggis is in Dan the butcher's shop ; the venison is dressed looking tempting to buy ; and a nice juicy trout looks at you from its cold, cold slab—with cod-like eyes !

All told you murmur *Slàinte Mhath!* For indeed there is really nothing more appropriate you *can* murmur !

It may be of use to list a few special dates of Scottish events, so that our visiting friends can always furnish others, who may be thinking of making the journey, of what they can expect at certain times of the year in the world of 'sport' :

February	11	Salmon fishing begins
November	1	,, ,, ends
March	15	Trout fishing begins
October	6	,, ,, ends
August	12	Grouse shooting begins
December	10	,, ,, ends
September	1	Partridge shooting begins
February	1	,, ,, ends
October	1	Pheasant shooting begins
February	1	,, ,, ends
September	1	Deer stalking (for stags) begins
October	12	,, ,, ,, ends
November	10	Deer stalking (for hinds) begins
March	31	,, ,, ,, ends
August (the last Thursday)		Skye Highland Games at Portree
May (the last week)		'Skye Week'
June		Skye Provincial Gaelic Mod
August		Gairloch Sheep Dog trials
January	25	Burns' birthday
November	30	St. Andrew's Day—patron saint of Scotland

December 31   'Hogmanay', when all true Scots bring in the New
                    Year with customary high 'spirits'; and visit friends
                    ('first-footing')
January   1   Haggis season opens!
December 31   ,,   ,,   closes! an all-the-year round love.

There is good fishing of some kind available every month of
the year in Scotland, and game fishing—for salmon, sea trout or
brown trout—can be enjoyed somewhere in the country for
more than ten months of the year.

CHAPTER II

THE KIRK

I N dealing with the Highlands of Wester Ross, and of the folk
here, I must, of necessity, devote more than a little space to
'The Kirk'; for religion enters very fully into their lives.
One might say they are steeped in it.

Scotland as a whole is a Church-minded nation to a far greater
extent than England, so that in such a context the Church of
England is relatively the junior partner. Church membership in
Scotland is 2½ times what it is in England. It will appear galling
to some devout Scots ministers when the Church of England is
projected as 'the National Church in Britain'. In fact, only about
10 per cent of the English adult population can lay claim to full
Church membership; whereas the Church in Scotland can claim
66 per cent of the adult population to Church membership.
Rather staggering figures, surely? It is predominately Protestant;
and the smaller the religious denominations, the more loyal the
members. On a normal Sunday one million adults in Scotland
attend at least one service; sometimes two services.

Yes, Scotland—particularly the Highlands—has deep religious
nationalistic feelings.

The Free Church of Scotland and the Free Presbyterian
Church of Scotland strictly adhere to all that the Bible says.
Under the name of Holy Scripture—or the Word of God,
written—are contained all the Books of the Old and New Testaments; all of which are given by inspiration of God, to be the
rule of faith and life. The Books, commonly called Apocrypha—

not being of divine inspiration—are no part of the canon of the scripture, they maintain ; and therefore are of no authority in the Church of God.

The authority of the holy scripture dependeth wholly upon God and therefore is to be received, because it is the word of God.

To become a 'member' of their Church (the Free and the Free Presbyterian) and to be able to attend and participate in the Communion, one has to undergo a very strict test of faith. 'The Confession of Faith'—which one could term as their acknowledged Text Book—deals exhaustively with every aspect of scriptural life from the Creation to the last Judgement ; agreed upon by the Assembly of Divines at Westminster as a part of the Covenanted Uniformity in Religion betwixt the Churches of Christ in the Kingdoms of Scotland, England and Ireland, and approved by the General Assembly in 1647, and ratified by Acts of Parliament 1649 and 1690, as the public and avowed Confession of the Church of Scotland. . . .

> And these words, which I command thee this day, shall be in thine heart : and thou shalt teach them diligently unto thy children, and shalt talk of them when thou sittest in thine house, and when thou walkest by the way, and when thou liest down, and when thou risest up.—Deut. vi, 6, 7.

For the assistance of those seeking membership in their Churches, there are the Larger and the Shorter Catechisms ; the former Directory for Catechising, such as have made some proficiency in the knowledge of the grounds of religion ; the latter for those as are of weaker capacity—both approved in 1648 by the General Assembly of the Church of Scotland. So it will be gathered that an infinitely stricter viewpoint is placed on religion than is the case with the Church of England.

The Old Testament in Hebrew (which was the native language of the people of God of old) and the New Testament in Greek (which at the time of the writing of it was most generally known to the nations) being immediately inspired by God, they hold to be authentical, being by singular care and providence kept pure throughout all the ages.

Although they acknowledge all things in Scripture are not alike plain in themselves, yet in searching through The Book, one will come across, in some place or another, a clear understanding of the word.

Remember the sabbath-day, to keep it holy.

Yes, the fourth commandment is rigorously observed in the Highlands. One whole day in seven was surely appointed in the scriptures. This was the seventh, or the last day of the week, from the beginning of the world to the resurrection of Christ ; and the first day of the week ever since, which in scripture is called The Lord's Day ; and so it will continue to the end of the world as the Christian Sabbath.

It is not so very long ago that the Scots Sabbath was, in a vast majority of households, consecrated to nothing but worship. The blinds were drawn in many homes ; there was neither cooking of food nor cleaning of shoes, nor washing of dishes on the Day of Rest ; the first two duties being discharged on the Saturday ; the other left over till the Monday. Such strictness exists even today in these parts of Wester Ross ; for it is conforming to one particular paragraph in 'The Confession of Faith' which says :

> This Sabbath is then kept holy unto the Lord, when men, after a due preparing of their hearts, and ordering of their common affairs before-hand, do not only observe an holy rest all the day from their own works, words, and thoughts about their worldly employments and recreations, but also are taken up the whole time in the public and private exercises of his worship, and in the duties of necessity and mercy.

(The underlining of these two words is mine ; the reason will be seen later.)

In the autobiography of the Rev. Thomas Guthrie, this extract (taken from H. V. Morton's *In Search of Scotland*) will surely be read with interest. That minister writes : 'On first going to Ross-shire to visit and preach for my excellent friend Mr. Carment, of Rosskeen, I asked him on the Saturday evening before retiring to rest, whether I would get warm water in the morning ? Whereupon he held up a warning hand, saying, "Whisht, whisht !" On my looking and expressing astonishment, he said with a twinkle in his eye, "Speak of shaving on the Lord's day in Ross-shire, and you need never preach here more !"' Continuing, the reverend gentleman says, in that same county (Ross-shire) Sir Kenneth Mackenzie—the Laird of Gairloch then—directed my attention to a servant girl, who, if not less scrupulous, was more logical in her practice. She astonished her master, one of Sir

Kenneth's tenants, by refusing to feed the cows on the Sabbath. She was ready to milk, but would by no means feed them ; and her defence shows that though a fanatic, she was not a fool. "The cows," she said, "canna milk themselves, so to milk them is a clear work of *necessity* and *mercy* ; but let them out to the fields, and they'll feed themselves.'''

Even in some nearby hamlets I hear of cases where Monday's newspaper will not be bought, let alone read, because it is maintained the paper is printed on a Sabbath for Monday's delivery ; and therefore violating the Lord's Day.

It is not for us, let alone me, to pronounce judgement on the justice or injustice, the wisdom or unwisdom, of such widespread national habits. The fact that they have left abiding marks on Scottish life and character is dramatic enough ; and whilst it might be said by the Lowlanders that two sects of Scottish religion are very narrow in their views, I cannot—for myself—but mete out praise, and full praise, to their unfailing belief and the courage of their convictions ; for have I not already unreservedly said, these people can be reckoned amongst the great people of these isles ? And I mean it.

Even as late as the spring of 1934 most of the Presbyteries, and many public authorities in the extreme north of the country, saw fit to protest before the Traffic Commissioners against the granting of licences to motor-bus companies to run Sunday excursions from the Lowlands into their territories.

I can well remember the time up here in the late 1920's, when wooden barriers were put up across some minor roads with the words chalked on, 'No motors on the Sabbath'.

When the Gospel was first sent to the Highlands, Popery claimed the whole region as its own, although its dogmas were not generally known, nor its rites universally practised. Fearing no competing religion, the priesthood had been content to rule the people, without attempting to teach them. His ignorance and superstition made the Highlander all the more manageable in the hands of the clergy and they, therefore, carefully kept him a heathen. He believed the priests were as powerful as the fairies, and he brought venison to the bishop and thus rendered her due of faith and of practice to the Church. In exchange there was given to him all the wild licence which he craved. Thus 'savage heathen' could everywhere be found ; trained Papists in very few places when the light of the Gospel first shone on the North.

There were then in the Highlands, clans, each with its chief ; as well as congregations, each with its priest. The influence of the castle had never been displaced by that of the chapel, anxious though the Romish hierarchy ever were for a monopoly of power. Had the clergy attempted to supersede the chieftains, they would have assumed the attitude of rivals before them and this would indeed have provoked the Highlands to a trial of strength. Even if they had endeavoured to check them, they might have become unmanageable.

Wisely, therefore, they gave them rein, being careful only to direct them. The chief sent his clansman, with blood on his hands, for peace to the priest ; and the more guilty the devotee had become in the service of the former, his fear made him all the more servile in the hands of the latter. The priest sent his penitent, with an indulgence, to the service of the chief ; and the more the serf placed his trust in the powers of the Church, all the more boldly could he fight the future battles of his clan. The two thus helped each other ; and combined, they bore with the pressure of a double despotism on the deluded people ; the chieftain using all his influence to keep them serfs and savages, and the priest doing his utmost to keep them dupes and fanatics.

It was in 1563 the first ray of Reformation light broke through the darkness of Ross-shire. This Reformation found the Highlander an utter heathen in ignorance, a very fanatic in superstition and in his habits a lawless savage, rioting in the wild excitements of the chase, in the perilous adventures of plundering raids and in the fierce fights of rival clans and chieftains.

In 1574 ten ministers and twenty-five readers were labouring in Ross-shire, the county being divided into ten districts, each containing several charges. To each district a minister was appointed, and so far as the supply afforded, a reader to each charge.

The Bishop of Ross, one of the Tulchan bishops (those appointed by James VI of Scotland on the express condition that they surrendered part of their income to the King) was deposed by the Assembly in 1638. He was one who was likely to use all his influence in suppressing the truth, and in oppressing the people who loved it.

On the re-establishment of Presbytery—after the days of the Tulchans—the people were found to be still grossly ignorant and superstitious and the state of their morals extremely low. The sacrificing of bulls has already been mentioned. During a tour of visitation by the Presbytery in 1656, even in Gairloch itself, this killing of beasts was also in practice, and it is minuted in the Kinlochewe records (6th September 1656) of the 'abomination within the parish of Gairloch in sacrificing of beasts upon the 25th August as also in pouring of milk upon hills as oblations. . . .' Some years after the Restoration in 1660 (the re-establishment of monarchy by the return of Charles II)—in 1690 to be precise— the Presbytery began to resume possession, but only slowly could it do so. There were few ministers to whom places, occupied by them before the Restoration, were open. The reoccupying of the county of Ross-shire was found to be more difficult than to take possession of it at first. A strong political feeling was aroused and directed by the Jacobite chieftains, against the reigning sovereign and against the Church, which he had been the means of restoring. The number of people who rejoiced in the restora- tion of the Gospel to their land was small. In several parishes the first presentees had much opposition to encounter.

In 1716 the minister of Gairloch was compelled to leave his parish, owing to the ill-treatment he received at the hands of both the laird and the people. His crops were destroyed, his home robbed and he and his family were reduced to starvation.

It was only after about 1725 that the best days of Ross-shire began. At the climax of Ross-shire's spiritual prosperity the cruel work of eviction began to lay waste the hillsides and valleys of the north. The peaceful, virtuous peasantry began to be driven off by ungodly oppressors, to clear their native soil for strangers, red deer and sheep. The owners of the soil acted as if they were the owners of the people and they treated them without respect to the requirements of righteousness or to the dictates of mercy. Families by the score were driven across the sea. Wholesale eviction wastes were formed for the red deer, so that the gentry might indulge in the sports of the savages of three centuries before.

One of the (many) great ministers of Ross-shire in those days was Mr. John Porteous, whose ministry in Kilmour (situated between Tain and Alness in Easter Ross) extended over forty- three years ; and his preachings were often quoted. He very often talked in allegories in order to arrest the attention of his listeners ; and here is one that prominently stands out :

A traveller, while passing through a desert, was overtaken by a storm. So violent was it, that he at last despaired of survival. Just as hope was dying within him, he caught sight of a light in the distance and hastened to reach it. Arriving, he sees an open house and entering it finds himself in a room, a fire on the hearth and a seat beside it. He sat down, making himself comfortable, feeling happy at his escape from the raging storm. There appeared to be nothing, or no one in the room, but towards midnight, on chancing to look around, he saw a dead body lying in one corner of the room. As he looked at it, the corpse began to rise and the poor man, being awestruck and frightened as the dead was rising higher and higher, rushed to the door to fly from the house. But the storm was still so violent that he dared not venture out and so had no choice but to return to the fireside. For a while the corpse remained at rest, but he could not take his eyes off the spot where it lay ; and as he looked, it began to rise now higher than before. Again he sprang from his seat, but this time instead of rushing to the door, he fell on his knees. As he knelt, the dead body lay back again and he ventured back once more to his seat by the hearth. Not long after, the corpse began to rise again ; this time higher than before and so once again he fell on his knees. Noticing that only while he was kneeling the dead body lay still, he did not rise up from his knees until daybreak, and the shadows melted away. . . .

Later on in this chapter I refer to another great Highland minister, Mr. Lachlan Mackenzie, of Lochcarron, Ross-shire.

Other than the ministers of Ross-shire, there were 'The Men' of Ross-shire. 'The Men' were so named, not because they were not women, but because they were not ministers. It was necessary to distinguish between the ministers and the other speakers at a fellowship meeting when notes of their addresses were given. And the easiest way of doing so was by saying 'one of the ministers', or 'one of the men' said so ; hence the origin of the designation. In these days the designation has—in general— been changed to that of 'missionary'.

In these days of 'Freedom' some women turn up for a wedding in English churches without hats, and think nothing of it, seeing it is a week-day and not a Sunday.

This would not be dreamed of in Wester Ross.

There may be no reference in the Kirk books, to week-days,

saying a woman must wear a hat in Church, but it is a convention strictly observed by Scotch womenfolk, and backed by the First Epistle to the Corinthians, chapter xi, verses 5 and 7, in which St. Paul says, 'But every woman that prayeth or prophesieth with her head uncovered dishonoureth her head : for that is even all one as if she were shaven' ; and 'For a man indeed ought not to cover his head, forasmuch as he is the image and glory of God : but the woman is the glory of the man'. Whilst the Free Church and the Free Presbyterian Church hold strictly to the Bible, the ruling is clear and uncompromising. But some say, did not St. Paul refer only to Sundays ? In Fife recently the minister turned away the bridesmaid's mother at a week-day marriage service because her head was not covered, even by a headscarf.

The lonely, barren, treeless Island of Iona, situated about 1 mile off the south-east extremity of Mull, is the cradle of Scottish Christianity, for in the year A.D. 563 St. Columba landed here from Ireland with two companions (disciples), established a monastery, and used the island as a base for his evangelistic journeys.

One of the most significant events in Scots ecclesiastical history was the *Disruption of 1843*, when what came to be called the Free Church split from the Church of Scotland on the ancient and sorry issue of patronage. That was an event of a most dramatic order, the ministers so opposed sacrificing their livings with selflessness that must be respected ; and congregations suffering forms of martyrdom—if only mild—for the sake of a conception of religious liberty. The people rebelled when worthless men were appointed to big parishes by lay patrons, quite regardless of their being suitable or unsuitable.

In Scotland it is held that Church history should take into consideration that the origin of the Church in the world came directly from God, and that He commanded Moses to do all things according to the pattern shown him on the Mount. This Moses did. But as time went on, the leaders of the people both in temporal and in spiritual matters departed from the prescribed worship by uniting it with the idolatrous mode of worship observed by the heathens around them. Every time they had, by their own policy, strayed from the worship originally ordained they were plunged into wars, famines and pestilences, and were brought into untold miseries by one nation after another. Whilst great men were to come forward to deliver them from their enemies, they could not for long be kept from idolatry, until at long last they were banished to Babylon for seventy years. Whilst this cured them of idolatry it did not cure them of mixing their own policy with the Word and worship of God, and so at last they were thrust out of their own land. The history of the Church reveals that, even during the lifetime of the Apostles, heresies began to appear. The letters to the Seven Churches of Asia, recorded in Revelations, show how far some of those Churches had departed from the faith and purity of worship.

Coming on to later days, the removal of the Emperor Constantine from Rome to Constantinople gave the Bishop of Rome a position of which he took all the advantage possible. After a long struggle for the ascendancy, he was duly acknowledged Pope. So Anti-Christ was set up, and the Church of Christ became an idolatrous organisation.

This was the Babylon into which the Church was banished for her infidelity and idolatry, and in which she lay under persecution and in bondage till the Reformation. This period of the Church's history is called the Dark Ages. Europe was sunk in immorality, ignorance, idolatry and superstition, until 'labourers' came forth to work. These reformers went to work with God's Word as their guide on how the Church should be ruled, and those Reformers of Scotland set up the two offices of elders and deacons as prescribed in the New Testament. They would not tolerate bishops ; and in all this they suffered twenty-eight years of persecution.

The Free Church of Scotland, at her separation in 1843, claimed that she adhered to the Creed and Constitution of the Established Church of Scotland in their entirety, and that she *had to separate* on account of the intrusion of the Civil Courts into the spiritual jurisdiction of the Church Courts, in order to maintain the lawful rights of the Established Church of Scotland. In one word, that she was the Church of Scotland, *free* ; following the Church's original Calvanistic preachings to the letter.

When the Disruption took place in 1843, the party who contended for the spiritual independence of the Church of Scotland— for the non-interference by the civil courts (magistrates) in matters belonging to the spiritual jurisdiction of the courts of the

Church—took every precaution to make their position crystal clear. The Claim, Declaration and Protest of 1842, regarding the encroachment of the Court of Session, leaves no doubt that the Disruption Fathers contended for the rights of the Church of Scotland as established by law. The two main claims put forward were (1) that 'there is no other head of the Church but the Lord Jesus Christ', and (2) that 'the Lord Jesus, as King and Head of His Church had appointed a government in the hands of church officers distinct from the civil magistrate, which government is ministerial, not lordly, and to be exercised in consonance with the laws of Christ, and with the liberties of His people'. In the law of Scotland the spiritual courts of the Church and the secular courts were co-ordinate, not subordinate the one to the other, in their own spheres of action.

The *Free Church* held this view unimpaired when she had in 1843, for truth and conscience's sake, to give up all the churches, manses, glebes and salaries, and all the remuneration which accrued to her from State connection, in order to maintain Christ's right to rule in His own Church by His Word in the hands of her own office-bearers. Those who fought for these rights recorded explicitly that they were compelled to relinquish State connection on account of the intrusion of the Civil Courts into the spiritual province of the Church by forcing ministers on congregations contrary to the wishes of the people and in defiance of the Church's courts, and *not* because they ceased to hold the doctrine of the Establishment of Religion by the State to be a Scriptural doctrine and highly valued by them.

This then was the position of the Free Church at the Disruption.

All office-bearers in the Free Church, when ordained to their respective offices as ministers and elders, bound themselves to ordination vows and solemn declarations as being equivalent to an oath.

There were certain obstacles existing between the Free Church and the United Presbyterian Church (another body that had welded together certain other 18th century seceders, anti-burghers and such-like—burghers being the name of a sect of seceders from the Church of Scotland) and at the General Assembly of the Free Church in 1863 a large committee was appointed to see whether these obstacles could be removed so that a Union of the two bodies might come about.

Much bitter feeling arose in discussions, so much so that at the Assembly of 1867 five members of the Free Church committee resigned. There then arose two parties opposing each other known as the *Unionists* and the *anti-Unionists*, and as time went on these divergent positions and views began to unfold themselves. The Free Church party was led by Dr. Begg of Edinburgh and Dr. Nixon of Montrose ; whilst the other party who were more for adopting a compromising solution was led by Dr. Rainy and Dr. Candlish.

Strife entered into the very heart of the Free Church. Instead of the Union that was contemplated in 1863, and so much desired, internal discussions and strife originated which at last broke up the Church into fragments.

A minority deplored the baneful effects of the union controversy on the peace and spiritual prosperity of the Free Church ; of the Free Church being rent into two opposing camps.

It was in *May 1893* at the General Assembly that the Rev. Donald Macfarlane of Raasay, making strong protests over past events, separated from the Free Church and many applauded and followed in his bold step, and upon his preaching to a congregation worshipping at Millhouse, Kames, formed itself into the first congregation of what was to be known afterwards as the *Free Presbyterian Church*.

On his return to Raasay, Mr. Macfarlane received much encouragement and many meetings were subsequently held in different parts of the West of Scotland, when it was decided that immediate steps be taken to form a Presbytery. In July 1893 the Revs. Macfarlane, D. Macdonald (Shieldaig) and Mr. Alex. Macfarlane (Schoolmaster, Raasay) met and formed ' *The Free Presbyterian Church Presbytery of Scotland* '.

At a meeting on *14th August 1893* at Portree, the Presbytery adopted the Deed of Separation. At a further meeting that month (30th August) a call was moderated to Rev. John R. MacKay ; and MacKay's ordination and induction took place at Gairloch in the golf-course hollow (mentioned in 'The Great Silence' chapter) —the *Leabaidh na bà Baine*—on 11th October 1893.

He was the first minister ordained in the Free Presbyterian Church.

This, then, was the small beginning of the Free Presbyterian

F

Church taken out of the Free Church. The F.P. Church then had but two ministers and a few students only.

On *30th October 1900*, the Union Act was passed ; *i.e.* the Free Church duly united with the United Presbyterian Church, becoming known as the United Free Church of Scotland—or the present Free Church ; a famous union and it produced the notorious litigation which gave the 'Wee Frees' their historical fame and which vested in this Union the bulk of the funds of the old Free Church proper.

The House of Lords declared in August 1904 that those who adhered to the Free Church were the 'True Free Church of Scotland' and therefore the rightful owners of all the property and funds.

This Union was heralded as one of the greatest blessings which had come to Scotland for years.

There still remained another union to be formed, the greatest of all, viz. : that of the authentic Church of Scotland and the United Free Church in 1929.

So much for a brief history.

It might be well to summarise as follows :

1. The *Free Presbyterian Church* came into separate existence in 1893.

2. It was owing to the passing of the Declaratory Act of 1892 that those who formed it felt in conscience they could no longer continue in the so-called Free Church. The Declaratory Act's effect on the Constitution of the Free Church, the Free Presbyterians said, was that it seriously affected the constitution in the explanation it offered of the Confession of Faith. With no uncertain sound, it was declared from pulpit and platform, that if the Act became law, the Free Church was gone as the 'Free Church'.

3. The present *Free Church* came into separate existence at the Union between the majority in the Free Church and the United Presbyterians in 1900. Had there been no union there would have been no body taking up the position of the present Free Church. There is, therefore, the greatest difference between the constitutional standing of the two Churches ; F.P. and Free. The former came into separate existence through the passing of the Declaratory Act.

4. According to the case presented by the Free Church to the

Law Lords, if it had not been for the Union no claim could have been made for the property, and that the majority with the minority would have remained in possession of the property and be recognised as the *legal* Free Church.

5. The Barrier Act (a self-explanatory Act), passed in 1697, enabled the Declaratory Act to be passed in 1892. The Free Presbyterians agree with the Free Church in saying that this Act was *ultra vires*, but hold that having been passed into law under the Barrier Act, it became a binding rule and constitution. It is this distinction really that made the division in 1893, and caused a separation that has not been healed.

6. Again, the present Free Church hesitated to rescind the Declaratory Act for a number of years after it came into separate existence (1900), simply because by so doing it might invalidate its claim to the property. The Declaratory Act was subsequently rescinded in 1906.

7. As regards Open Communion, all the Presbyterian bodies with the exception of the 'Reformed Presbyterians' and 'Original Seceders' hold the principle of Open Communion.

Concluding, it will be seen the Free Presbyterian Church and the Free Church accept the Bible as the infallible supreme standard ; and the *whole* doctrine of the Confession of Faith as the subordinate standard because it is believed to be founded upon God's Word ; and it is the desire of both these denominations to hand down their priceless heritage to their children and their children's children unimpaired.

I have said the Free and the Free Presbyterian Churches take the Bible very literally.

In the spring of 1961 another new Bible was published. This, *The New English Bible*, was a fresh translation of the New Testament by British scholars who started work on it thirteen years ago.

Originally the Bible, as we know it, was written by more than thirty-five writers, distributed over sixteen centuries and therefore it was impossible for them to have a mutual understanding as to the purpose of the Book and their own particular section as it was related to the whole. Only a few of the writers of the Bible were of sufficient scholarship to write ; the majority were unlettered and incompetent to write any manuscript.

There are thirty-nine books in the Old Testament, written primarily in Hebrew, and twenty-seven in the New Testament, written in Greek ; sixty-six in all. Each of the writers were so 'inspired' to write so that each book fitted perfectly into the remainder. Some of the scribes never possessed a copy of any of the other sixty-five works ; so there could be no collusion at all. Time does not leave its mark on this great Work and so it retains its perennial freshness.

(The arrangement of the books is not strictly in chronological order. Nehemiah, for instance, is placed ahead of Job ; but actually Job lived hundreds of years before Nehemiah.)

A term employed in connection with the origin of the Bible is *canon*—meaning 'standard' or 'rule' ; and apart from the sixty-six books which originally passed the test for divinely inspired writings and so are included in the Bible, there were found to be some fourteen in the Old Testament like Esdras, Judith and others that did not pass the test of 'canonicity' ; and this group is known as the Apocryphal books—valuable as ancient history, but not in the class of Scripture. (The Roman Catholic Church has included them in its Rheims and Douay versions.)

All of the original manuscripts were written by hand on fragile papyrus or animal skins, and each new copy had to be reproduced by hand; the manuscripts of the early writers were held in sacred trust by Jewish scribes from one generation to another.

One of the first attempts at putting portions of the Bible into Anglo-Saxon occurred about A.D. 650. The first *complete* Bible was made by John Wycliffe in 1382, copies being hand-written. He made his translation from the Latin Vulgate, which was a translation from the Hebrew and Greek ; thus his work was a translation from a translation.

The first *printed* English New Testament, by William Tyndale, appeared in 1525 ; and the first complete printed Bible came out in 1535 by Miles Coverdale.

The 'Unity' of the Bible is truly remarkable. Written, as I have said, by some thirty-five different persons over some 1600 years ; written in many different languages in many different countries by people in every walk of life—herdsmen, fishermen, scribes, preachers, politicians. Written under all sorts of circumstances and conditions, yet all blending in unity of thought. One can only conclude by saying that all these writings were inspired by a Master-mind ; a Master-Architect.

Certainly a unique feature of the Scriptures is the great number of prophecies ; the fulfilment of hundreds of such prophecies is recorded in subsequent history. Even the Old Testament writers describe the Master in language that perfectly matched the descriptions of biographers and eye-witnesses at the time. How does 'it come to pass' these writers described the birth, trial, crucifixion and resurrection so many hundreds of years before these events came into being ? For nothing in history in their time could aid them in such descriptions. There can be but one answer ; their writings were 'inspired', and behind the Book was surely a 'Person'. Everywhere in the Old Testament there was preparation for and expectation of a Master ; in the Gospels there was manifestation ; and from the Acts to the Apocalypse, realisation.

The translation of the Bible most commonly used today is that known as the Authorised or King James Version. This translation was promoted in 1603 by James VI of Scotland, who came to the throne of England as James I. It was undertaken by a group of fifty-four men ; some of the best-known scholars of that day, and they completed their work in 1611.

This 1611 edition contained a number of typographical errors ; one verse used the word Judas instead of Jesus and printer's errors continued for many years, reaching a climax in the 1631 edition which left the word 'not' out of the seventh commandment, making it read 'Thou shalt commit adultery'. This particular edition was known as the 'Wicked Bible'.

By 1644 the King James version had become the general Bible of the English people ; and for over three centuries it has made its impact felt upon the life, culture and institutions of the English-speaking peoples. Those who may be indifferent to its spiritual message, bow to its literary beauty.

These various scriptural writings are from the East of by-gone days. Living amongst the Eastern races so long, I know they love to weave stories *ad lib.* and to go into extraneous detail, even though it simply entailed a plain 'yes' or 'no'. Therefore it is reasonable to understand that in the handing down of incidents from generation to generation, differences should arise, which over the ages produce further differences. Many meanings apparently, in the light of Biblical research, can be placed on various words and sayings ; the 'literal' interpretation must not always—

according to some quarters—be taken 'literally'.

At the orthodox Christmas season one often hears the saying 'Peace on earth and goodwill towards men'—taken actually from St. Luke, Chapter ii, verse 14 ; whereas in reality the message of the Angels on the occasion of the Nativity was meant to imply 'Peace on earth to men of goodwill'—which is what the Douay version has. *The New English Bible* (published early 1961) translates the verse as 'Glory to God in highest heaven, and on earth his peace for men on whom his favour rests'.

In almost every village of importance in Ross-shire there are to be found, as a rule, two separate churches ; the Church of Scotland, and the Free Church of Scotland ; and in some villages, three kirks, the extra one being the Free Presbyterian Church.

In Gairloch, three such churches exist ; three distinct denominations ; three faiths. With three churches in a tiny village ; three houses of prayer, convenient to the reach of everyone, I am prone to give the following verse inspired many years ago by Robert Murray M'Cheyne—of Dundee fame—who did wonderful ministerial work.

> Give me a man of God the truth to preach
> A house of prayer within convenient reach ;
> Seat-rents the poorest of the poor can pay
> A spot so small one pastor can survey.
> Give these—and give the spirit's genial shower
> Scotland shall be a garden, all in flower.

The cemetery mentioned in the Gairloch chapter is a common burial-ground for all denominations.

The Church of Scotland's service is similar to the Church of England. The other services are conducted in English and Gaelic ; and as a rule the first question at the Kirk Session to a new minister (in the Free and Free Presbyterian denominations) is '*Bheil Gàidhlig, Agaibh, Urramaich?*'—'have you the Gaelic, reverend sir ?'

There are many different religions throughout the world ; many indeed ; but through most—if not all—runs a single theme, expressed in very similar forms ; and I quote six of the leading ones :

BRAHMANISM : This is the sum of duty ; Do nought unto others which would cause you pain if done to you.—Mahabharata 5 : 1517.

BUDDHISM : Hurt not others in ways that you yourself would find hurtful.—Udanavarga 5 :18.

CONFUCIANISM : Is there one maxim which ought to be acted upon throughout one's whole life ? Surely it is the maxim of loving kindness : Do not unto others what you would not have them do unto you.—Analects 15 : 23.

JUDAISM : What is hateful to you, do not to your fellow man. That is the entire Law ; all the rest is commentary.—Talmud Shabbat 31a.

ISLAM : No one of you is a believer until he desires for his brother that which he desires for himself.—Sunan.

CHRISTIANITY : Therefore all things whatsoever ye would that men should do to you, do ye even so to them : for this is the law and the prophets.—Matthew 7 : 12.

However their religions may differ, each sect has its own way of things ; its own way of life—'Each in his own tongue' so to speak. And in this connection I would quote an anthology published in *The Book of American Poetry*, entitled, appropriately enough, 'Each In His Own Tongue', which I came across abroad nearly half a century ago. The author was one William Herbert Carruth, and it is surely very profound in all its references to Evolution, Autumn, Longing and Consecration. Very old, but very true.

> A fire-mist and a planet—
> A crystal and a cell—
> A jellyfish and a saurian,
> And caves where the cave-men dwell ;
> Then a sense of law and beauty
> And a face turned from the clod ;
> Some call it EVOLUTION,
> And others call it GOD.
>
> A haze on the far horizon,
> The infinite, tender sky,
> The ripe, rich tint of the cornfields,
> And the wild geese sailing high ;
> And all over upland and lowland
> The charm of the golden rod ;
> Some of us call it AUTUMN,
> And others call it GOD.
>
> Like tides on a crescent sea-beach,
> When the moon is new and thin,

> Into our hearts high yearnings
> Come welling and surging in ;
> Come from the mystic ocean,
> Whose rim no foot has trod ;
> Some of us call it LONGING,
> And others call it GOD.
>
> A picket frozen on duty—
> A mother starved for her brood—
> Socrates drinking the hemlock,
> And Jesus on the rood ;
> And millions who, humble and nameless,
> The straight, hard pathway plod ;
> Some call it CONSECRATION
> And others call it GOD.

I feel sure readers will agree, this is a beautiful devotional piece of poetry—one worthy of being hung in every devout Highland home ?

I have indicated that both the Free and the Free Presbyterian Church are fervently set in their views and doctrines. There are, naturally, to be found in all walks of life some who do not always hold on rigorously to the absolute spirit and letter of the teachings. One instance I readily call to mind.

In one hotel privately owned by a dear lady of strict religious principles, there is a cocktail bar that she begged me to come and see one day in mid-winter when I happened to be passing and had dropped in for a meal and a 'Glayva' to warm me up. The bar was in the process of being reconditioned. 'What do you think of it ?' she said. 'Lovely,' said I. 'Pitch-pine ; fancy that ; very difficult to come by surely ?' I said. 'Yes,' she replied, 'but whisht ! don't say a word to anyone ; all this wood for the bar counter, sides and walls came from the pews of the Free Presbyterian Kirk !'

So when you have a drink and *Slàinte Mhath* at that hotel (and naming it would be telling tales out of school !) you are leaning up against and supporting the Free Presbyterian Kirk of that village !

Many years ago when I took those early holidays in Arran, I learnt the following verses. I believe there were more than the two I give, but I have forgotten the rest :

> There was a Presbyterian cat,
> Went searching for its prey ;

It caught a 'moose' within the 'hoose'
Upon the Sabbath Day.

The minister was horrified,
And to that cat did say,
You poor perverted pussy-cat
To spoil the Sabbath Day.

It is a strange thing, but very few cats up in the Highlands—a Highland-brought-up cat, that is—will kill, let alone eat, a robin redbreast. I wonder why ? Perhaps the concluding paragraph of this chapter may have some significance ?

The Free Church and the Free Presbyterian Church set aside special dates for their Communion weeks. In Gairloch they are held the fourth Sunday in June and the second Sunday of October; the so-called fast weeks commencing on the Thursday and carrying through till the Monday forenoon. All observe them strictly, shops closing, schools on holiday and a general 'break-down' in everyday practices. Some of those ardent worshippers who can manage the time visit other parishes where *their* fast weeks are being held ; going to worship there, meeting friends, and staying a few days.

In the old days I remember witnessing these communions which were held in the open in the famous hollow at the Gairloch Golf Course, the *Leabaidh na bà Baine* (Bed of the White Cow, mentioned earlier), and thousands from near and far (50 or 60 miles even) came to join in the service. Days before the fast days every spare hole and corner was got ready to accommodate the throng of folk ; every hut or shed with a roof over it was got ready by strewing it with straw to act as bedding during the five or six nights of their stay. Undressing or washing was never thought of. This hollow, a deep oval, was ideal for such a gathering and at one end was the preacher's 'box' affording him shelter from wind, sun and rain, so that his voice could be heard distinctly. It was never rain-sogged, for the soil was of pure, porous drifted sand ; and the sheep saw to it that the grass was short. This hollow accommodated as many as 3000 people ; and any stranger passing by, hearing these voices floating up out of the hollow, chanting beautiful and ancient Gaelic psalms, could not fail to be charmed with such utter solemnity ; purely reminiscent of our Lord's time ? Unhappily this practice has ceased these many years, the services now being held indoors in the respective churches. Yet, as I have said, some today travel many miles attending other parish communions.

When the communion is held at Shieldaig—near Applecross—some 15 miles as the crow flies, but nearly four times that distance by road via Loch Carron, a party from Gairloch will hire a motor-launch and set out from the pier in the early hours of the Sabbath for the long sea-journey, worship there, getting back again about 10 o'clock that self-same night. Others will go by car the sixty-odd miles, early ; also returning late. And it is not to say those who make the journey are young. There are many old ladies I know in their 70's, and some not in good health, who insist on participating in the Faith at such times. They even travel as far afield as Staffin—near the northern tip of Skye—taking the mail-bus from Gairloch (a day or so before the Sabbath) to Achnasheen ; then train to Kyle of Lochalsh ; thence by boat from Kyle to Portree and then finally by bus to Staffin. Many hours and many miles of a journey.

Men and women come to worship at the Gairloch Free and Free Presbyterian Churches from villages as far away as 8 miles, and have to hire a car, costing them several shillings each, to bring them and take them back. I cannot point to any similar practice in the places I have lived in England, or that I have spent Sundays in, in different parts of Britain. Paying for a car to go to church ; Sunday after Sunday ? Unbelievable! Yet here, in Wester Ross, it is a custom that is as old as the hills ; a tradition that neither time nor age will ever alter. And why ? Because it is part of their life.

Yes ; these people are devoutness itself. All honour to them. Where would you come across such devotion in all England ? And echo answers, 'Where ?' And in their homes the Grace is always said at the beginning and end of every meal ; no matter whether it be just a cup of coffee and a biscuit.

Did I say a great people ? Surely a great people. They have taken unto themselves for protection the shield of faith. The Word of God is the acid test. It makes the likes of others sit up and take notice ; and I for one—in my humble way—proudly *do* take notice and think within myself, there is more to life than earthly possessions. And I feel sure I am not alone in these thoughts.

I chance to wonder what some would say to seeing a pack of

playing-cards spread out on a pew at a Sunday service ? I feel
that even when folk around these parts hear the story I am about
to relate, they may but say 'aweel'—and let it go at that ?

The incident is a true one ; told me by one Hugh O'Brien,
the American film star of 'Wyatt Earp' fame, who was next to
the soldier in question.

It all happened in Korea at the time of the Korean War (after
the Second World War) when several of the troops went to
church one Sunday, but one lad had no prayer-book or Bible in
his kit—only a pack of cards, which he spread out before him on
the pew top. The sergeant, spotting this terrible offence, duly
brought the soldier before the provost-marshal, who took a
serious view of the matter until the G.I. explained as follows.

He said he had no Bible or prayer-book at hand ; only a
dirty, worn pack of cards.

'I laid them out,' he said, 'and looked at the ACE, which
reminded me of there being but one God ; then the TWO, that
the Bible was divided into two parts, the Old and the New
Testaments ; the THREE made me think of the Holy Trinity,
the Father, the Son and the Holy Ghost. The FOUR, the four
evangelists, Matthew, Mark, Luke and John, who went abroad
preaching the Gospel ; the FIVE reminded me of the five wise
virgins who trimmed their lamps—there were really ten, but
five were wise and saved, whilst five were foolish and shut out.
And when I came to the SIX I recalled that in six days
the Lord made Heaven and Earth, and on the SEVENTH, He rested.
The EIGHT denoted the eight righteous people whom God saved
when he destroyed the earth—Noah, his wife and their three sons
and three wives ; and the NINE told me of the lepers that were
cleansed, but nine of the ten did not even thank Him. When I
look at the TEN,' he said, 'I think of the Ten Commandments
God handed out to Moses on a tablet of stone ; and the JACK is
the knave or devil. The QUEEN is emblematic of the Virgin
Mary, and the KING again reminded me of there being but one
King of Heaven, God Almighty.

'Not only that,' he said, 'when I count the number of spots
on the fifty-two cards (including the "Joker" as one, the Jack as
eleven, Queen twelve and King as thirteen) they total up to
three hundred and sixty-five—the number of days in the year. There
are *fifty-two cards*, the number of weeks in the year ; there are

thirteen tricks, the number of weeks in a quarter ; there are *four suits*, the number of weeks in a month ; and finally there are *twelve picture cards*, the number of months in a year.

'So you see, Provost-marshal,' he said, 'my pack of cards serves me as a Bible, an Almanac, and a Prayer Book.'

Surely there is no comment one *can* make on this.

In the very olden days ministers preached 'Fire and Brimstone' from the pulpit, and it was perhaps well that the Big Book was heavy by reason of it being well bound with brass hinges and lock, or else the preacher might often have dislodged it as he got so carried away with his sermon.

There are some, of course—as there are in all religious bodies— that are ultra, ultra narrow in their outlook and behaviour, and yet like to pry into other people's affairs *ad lib.* ; they belong to an association called the 'Unco Guid'. To quote the words of Rabbie Burns :

> O ye wha are sae guid yoursel,
> Sae pious and sae holy,
> Ye've nought to do but mark and tell
> Your neebour's fau'ts and folly !

and it can be very true.

I knew one such 'unco guid'' working in a Highland hotel, who was righteousness itself, yet must pry into other's business. Suspecting one of her neighbour's sons—outwardly a pillar of the Kirk—was having a drink in the public bar, she went along and bent down to 'keek' through the keyhole to confirm her suspicions. However, she could only see the 'middles' of the men inside, not their faces. Not being thwarted she went round to the other door behind the bar counter, opened it, saying to the barman, 'Can you give me change for half a crown, Donald ?' Whilst he busied himself giving her small change, she rapidly looked round—nonchalantly, if you please—taking stock of all who were imbibing. Then with her change—which of course she didn't want—she went on her way rejoicing !

There are, of course, many stories of the Kirk told in lighter vein. One is of the preacher who made it a rule never to take a meal before he preached a sermon. Whilst he was preaching away from his parish, he had the utmost difficulty in dissuading his kind hostess from giving him lunch before he took the afternoon service. 'Many thanks,' he told her, 'but it would affect my preaching.'

She stayed at home while the preacher and her husband went to church. When they returned she asked her husband privately, 'How did he go on?' 'Well,' said he, 'thou might as well have given him his dinner!'

And of another, of the aged minister who found the burden of preparing two sermons every week becoming too much for him. He solved the problem most ingeniously. He prepared only one sermon, which he duly delivered on the Sabbath morning. He delivered it again in the evening—but that time without his false teeth!

One old minister who had a faithful old retainer looking after his manse and garden, and whom he often had occasion to reprove for drinking, had reason to thank him for something special he had done; and as it was a cold day and he was feeling the need of a little stimulant, offered Donald one out of his bottle, at the same time saying to him that he should remember that 'every dram you take, Donald, is a nail in your coffin'. 'Well,' said Donny, 'seeing as you have the hammer in your hand now, there'd be no harm in giving the nail a few more knocks!'

In the Highlands many a man is known by a nickname. There are so many Frasers, Mackenzies, MacLeods, MacIvers, etc., so that calling a person by his Christian name and adding a nickname serves an easy, simple way of knowing who is meant. (I have often tried to find out what my nickname is, but without success!)

The lay preachers in the Free Presbyterian Kirk who go and deputise to a church who may be without a minister, are called missionaries. There was one such missionary, and there was a member of his congregation living some miles away, nicknamed 'Satan'; why, I could not say.

It so happened one Saturday night 'Satan' took more than was good for him, and creating a disturbance outside the bar, was promptly put in the local cell to cool off during the week-end. The missionary was due to go over to preach at that same parish where 'Satan' was a staunch member, but when all this occurred on the Saturday, a close friend of the 'offender', having a sense of humour, hurried along to the missionary's house, knocked on the door and said to the wife 'You can tell your guid man there's no need for him to go over to Achnatilt tomorrow to preach, because Satan's locked up for the week-end!'

Certainly a little humour now and then helps life along. Those who take religion seriously, generally take life seriously.

At a wedding, neither the Free Church, nor the Free Presbyterian Church minister, as a rule, stays on, once the meal is over ; for it is then that 'conviviality' commences to reign.

In some girls' schools the teachers will not permit of any pupils having their hair cut short ; and if it came to be known that a child had been sent to buy a Sunday newspaper—then the parents would soon be taken to task over such an offence.

I can recall the days of long ago when the receptionists in a Ross-shire hotel were not allowed to wear dresses with short sleeves. The manager was consulted on one such occasion, as one of the girls had bought a black dress (always it had to be black) with short sleeves, and he told her if she wanted to wear it, she must put on a black, full-sleeved cardigan. What a revelation awaits one now when I visit that same hotel and see the girls behind the counter—teenagers sometimes—all decked up in 'come-hither' dresses, pencilled eye-brows, shaded eye-lids, and eyelashes caked with mascara. All that, plus ear-rings, bracelets and brilliantly painted finger nails. Undoubtedly 'Time marches on' ; and indeed 'it came to pass'.

'Summer-time' always ends officially at 2 a.m. on a Sunday, and clocks are put back or forward as the case may be. But as regards *that* Sunday's service, the clocks are *not* altered on the Sabbath here. They are altered on the Monday. So if the morning service is at 11 a.m. and you *did* chance to put your own watch back one hour, and you went along at *your* correct 11 o'clock time, you would find the service was over, for you would be arriving at 12 noon.

Among the Highlanders of Ross-shire, the name of Mr. Lachlan Mackenzie, the minister of Loch Carron (over the Torridon range and near Strome Ferry) was very fragrant, and even today there may be some to whom 'the great Mr. Lachlan' is a pleasant name. He was a minister of the old school. Of all the eminent ministers in the Highlands none is more famous than this Divine.

Mr. Lachlan—as he was invariably called—had an extraordinary influence over his people. Preaching on one occasion against the sin of lying, he counselled his hearers to refrain in all circumstances from prevarication and falsehood, saying they would find it the best policy as well as their safest course for eternity.

One of his congregation, conscious of having often told a lie, and finding it impossible to believe that it could always be wise to tell the truth, went to speak to him on the matter.

He was a smuggler and told Mr. Lachlan, 'Surely if the Exciseman should ask me where I hid my whisky, it would not be wrong that I should lead him "off the scent"? But Mr. Lachlan would not allow this was a case to which the rule he laid down was not applicable and advised him to tell the simple truth.

The smuggler was soon afterwards put to the test.

While working behind his croft by the wayside the following week, the Exciseman came up to him and said, 'Is there any whisky about your house today?' Remembering his minister's advice the smuggler at once said, though not without misgivings as to the result, 'Yes, there are three casks of whisky buried in a hole under my bed, and if you will search for them there you will find them'. 'You rascal,' the Exciseman said, 'if they were there you would be the last to tell me'; and walked away.

As soon as he was out of sight and the smuggler could breathe freely again, he ran to the minister and said, 'Oh, Mr. Lachlan, you were right as usual!'

In a later chapter (Christmas and New Year) I refer to the practical non-observance of Christmas up in the Highlands; there is also no children's pent-up excitement over Santa Claus in the Free and Free Presbyterian households such as there is in England.

The 25th December—a set calendar date—is not acknowledged as the birthday of Christ; for no such specific date is recorded in the Bible. 'Whilst shepherds watched their flocks by night' could not, they say, be the month of December; for then both shepherds and flocks would not be out in the open fields. What *is* observed is the ascendancy of Christ; Christ risen from the dead; and this is observed every Sabbath throughout the year; not as the Church of Scotland and Church of England do only at Eastertide.

On the morning of each New Year's Day, be it a Sunday or a week-day, the Free Church and the Free Presbyterian Church hold a service, which is more in the nature of a 'Lecture' than of an ordinary Sabbath-day worship service ; a means of bracing and fortifying oneself for the coming twelve months' worldly affairs and pitfalls of life.   The Church of Scotland and Church of England do not hold such a service.

At certain times when I have had occasion to visit local friends early in the mornings, I have seen through the windows the whole family kneeling in prayer ; and so waited silently till their meditations were over and then knocked on the door. I have used the phrase 'where else would you find . . .', but the parallel bears repeating ; namely, you would not find such devotion in places other than the Highlands of Scotland. Certainly it is not commonplace in England.

The Free and the Free Presbyterians have no stereotyped form of Common Prayer or Common Worship, such as in the English Churches. Only the Bible and the Psalms (standing at prayer and sitting whilst singing the Psalms to metre) and the 'Confession of Faith' agreed upon by the Assembly of Divines at Westminster; as I have said previously. As to Santa Claus, the view is held that, since this is a myth—a fairy-tale—it is not fit for the young to be brought up in any such 'false' faith ; for, when all is said and done, lovely as it may be in all its general idea and trappings, it *is* a fairy tale.

Yes, as readers will have gathered through these lines, the Free and the Free Presbyterian congregations get strong advice from their preachers ; and the law of the Sabbath must be upheld.

I remember hearing tell, many years ago, of the Free Church minister who lived at Aultbea and who travelled once in a while to Gairloch to preach ; and as travelling was slow in those days he had to stay overnight in Gairloch, returning to Aultbea on the Monday. He was a very 'strenuous' preacher, and perspired freely, so much so that he needed a change of underwear upon retiring for the night, after preaching two 'heavy' sermons.

He could only be sure of this change if there had been an opportunity during the preceding week of getting his small brown-paper parcel containing his shirt, vest, etc., over to Gairloch ; for though he drove to church in his own horse and trap, he would not dream of carrying this little parcel in his trap on the Sabbath.

There is also the story of a fishing-boat returning from a two-week's absence and being delayed by storm and wind, did not manage to reach Gairloch till the Sunday morning a few hours before churchtime. The skipper was an elder in the Free Kirk and so had to decide which would be the greater sin, namely, to shave off some of the fortnight's growth of beard to make themselves look more respectable for the Sabbath, or not to go to the Kirk. In the end, it was decided that as shaving on the Sabbath was an unforgivable sin, it would be less wicked to stay away from Kirk! And this they did.

There is no doubt at all but that many prophecies mentioned in the Bible have 'come to pass'—as time has also passed.

Dr. Cyrus Hamlin, a man of great Scriptural learning, was in Constantinople (as the Turkish capital was then called) soon after the Crimean War, and a colonel in the Turkish army calling on him said, 'I want to ask you one question. What proof can you give me that the Bible is what you claim it to be, namely, the Word of God?'

Dr. Hamlin, evading the question, drew him into conversation, during which he learned that his Turkish friend had travelled widely, especially in the East in the region of the Euphrates.

'Were you ever in Babylon?' he asked him.

'Yes, and that reminds me of a curious experience I had there,' the Turk said, 'I am very fond of sport, and having heard that the ruins of Babylon abound in game, I determined to go there for a week's shooting. Knowing it was not considered safe for a man to be there except in the company of several others—and money being no object to me—I engaged a sheik with his followers to accompany me for a large sum. We reached Babylon and pitched our tents. A little before sundown I took my gun and strolled out to have a look around. The holes and caverns among the ruins are infested with game, which is rarely seen except at night. I caught sight of a few beasts in the distance, and then retraced my steps toward our encampment, intending to begin my sport as soon as the sun had set. What was my surprise to find the men striking the tents! I went to the sheik, protesting most strongly. I had engaged him for a week, paying him handsomely, and here he was starting off before our contract had scarcely begun. Nothing I could say, however, would induce him to remain. "It isn't safe," he said, "No mortal flesh dare stay here after sunset. In the dark ghosts, goblins, ghouls and all manner of things come out of the holes and caverns, and whoever is found here is taken off by them and becomes one of themselves." Finding I could not persuade him, I said, "Well, as it is I am paying you more than I ought to, but if you'll stay, I'll double it." "No," he said, "I couldn't stay for all the money in the world. No Arab has ever seen the sun go down on Babylon. But I want to do what is right by you. We will go off to a place about an hour's distance and come back at daybreak." And they went. And my sport had to be given up.'

As soon as the Turk had finished recounting this episode, Dr. Hamlin took out his Bible and read to him from the 13th chapter of Isaiah :

And Babylon, the glory of kingdoms, the beauty of the Chaldees' excellency, shall be as when God overthrew Sodom and Gomorrah. It shall never be inhabited, neither shall it be dwelt in from generation to generation ; neither shall the Arabian pitch tent there ; neither shall the shepherds make their fold there. But wild beasts of the desert shall lie there ; and their houses shall be full of doleful creatures ; and owls shall dwell there, and satyrs shall dance there. And wild beasts of the islands shall cry in their desolate houses, and dragons in their pleasant palaces ; and her time is near to come, and her days shall not be prolonged. . . .

'That's it exactly,' said the Turk, 'but that's history you have been reading to me.'

'No,' said the great Doctor, 'it's prophecy. You, as an educated man know that the Old Testament was translated into Greek some three hundred years before Christ. And the Hebrew was given at least two hundred years before that.' 'Yes,' he said. 'Well,' said the Doctor 'wasn't this written when Babylon was in its glory ; and isn't it prophecy ?' 'I must have time to think this over,' said the Turk. But apparently he never came back with his answer. He must have accepted the truth.

The modern and wonderful medicine 'penicillin' was anticipated in Biblical times. Penicillin is derived from a plant mould ; and this mould is that of decaying hyssop. And in Psalm 51, verse 7, King David says, 'Purge me with hyssop, and I shall be clean'.

Jealousy is not countenanced in the true Christian faith. There is the fable of an eagle which could outfly another ; and the other did not like that. So this one happened to see a sportsman one day and said to him 'I wish you would bring down that overproud eagle'. The sportsman said he would do so if only he had some feathers to put into his arrow. So the eagle pulled one out of his wing. The arrow was shot, but didn't quite reach the rival eagle for it was flying so high. The envious eagle pulled out more feathers and kept pulling them out until he lost so many that he couldn't fly. And then the sportsman turned on him and killed him.

I have dwelt most of my life in the East, and they have a saying there, that as the tares and the wheat grow, they show which God has blessed. The ears that God has blessed bow their heads and acknowledge every grain ; and the more fruitful they are the lower their heads are bowed. The tares which God has sent as a curse, lift up their heads erect, high above the wheat, but they are only fruitful of evil. As the lark that soars the highest builds her nest the lowest ; as the nightingale that sings so sweetly, sings in the shade when all things rest ; as the branches that are most laden with fruit bend lowest ; as the ship most loaded sinks deepest in the water—so those most holy are the humblest.

In these days of probing outer space and of men being shot into orbit, one wonders if theologians give thought to the possibility of there being life on other planets ? I am of opinion that many of the devout Highland folk do go *outside* space each time they are in earnest prayer—into the eternal realm, 'Heaven' ; for do they not believe in two worlds, spiritual and physical ; and in that belief there is surely immensity of space ?

My first introduction to the Free and the Free Presbyterian Churches here in Gairloch was in winter ; the roads icy, the Torridon and Flowerdale Hills clad in snow—as was all Skye.

Whilst the minister preached in English, the psalms (46th and 23rd) were sung—seated of course—in Gaelic, led by two precentors who alternated the lead.

Never before have I heard such a warmth and depth of song coming from a congregation ; so very different from English churches where few, if any, appear wishful to sing aloud and lift up their hearts thereby.

It was truly emotional to hear 100 voices singing so lustily ; an inspiration to any luke-warm Christian. The absence of an organ or any form of musical instrument (which invariably seems

to make a point of 'drowning' any singing in English churches)
allowed the congregation full scope to raise their voices heaven-
wards. The singing of the psalms in Gaelic is profoundly more
impressive, more heart-moving, than when sung in English. And
in the Kirks in the Island of Lewis and other Outer Hebridean
isles, the Gaelic rendering can be termed as sensational.

And so, in all humility, I draw this chapter to a close. For all
these past 2000 years, however, with its constant wars and rumours
of wars, I am afraid no nation can as yet sound any true note of
self-congratulation. A great deal of self-satisfaction notwithstanding appears in many quarters—like a decaying house, proud
of the tablet commemorating that somebody great once lived
there. But we must needs get rid of this ruinous self-complacent
attitude. Whilst the past may give some measure of heartening
in certain directions, the future presents a great challenge, with
tremendous tasks ahead.

Up in the Highlands, the people say the WORD must succeed
where the SWORD failed ; and their preachers must appear before
men with an arresting 'Thus saith the Lord'.

With so much nuclear development, we should not only ask
ourselves '*quo vadis ?*'—'whither goest thou ?'—but more con-
cernedly '*quo vadistis ?*'—'whither goest thou who art on the
other side ?'

Whilst the old Scottish theological principles date from John
Calvin (the French Protestant reformer, 1509–1564) and John
Knox (1505–1592, the Scottish Calvinist reformer) and as these
teachings are for the most part observed—more than strictly
observed in these parts—I was confounded that the 73-year-old
Moderator of the Church of Scotland General Assembly, the
Rt. Rev. Dr. A. C. Craig, should have been received in audience
by the Pope at the Vatican when he visited Rome in March 1962.
All the more strange it is to me at any rate—albeit I am English—
that he did so with the sanction of the General Assembly. Such
an action as this would have been undreamt of long ago, when
the Protestant Church separated from the Roman See. Surely
there is not a change of wind springing up ? Surely 'The Kirk'
will remain the Church of Calvin and Knox ?

I can hear these good old Highland folk quoting a line from
Tennyson every Sabbath, 'Pray God our greatness may not fail'.

To which, in my own humble way, I would add a loud AMEN ; 'so let it be'. And may the Church of Christ in Scotland always appear 'Fair as the moon, clear as the sun, and terrible as an army with banners'. There can well be Christian fellowship, but certainly no unity with Rome.

The greatest drama of all, the Crucifixion, has inspired all great painters down the ages. Even so, I need no great painting, or indeed any great preacher, to bring my mind to a simple, religious childhood tale—the story of a little bird hovering and fluttering above the Cross.

It saw the agonised brow pierced by the crown of thorns ; the sacred blood streaming down. Seeking to ease the pain, it tried to pull out the thorns. . . . And I recall that story whenever I see the red glow on the breast of a robin.

A sweet story ? A precious thought ?

———————————

I have just referred to a 'change of wind.'

As this book goes to press, one wonders if there is not another wind blowing up of hurricane effect ? I allude to a move by certain members of the General Assembly, to re-write the Westminster Confession of Faith in 20th century terms. This Faith is one of the Kirk's basic documents ; it has for 300 years been second only to the Bible. The Lord in His sovereign pleasure inspired its articles, for which the Kirk's Presbyterian fathers fought and died.

Those advocating this change do so in the light of the enormous changes of thought, in scientific discovery and so forth during the last 100 years. Some of the 17th century ideas, they say, are now out of date.

I am of the firm opinion this will not be tolerated as a whole ; certainly not by the Highlanders. Here, the principles of Presbyterianism are steadfastly held, and any change in the faith of their forebears will never be countenanced. They will not stand for any disclaimer of such courageous men as Knox and Calvin. No Presbyterian tenet would be sacred—or safe—if their Confession were to be trifled with in any degree.

These people stand cast iron in their firmness on fundamentals; and are not afraid to say so.

CHAPTER 12

THE STONE OF DESTINY—'LIA FÀIL'

THIS is a true story of a young girl of daring Scottish Nationalistic views, who lives near Gairloch who was a 'partner-in-crime' to the stealing of the Stone of Destiny from underneath the Coronation Chair in Westminster Abbey on Christmas Day 1950.

Chief-Inspector Paul Lochart sat at his big oak desk in Scotland Yard, closeted with his assistant, Jock Macleod, with a pile of papers and files at his finger-tips. Whilst both were wearing serious looks, Jock's mind seemed to be thinking of a far-away place, Slattadale, on the shores of Loch Maree, where for many months he had been billeted whilst being assigned to a special task, known as 'Operation Pipes'; and during that time had fallen for a wee lassie working in a near-by bank who obviously needed someone like Jock's 'manly frame' to cuddle up against for protection from life's worries and from the wintry storms and snow-bound roads. At least that was as good an excuse to her as any other!

Paul Lochart was considered a very adroit character, with a keen scent that invariably put him on the track of a criminal streaks ahead of others who had only had time to read through the dossiers of a case. He prided himself a canny Scot, but although neither of his parents were Scotch, he imagined he had *some* Scotch blood running through his veins seeing that the first four letters of his surname spelt LOCH.

Suddenly a knock came to the door. (In all such literary phrases, no one seems to have yet told anyone just how a knock *could* come to a door?) A smart commissionaire, wearing a string of medals, came in, saluted and handed the Chief a telegram; went out and shut the heavy oak door.

Lochart read it. He read it again; then jumping up out of his chair as though jet-propelled, waved the form at Jock (just as Prime Minister Chamberlain had waved his piece of paper in 1938, after returning from Munich) and bellowed out one Greek word EUREKA—'I've found it!' just as Archimedes exclaimed in 250 B.C. when he discovered a method of detecting the amount of alloy in Hiero's crown—though Jock, thinking it was some Gaelic ejaculation, was trying hard to understand what his chief was meaning. 'I've found it, Jock ; it's in Gairloch, Wester Ross ; or if not in Gairloch itself, certainly in Gairloch parish,' said Paul Lochart proudly and triumphantly.

And that's how this story, in a manner of speaking, 'came to pass'. The stolen Stone of Destiny indeed ; well perhaps not *exactly*, but at any rate something concrete leading to its recovery.

But before relating this local story, it might be well to refresh one's memory as to this Stone and Scottish Nationalism generally.

The Stone of Destiny is probably the oldest relic of Scottish royalty. It was kept at *Scone* (pronounced SKOON) near Perth, and Scottish kings were seated on it at their coronation.

It is nothing much to look at. Just a rough and cracked rect-angular three-hundredweight block of yellowish sandstone, 26 inches long, 16 inches broad and 10½ inches deep.

The top is flat and bears the marks of chiselling.

The theories concerning the origin of the Scots Coronation Stone are almost as complicated as the legends which cling to it.

A general notion prevails that it is of Irish origin, and that it is actually the '*Lia Fàil*', or Stone of Destiny, spoken of in Irish tradition which was brought to Scotland by conquering Irish Scots from the Hill of Tara.

The Coronation Stone, as we know it, can most definitely be proved to have been situated in the Royal Scottish demesne at Scone in the 13th century, until it was removed to Westminster Abbey by Edward I ('Hammer of the Scots') in 1296. The memory of Edward I, one of the early Norman Kings of England, is one which is not easily erased from Scottish minds. He brought slaughter to a peaceful Scotland which, although betrayed by its national leaders, its fields and burghs desolated, fought back to secure its liberty and vindicate its ancient rights. Folk-lore has a longer memory than history, and neither history nor folk-lore forget the rape of Scotland in 1296.

But to return to history. In all likelihood the Stone had been at Scone from still earlier times ; the year A.D. 838 is even named. The last Scottish king to be crowned on it was Alexander III in 1249.

Some historians have suggested that it was really a portable altar, belonging to some early Celtic saint, perhaps St. Columba.

Geologists who have examined the Stone are in agreement that it was quarried at or near Scone, as its composition reveals.

One legend, however, has it that it was the stone which the patriarch Jacob used as a pillow at Bethel.

An ancient Latin rhyme about it is translated :

> Unless the fates shall faithless prove
> And prophets speak in vain ;
> Where'er is found the sacred stone
> The Scottish race shall reign.

This prophecy is supposed to have been fulfilled when James VI of Scotland became James I of England.

Another legend is that it was taken from the Holy Land to Spain, then to Ireland, thence to Scotland.

When Edward I annexed Scotland in 1296 he seized the Stone, together with other symbols of Scottish nationality, and it was he who had it placed in the Coronation Chair (specially made to contain it, at Westminster Abbey), on which English kings have since been crowned. He believed it to be inhabited by a spirit who advised the Scots how to wage war successfully.

Scotland, regarding the Stone as sacred and the symbol of her independence, saw its going as her greatest humiliation.

When King Robert Bruce won back Scotland's independence from Edward III, he demanded back the Stone, for he knew of the superstition in Scotland that his land could never be prosperous until the Stone was returned, and in 1328, by the Treaty of Northampton, it was agreed that it should be sent back to Scotland with the other stately belongings that were taken by Edward I ; but the bargain was never kept. As it was being conveyed through London the mob made so threatening a demonstration that its bearers were compelled to return it to Westminster Abbey.

Up till 1950, when it was stolen, it only left the abbey once— when Cromwell as Lord Protector sat on it in the adjacent hall. But around the Stone much strife has gone on.

During the Suffragette troubles a bid was made to destroy the Coronation Chair with a bomb ; but only slight damage resulted.

In 1934 Mr. David Kirkwood, M.P., was given leave to bring in a Bill to transfer the Stone to Holyrood Palace. Nothing came of it.

In 1936 came the first 'plot'. The Dean of Westminster revealed the projected attempt to take the Stone away, Scottish Nationalists being blamed. And in that year, the Wallace Sword was stolen by four masked men from the Wallace Monument, Stirling. The sword was found later at the bottom of a well in Bothwell.

In 1939 a super burglar alarm was installed in the Abbey, and later an invisible ray alarm was built to guard the Chair and the Stone.

So much for the Stone.

But still holding readers in suspense regarding the 'story proper', I would crave a little more indulgence whilst I make some passing references to *Scottish Nationalism*, for it is so closely tied up with the removal of the Stone.

To the Scottish Nationalists the Stone of Scone, as I have stated, was fundamentally a symbol of Scottish independence ; and a little group formed the idea of seizing the Stone and conveying it to Scotland in order to draw public attention to their grievances.

The past was glorious. 'Here's tae us, wha's like us?' One might well sustain the thesis that even the impulse behind Scottish Nationalism is a last despairing effort to get back the land lost long ago whether with the Reformation, the Act of Union (1707) or the discovery of coal and iron in Lanarkshire. Scottish Nationalism, in the political sense, is but the last ditch expression of the will that the country should not lose its cultural identity.

Scotland and England became united under one crown in 1603, through a Scottish king succeeding to the English throne. Before that, there had been many wars between the two countries, with Scotland determined to maintain her independence. Union under one crown did not mean the end of strife between the neighbouring countries situated on one main island. Scots and English sometimes took different sides in the dynastic troubles of the United Kingdom. Scots and English were rivals for world trade and conflicts abroad led to bitterness at home.

It was to put an end to these continual disputes that the Parliaments were united, as I have stated, in 1707, against the wish of many Scots, however.   The Union was to create a new nation called Britain, but English nationalism unfortunately encouraged its Scottish opposite.   The Stuarts, attempting to regain the throne, exploited the dislike of the Scots, especially of the Highlanders, for the new arrangement ; and many Jacobite warriors of 1745 had 'No Union' engraved on their swords as they went into battle.   That was the last rising against London authority, but the rumblings of discontent with centralisation of rule in the South continued.   Whenever there were bad times in Scotland in those days, the tendency was to blame 'centralisation'.

Bad times led to the development of a strong Socialist movement in the industrial belt, especially on Clydeside around Glasgow.   Many of these Socialists were also Scottish Home Rulers. Keir Hardie was numbered with them.

After the First World War, Scottish nationalism became more vocal and it was intensified by the depression which affected the Scottish shipyards, coalfields, iron, steel and engineering works. Scottish unemployment became proportionately higher than English and all these points were driven home by Nationalist propaganda.

The National party of Scotland began in the 1920's and soon there was a rival organisation, the Scottish Party, with many distinguished members.

One of Scotland's most fervent advocates of 'Home Rule' was Dr. John MacCormick, who died in Glasgow in October 1961 aged but 56 years.   He was a lawyer by profession and one of the greatest orators Scotland has produced this century.   On his father's side, he claimed descent from Cormick, an Irish princeling who followed St. Columba (in Latin 'a dove').   His roots were deep in the thin soil of Mull and Iona.

Casually one September night in 1927, he and two friends gave expression to their innermost feelings by founding the Glasgow University Scottish Nationalist Association in a Sauchiehall Street café.   It was a meeting of moment ; the beginning of the beckoning road that, however, ultimately led to nowhere. The minutes of that meeting were recorded on the back of an envelope !

Out of nationalistic diversity in April 1928, the puny Uni-

versity Association moulded the Scottish National Party, and the
objects were to foster and maintain Scottish Nationalism by (1)
securing self-government for Scotland, and (2) advancing the
ideals of Scottish culture within and without the University.

In 1947 churchmen, councillors, trade unionists, business
leaders, representatives of every sort of public organisation,
poured into Glasgow to an unprecedented national assembly ; all
pledging themselves to a Scottish Parliament.

Some of his dubious friends said to MacCormick, 'Home
Rule for Scotland indeed ?—that died at Culloden and you'll
be daft to throw your future to the winds chasing that old
dream.'

However the movement went from strength to strength.
MacCormick was knicknamed 'King John', and he might con-
ceivably have become Prime Minister of Scotland, for he then
found a country marching behind him.

On 29th October 1949, the climax came in a moment of
dedication in the Assembly Hall in Edinburgh, when the Duke of
Montrose—descendant of the great Marquis who had signed the
first covenant centuries before—put his pen to a sheet of paper,
closely followed by Dr. John. At this meeting the Covenant for
a Scottish Parliament was launched.

Over two millions signed this Home Rule Covenant, pledging
themselves to do all in their power—in loyalty to the Crown—to
bring about Scottish self-government.

But gradually the dream faded and the flood of Nationalism
subsided as the various 'lieutenants' melted away.

He was a brilliant man and none will deny he has his place in
history with the great patriots of Scotland.

In short, he was a Wallace of the Word.

Today, however, 'Home Rule for Scotland' is rather a dis-
creditable political slogan—more of a music-hall joke. I would
very much doubt now if there are but one per cent of the whole
population so inclined.

In the aforementioned year of 1927, the affairs of Scotland
were in the charge of the Scottish Secretary who occupied a mean
and indeterminate place in the ministerial hierarchy, and whose
work was wholly carried on from Whitehall. Today we have
both a Secretary of State and a Minister of State of full Cabinet

rank and almost the whole machinery of Scottish administration centred in Edinburgh.

The North of Scotland Hydro-Electric Board has transformed (and continues to transform) the face of the Highlands, harnessing power which Nature has given us. A host of non-political organisations are building up Scottish economy and achieving fine results in advertising Scottish products and making the name of Scotland known abroad. The Edinburgh Festival Society which has sprung up since the war has already made Edinburgh once again a cultural capital ; and in Glasgow, the Citizens' Theatre is actively and successfully promoting Scottish Drama.

In the 1920's, a Scottish flag was a rarity. During the Coronation celebrations in 1953, the flag of St. Andrew flew proudly above nearly every building in Scotland.

Therefore, since those early days of 1927, I think we can safely say the 'wind of change' has come about, and Scotland is being given more and more consideration—I would say every consideration—and respect from Westminster ; so that the early cry of self-government—a free Scotland in a Federal United Kingdom—is surely now a thing of the past to every broad-minded citizen.

One point should be borne in mind, however. Most Nationalists—whatever party they may have assigned themselves to—are loyal in their feelings towards the Queen. They disagree with the numeral 'the Second' in the Queen's title for historic reasons, as the first Queen Elizabeth was *not* a Queen of the United Kingdom. As to the 'British Federation' aforementioned—in which a series of Parliaments would look after Scottish, Welsh, North of England and South of England affairs, while a central Parliament would deal with foreign affairs, general trade questions and defence—this whole set-up would be unthinkable, unworkable. In short, crazy.

It was on 20th March 1948 that proposals for the establishment of a Scottish Parliament were approved by the Scottish National Assembly and they have been, ever since, the basis of the Scottish Covenant campaign. The 'Covenanters' said they were fighting not against oppression from without, but against the private ambitions and narrow partisanship of their own politicians.

Briefly the proposals were :

(1) To establish in Scotland a Parliament which would have the final legislative authority in all matters as they affected Scotland.

(2) It would consist of a simple chamber composed of two members elected by each of the constituencies returning members of parliament to Westminster.

(3) It was to have full power to repeal, alter or amend any Act passed by the Scottish Parliament before 1707 or by the United Kingdom Parliament thereafter, in so far as affecting Scotland.

(4) The Scottish Parliament would have power to alter its own constitution.

(5) During the first two years after the setting up of the Scottish Parliament, there would continue to be sent to represent Scottish interests at Westminster, the number of members who, at the time of the establishment of the Scottish Parliament, represented Scottish constituencies in that Parliament and 16 representative Peers in the House of Lords in that Parliament. These Scottish representatives would not take part in any proceedings of Parliament dealing solely with English or Welsh domestic affairs.

For the adjustment of financial balances between the Scottish and the United Kingdom Governments, a joint Exchequer Board was to be established, two from the Scottish Ministry of Finance, two from the U.K. Treasury, and an independent Chairman.

Widespread matters were to fall within the exclusive legislative power of the Scottish Parliament, except those relating to Defence, Foreign and Dominion affairs and currency.

The Postal, Telegraph and Telephone services, lighthouses and harbours were to be dealt with partly by the U.K. and partly by the Scottish Parliament. Income Tax, Estate Duties and the like, were to be wholly in the hands of the Scottish Government.

Thus it was to be.

Today, Scotland is still having to rely more and more on industrial development to stay alive ; and much has come about in this direction in the Midlothian area.

Whilst Scottish industrialists cry aloud for English aid it is a fact that much private investment finds its way 'South of the border, down Mexico way !'

The character of the nation is tough and resilient, veined with the humour that makes little of adversity. There are people of genius and drive in Scotland still. But inspired action, a stimulant (other than whisky!) is constantly required to send the adrenalin once more coursing through its veins. It does *not* require Scottish Nationalism to affect all this; the ability to do anything is within us, and the strength to achieve it comes from an inner force which is also within us, and will work for us if it is allowed to do so.

The Psalmist knew there was literal truth in the words 'lifting up our eyes to the hills'. To look up, is to get a feeling of strength and power; to realise we are part of a pattern, so vast that our own little struggles slip back into proportion.

So much for the Stone.

So much for Scottish Nationalism.

Now for the story!

The Coronation Stone was stolen from underneath the Coronation Chair in Westminster Abbey, as I said at the outset, on Christmas Day 1950; and the girl, who was the only woman in the party of four in the 'raid', lives quite near me in Gairloch.

I know her as 'Kay' (Katrine); her full name, address and photo, were blazoned across the front pages of all the national newspapers at the time; so there is no need for me to enlarge on that score.

She is small, dark, with large brown eyes; discreet, and although at the time reporters said she was as remote as a Hebridean island, I beg to differ with that very much; for I have found her to 'open out' quite a lot; to be full of humour and to appreciate a joke most heartily. It's 'not what you say, but how you say it' is a very true maxim, and speaking for myself I have found—both at home and abroad—that that truism has stood me well through many, many occasions! And the personal touch counts for far more than anything else.

She was then 21 years of age. Now, still beautiful and attractive, and single at 33 (though I don't know why; unless it is the local boys would feel she would 'Rule' the home in view of her 'Home Rule' principles of over ten years ago!) she still lives on the shores of Loch Ewe at a mountain-shadowed croft house, surrounded by barren hills, with her aged mother and teaches domestic science, P.T. and Gaelic at Achtercairn School in Gairloch. She hails from the ravaged Highlands with their long memory for oppression and clearances ; speaks with the quiet Highland tongue that knows English only as a second language. The last time I went over to see her (one storm-tossed wintry day) she had on a seaman's oilskin and Wellington boots, holding a ladder for the man who had come to look at, and sweep, the chimney of their whitewashed house that lies on a spit of land jutting into the waters of Loch Ewe and looking across at the famed Inverewe Gardens.

In 1950—the time of our story—she was a keen worker in the Scottish Covenant movement. She had come to Glasgow University to study and later became a junior domestic science teacher at Eastpark School, Maryhill, Glasgow.

It was on Friday evening, 15th December 1950, and Glasgow University undergraduates were celebrating 'Daft Friday' at the traditional ball in the Students' Union. Under the soft lights of the ballroom, she chatted earnestly across a table with a young fellow of 25 years of age—Ian Hamilton—a 3rd-year law student and a students' representative on the Covenant Committee. He had met her two months previously at a party given by Dr. John MacCormick, Chairman of the Covenant Movement, to celebrate the success of the Covenant Plebiscite in the Scotstoun by-election.

At last they rose, and with her companion, joined the dancers on the floor. In those few moments she had entered into the plot to remove the Stone of Destiny from Westminster Abbey ; the start of an exploit that was to set the world agog and wonder-ing—apart from setting Scotland Yard on one of their most intensive man and woman hunts. She surely had that night, received an 'invitation to danger'.

When her school broke up on 22nd December for Christmas holidays, she joined Hamilton on their journey to London on roads that were snowed up and icy, and where they met the other two in the conspiracy.

In short these four planned to bring the Stone of Destiny from the Abbey to Scotland on Christmas Day. But a certain amount of bad luck dogged them and finally when they moved the Stone it broke into two. Kay took the smaller part in her

car. Whilst travelling through the heart of London, it fell out
of the boot, at Hyde Park Corner of all places, but by super-
human effort she managed to lift the 90-pound weight back into
the car and made for Reading, then for Oxford and finally to
the Midlands—Birmingham—(a devious route since police blocks
had been set up and all cars were being searched) where she
left her part of the Stone hidden in a friend's house. The night
she called unexpectedly at that house explaining her purpose and
mission secretly to her girl-friend, it so happened they had a friend
in for supper ; and believe it or not, it was no other than the
recently retired Superintendent of Police of Birmingham ! What
a 'glow' Kay must have felt inside her ! Am sure it would have
made her look more radiant than ever. The next day she took
train to Glasgow and on to Ross-shire, to Inverasdale, near Gairloch. Later on it was planned for her to return to Birmingham
to bring back both the car and the half stone ; but in the end,
seeing a fairly accurate description of her was being broadcast—due to the keen eyes of a policeman who happened to
see her parked near the Abbey on Christmas Eve—one of the
others in the party went in her stead and safely brought her
'portion' to Glasgow.

It was intended Kay should be captured and that the others
should escape ; for the plotters believed that the capture
of a woman would attract much more publicity than that of a
man. As it turned out, they all got clear away. Kay was
also picked for the job since she was known to have a strong
belief in the cause of home rule, and also she could drive a car
expertly.

As to the other part of the Stone—the larger part—it was
taken by 'the lads' and hidden in the grassy bank of a sheltered
field near Rochester, and then six days later, 'unearthed'—
although, most amazingly, a gipsy's caravan was camped practically on top of the Stone when they went to dig it out—taken
up to Scotland via Glasgow to a house in Bearsden on New
Year's Eve 1950.

The two parts were successfully repaired in a little yard by a
mason, by joining the pieces with bronze bolts, and instead of
using sand in the cement, dust from the Stone itself was used,
so that the join and the drill holes were invisible.

The Stone lay in Bearsden three weeks until it was finally

decided to return it to Arbroath Abbey. (It was at Arbroath that the original 'Declaration' was signed.)

It was taken there by car by two of the male members of the plot and another keen outsider. The Stone was carried through the Abbey Gates, across what is now a carpet of green turf, placed in front of the High Altar and covered with the blue and white of the St Andrew's Cross. As they turned away, the leader seemed to hear the voice of Scotland speak as clearly as it spoke in 1320 . . . 'For so long as there shall be but one hundred of us remain alive we will never give consent to subject ourselves to the dominion of the English. For it is not glory; it is not riches, neither is it honour, but it is liberty alone that we fight and contend for, which no honest man will lose but with his life.'

Thus the Stone came to its resting place.

There was actually far more to it than what I have related, in so far as the Stone's actual journey and hiding-places from London to Arbroath ; far more than was ever known to the public or the police ; but as I promised to keep such secrets to myself I would never dream of betraying such trust placed in me for the purpose of this narrative.

During the 'episodes', it was decided to formulate a petition to the King (King George VI) and this was given into the hands of a Glasgow newspaper office. This was done to make clear the motives in removing the Stone and to assure the authorities (and the public) that the Stone was not in irresponsible hands. Later on it was thought they should make yet another appeal.

So Kay and Ian went through to Edinburgh and, under cover of darkness, nailed to the door of St. Giles' Cathedral the message suggesting that the future resting-place of the Stone should be considered by a National Assembly, called by the Scottish Covenant.

The note was fixed to the door with one of the nails brought from the door of Westminster Abbey to prove that it was a genuine appeal.

So the exploit ended. There was no prosecution. The stealing of the Stone had already brought enough signatures to the Covenant, and the Government had no desire to make martyrs, who might bring more signatures still.

The case was dropped ; and my dear Kay was not sent to jail !

It is the only case in modern Scottish legal history where clear

G

proof has existed and no prosecution has followed ; though the maximum penalty for sacrilege is fourteen years.

The conspirators have long since scattered. All, I believe, have lost interest in the affair. All except Kay who—although not so young as she was then—would, I fancy, do it again if it was felt that by so doing, great and far-reaching results would 'come to pass' for Scotland. But in this year of grace (1962) there seems to be no call for repeating this 'master-stroke'.

The police team which ran them to earth is still active in the West of Scotland.

And the Stone is back, snug in Westminster Abbey.

From that 'sensation', Kay went to be a junior teacher of Domestic Science at Duncraig school, Plockton, near Kyle of Lochalsh—where she was known locally as 'Clara'. From that appointment she went over to the Outer Hebrides, travelling between the islands of Eriskay, South Uist and Benbecula, teaching at the schools there. After that, she was transferred to Tobermory, on the Island of Mull ; and then later to her present-day post, teaching in the Gairloch School ; literally a stone's throw from me as I write—*not* the Coronation Stone of course!

During police investigations it was found that scratched on the gilt of the Coronation Chair, beneath which the Stone rests, were the initials J. F. S. These initials chance to be those of the old Pretender, James Francis Stuart, who died 195 years ago. They could, of course, have been meant then as a slogan, namely *Justice For Scotland*? But I am given to believe that this was *not* the work of Kay and her three compatriots.

I have said the party has scattered.

Of the quartet, only Kay, I learn, does anything active for Scotland now. In winter evenings she runs the local Gaelic Youth Organisation, tape-records old songs and poems from the local bards, and is compiling a place-name map of the district for the School of Scottish Studies.

In the summer she gives up her holidays to work at the Gaelic Youth Club camp at Tain—as a cook ! So saving the organisers money. She interests herself too, in injecting new life into the local crofts, mostly owned by old people incapable of doing heavy work such as fencing, stone clearing, drainage, etc., by organising work-parties.

As a relic of her Westminster Abbey foray, she wears—on special occasions—a golden locket round her neck, an heirloom from her grandmother ; and inside it is a fragment of the Stone of Destiny, which I have seen, touched and felt honoured in so doing.

It was said, at the time, that six medals were to be fashioned (struck by an Edinburgh firm) for Celtic Silver ornaments and jewellery for those who removed the Stone from the Abbey, sponsored by Scottish National Congress President, Mr. Mathew Somerville ; but whether this 'came to pass' or not I cannot say. Kay certainly never received one.

At the Annual General Meeting of An Comunn Gaidhealach (the Gaelic Association or League) in Stirling in October 1961, there was much talk of a 'wind of change' to whistle through the whole structure of the Association, to blow away out-of-date methods and ideas. It may be that this wind may blow from the north to the south rather than from south to north as has been the case previously.

Probably the most important of all, the Standing Committees of the Executive Council which deals with the Gaelic Youth (in whose hands lies the future of Gaelic as a living language and the whole Gaelic culture and way of life) elected their youngest Convener to the Executive Council for many years ; and the only Convener for quite some time who has been domiciled in the north.

That very person was Kay ; and what an honour it is to be sure, for this comparatively young girl teaching in her own Gairloch locality, which is considered to be one of the last strongholds of Gaelic on the mainland of Scotland.

It may well be, that a fresh, cold northerly wind blowing from Wester Ross will revive the warm, sluggish southerly wind from the Association's Glasgow headquarters ? A 'Gael' force wind perhaps to shake the whole movement.

From what little I have written, it must be freely admitted, Kay is a grand personality ; talented, and a practical worker for the country folk. In short, a patriot if ever there was one ; and certainly from what I can gather, the only real patriot of the four.

Yes, Kay is all that, and more—petite and pretty—and to her, and her large brown eyes, I say *Slàinte Mhath* in all sincerity.

That then is the story connected with a demure little Gairloch parish girl.

Who would have thought during that nation-wide hunt, one of the 'offenders' lived in outlandish, quiet-living, peaceful Wester Ross ? Being English, I am not a Scottish Nationalist. If I were, I would surely 'take off my hat' to Kay Matheson ; though not perhaps for this 'exploit' alone, but for all her other sterling qualities—and her beauty !

The theft of the Coronation Stone in 1950 stirred few Scottish hearts. It was described in the press as a shabby exploit, timed for a night (Christmas Eve) when the risks could be counted low. Scottish necks, it was said, grew red at the thought that the thieves were Scots !

Whilst, I suppose, Scotland would like to have her Stone of Destiny back, she would not have liked it back that way, I am sure, by the desecration of Westminster Abbey on a Christmas day. It would have been far better to have gone about it through 'diplomatic channels'—to use the parlance of the Foreign Office !

Extremist demonstrations of any kind shock the canny Scot's mind. When shame is added to shock, the damage is complete.

Bringing Scotland's future constitutional position right up to date, on St. Andrew's Day (30th November) 1961, an appeal for £100,000 by May 1962, to enable a plebiscite to be taken on this subject, was launched by fifteen distinguished Scots, including the Earl of Airlie and Lord Boyd-Orr ; the intention being to enable every adult Scotsman and woman to choose how their country should be governed.

These fifteen 'dignitaries' represent a wide section of Scotland's character and life ; and people were asked in the appeal to send donations to the Scottish Plebiscite Fund, Forfar, in Angus.

These prominent Scots offer three choices : (1) Dominion Status, like New Zealand ; (2) limited Home Rule within the framework of the United Kingdom (as in Northern Ireland) ; and (3) the present position. It will be noticed they do not offer the choice of a completely independent Scotland.

It will be interesting to discover whether enough people think this so vital a question that they will raise at least £100,000 among them ?

Personally I can think of many other, and more noble, purposes to which £100,000 could be put, than to a plebiscite !

CHAPTER 13

SCOTTISH HUMOUR

As long as there is a Scotsman who will say 'nae bad' when he means 'very good' there will be a humour completely Scottish.

In the old days there was little to do after work but talk and sing—the old-time céilidh, which nowadays has resolved itself into an informal concert in the village hall or school. In the Hebrides and here in Wester Ross, till the turn of the century, the men and lads—and the lassies of course—would gather during the winter evenings in a favoured house, where they would be sure of a welcome.

The man of the house would be well able to take the lead and tell the first tale, and everyone else was expected to contribute to the night's entertainment. There might be singing or playing, but the time was mainly spent in telling of stories and personal anecdotes, the asking of riddles and the quoting of sayings. So humorous story-telling became the thing. The Scot does not create a situation for humour, but takes the humour out of the situation. Thus, an Aberdonian woke up in the morning and found his wife had died in the night. Walking to the head of the stairs he called out to the maid, 'Jeannie, just boil one egg for breakfast today!'

Of course, to see a Scotsman come on wearing the kilt, the tartan, is quite enough on its own to gladden the hearts of an English audience. There is something about the dress that fascinates those south of the border. And the Highlander himself feels a glow of emotion wearing the dress that he wore so often when roaming the lonely glens or climbing the heathery hills of his beloved Scotland. The tartan of his kilt denotes the clan in which his ancestors fought against the invader in the renowned days of old ; and many is the hero who has lain down to die with his blood-wet tartan wrapped about him. It is the imperishable badge of bravery.

The kilt followed the belted plaid. It is thought that about 1720 the manager of an iron-smelting works in Glengarry introduced a garment made of one width of material sewn into pleats—the kilt—because the belted plaid, then worn by Highland workmen generally, was so unwieldy. The belted plaid may have been suitable enough for pastoral life, but not for heavy manual work.

Up to about twenty years ago Scots humour was so defined, so keen, that Harry Lauder and Will Fyffe were able to make it understood and popular all over the world. Today it is very rare for a Scots comedian to succeed in the south, as a lot of Scots humour depends on dialect. It is very regional really. Harry Gordon was more successful in Aberdeen than anywhere else.

Scots humour loved taking a rise out of people ; they laughed at what they feared, death and the Church ! It is broad humour and tough. A pawky one on death is the one of the corpse sitting up in his coffin saying he was hungry. 'You can have some ham,' one of the mourners told him, 'but you'll have to be quick about it because you're getting buried in two hours !' And this one of a dock labourer telling of the death of his Maggie. In her last moments she tells him, 'John, we havena' gotten on very weel a' they years, but I'd like you to ride tae the funeral wi' ma mither'. John pauses, purses his lips and says, 'Richt ye are. But that's aye you—spoilin' ma day agin !'

In the Highlands the humour is mainly about farming, fishing and sly stupidity. One such typical joke is of the farmer being visited by a Ministry of Agriculture official : 'What are you seeking ?' he asks him. 'How many people are employed here,' the official says. 'Well,' says the farmer, 'there are four, three of whom are well paid with £9 a week. The other gets 10s. pocket money and a new pair of trousers every three years.' 'I would like to see this underprivileged half-wit,' the official says. 'Carry on,' said the farmer, 'it's himself that's speaking.'

Audiences don't have the patience as of old. Harry Lauder could come out and sing a song and then go off-stage to change his costume and make up, leaving the audience to sing with the orchestra until he came back. But that patience is no more. As illustrated by the following : An Englishman was fishing from a boat on the loch. On the shore a local watched and watched. The Englishman fished for four or five hours, catching nothing.

All that time the local watched and watched. Coming ashore the angler said to the local, 'Why don't *you* try fishing?' 'Och,' said the local, 'I wudna' hae the patience for yon kind o' thing.'

Yes, Scots humour surely comes out of situation, out of Scots quick-wittedness; for instance, a man rushed into a shop and said, 'Can I have a mousetrap in a hurry; I've got to catch a bus'. 'What size of bus?' the shop man asked! And the Highland village policeman, after a bus accident, walks up leisurely-like and says, 'Did anyone see the accident? I want to know if the man was on the bus when he fell off!' And again, when a customer asked a jovial Scottish fishmonger for a hare, he thought he'd be a little humorous, and said to the buyer, 'Would you like one wi' brown eyes or blue eyes, madam?' but the customer was a real Scot deep down, and she said, 'I'll tell you what sort I'd like; I'd like one wi' round shoulders on it, so as to keep the pie crust up!'

Scotsmen are always thought to be mean, and many a joke there is they tell against themselves. For they are *not* mean; far from it. As a race they are careful; but mean? Never. Typical of this 'nearness' is the story of the young Scots lad who often gave his girl-friend lipstick for a present, because he knew he would get half of it back! Subtle?

As subtle as this one : A father took his son round the docks in Glasgow one day. The boy asked his dad what the plimsoll line was. Said the father, 'I dinna ken'. For an hour or so the boy asked question upon question, and every time the answer came, 'I dinna ken'. As they left and walked out of the dock gates homewards, the boy turned to his father and said, 'I hope, Paw, ye're no' angry wi' me askin' a' these questions?'; to which his dad answered, 'Oh no, son; if ye dinna spere, ye canna learn!'

This time it's the father's turn; so when they reached home he tells his son to nip round 'to ask how old Mrs. Fraser is today', for she had been ill. In less than no time, sonny is back, saying, 'Mrs. Fraser says it's none o' your business how old she is!'

A real Scotsman is very proud of his country—the land of his birth—and such a man who had gone down to a job in England arranged for a sack of his Highland village's soil to be sent down to him when his wife was expecting the first baby; and he sprinkled it under the confinement bed making sure that when his child was born it would be born on Scottish soil!

Och aye ; many a man comes oot his shell when his missis eggs him on !

Then there was the very drunk Glaswegian who, whilst staggering along Sauchiehall Street, stopped and asked a dear old lady the way to the Alcoholics Reform Club. She told him and said, 'I hope they will be able to help you, my guid man.' 'Help me, ma foot,' says he, 'I'm going there tae resign !'

Weddings are, of course, a happy hunting-ground for story-telling, and at Highland weddings many broad humorous anec-dotes are slipped in with the speeches, the minister (though not a 'Free, or a Free Presbyterian divine) generally starting the ball rolling, when he proposes the toast of the 'Bride and Bridegroom', with one or two having a biblical background. I remember at one such wedding the Church of Scotland minister was an easy, fluent speaker, and he recounted the story anent the feeding of the five thousand ; saying that an old clergyman had rather mixed up the reference by declaring at the time that his text would be the feeding of five men with five thousand loaves and two fishes. After the service and whilst walking out—as was his custom—with one of the chief elders, he asked him how he liked his sermon that morning ; and of course the elder very forthrightly told him—much to the minister's disgust—he had made a grievous mistake in the quotation and, as such, it was impossible to liken it to a miracle and that he would needs make amends next Sunday. Accordingly, after giving out the text correctly the following week, he paused for a moment, gazed down on the elder from his pulpit and said to him in a low voice, 'Got it right this time, Andra' ; and it sure is a miracle that even *you* must admit.' Back came Andra's comment, also softly, 'Oh! no, not a miracle minister, from what was left over last week'.

There are many minor roads up in the Highlands that just go to one or two villages and then stop there ; you cannot go any further, but have to go back all the way you came ; a 'dead end' so to speak. An English tourist motoring on one of such narrow roads, came across a crofter feeding his hens, stopped and said, 'Excuse me, I'm a stranger up here ; can you tell me if this road leads anywhere, or is it a "dead end" ?' 'Aweel,' said the crofter, 'in a manner o' speakin' it is and it isn't a dead-end.' 'What do you mean ?' enquired the puzzled motorist ; 'Well,' said the Highlander, 'it leads to the cemetery, ye ken !'

From the Sheriff's court comes the story of the couple that were up before the bench for some disorderly conduct, arising out of leaving the 'local' one Saturday night ; and they were duly fined. Before leaving the box and speaking earnestly to the Clerk, the latter turned to the sheriff and said, 'It seems, sir, they cannot pay the fine, but they'll take the fourteen days if they can have the last week in July and the first week in August!'

I hold the view that the secret of keeping 'young in heart' is to have a tremendous joy in living, coupled with a highly developed sense of humour.

Laughter is one of God's best gifts, and it is one of the surest solvents for the hardships of life. A sense of humour—which has been defined as 'the capacity for seeing the amusing side of the tiresome and trying events of life'—is a great asset on our journey.

The Bible is right when it says that 'a merry heart doeth good, like a medicine'.

CHAPTER 14

THE GAELIC—A' GHÀIDHLIG

THE words *Fàilte D'on Tigh So*, hang in my verandah—cut deep in a piece of elm—'welcome to this house'. Another plaque hangs, viz. *Slàinte Mhath*, 'good health'.

No book about the Highlands, however small or insignificant, could possibly omit references to 'the Gaelic'. I am far from knowing much about this language, but will try to make a few points for our visiting friends, who may be under the impression that nothing but a foreign tongue—Gaelic—is spoken up here!

In this connection Maclaren's Gaelic self-taught manual would be found helpful to anyone wishing to take up this subject in more detail.

There are, of course, varying dialects to be found all over the north and north-west of Scotland, like different words and phrases one may come across in passing from one Riding of Yorkshire to another. It is a living, and, therefore, a spoken language; though I am sorry to think fewer and fewer people speak it, despite early schooling aid and efforts.

It is said the difficulties to be surmounted in studying the Gaelic are not at all so formidable as they may at first sight appear. But of this, 'I hae ma doots'; very much so. To my mind pronunciation presents the greatest difficulty.

In the Gaelic alphabet there are only 18 characters : 5 vowels; 12 consonants; and 1 'h'—the sign of a breathing or aspiration only.

There is no indefinite article (nor is there in Greek or Latin for that matter) and there are only two accents, grave and acute. Some words are spelt the same, but the accent and pronunciation gives them a different meaning; *i.e.* BÀTA (a boat), BATA (a staff or rod). These accent marks are easier in Gaelic than in, say, the French language. Thus :

A, U, and I when given a long sound are written as à, ù, ì; sounding as in the English words dam, doom, and deem.

ó is like o in the English word tone
ò ,, o   ,,   job
É ,, A   ,,   say
È ,, E   ,,   get
s before E or I is pronounced as SH in the English word show.

This letter 'h' is rather intriguing. It is simply a breathing which modifies the letter into a *softer* sound, sometimes smoothing it away altogether. *B* when aspirated becomes a *V* and *S* when so aspirated, vanishes altogether. In short, the aspirate is to silence or euphonise the consonants when their initial sound would injure the easiness of flow ; and so this aspirate power and correct use is most important. This 'h' is not included as a letter in the alphabet and there is not a single word in the Gaelic language that commences with the letter 'h'.

It is an aid to inflexion and is also used to denote gender, number, case and tense. Thus in BEAN MHATH (a good wife) where MATH appears as MHATH the aspiration shows that BEAN (wife) is feminine ; and this aspiration may take place at the middle or end of a word.

The Latin word for *Mother*, MATER is MÀTHAIR in Gaelic and pronounced MA'UR, the original hard 'T' completely softened by aspiration. Gaelic is therefore a soft language ; harsh, hard sounds seldom occurring. The music of the Gaelic speech is due in large measure to the use of this 'aspiration', thus causing sounds to glide into one another.

The Gaelic *vowels* sound very similar to the continental vowels. Thus A (ah), E (ay), I (ee), O (oh), U (oo).

There is no silent final vowel, like the English *e*, as in home, house or give.

The *consonants* are sounded each in their own way, and it would take too long—and be very uninteresting here—to give them all. Just to quote a few examples :

       B is like B in boat, but tending towards a P sound
     BH is like a V ; BHA (VA)
      C is always hard like C in cat ; never like an S
     FH is always silent ; FHEAR (ER'R), meaning MAN
    MH like a V with a nasal touch ; MHATH (VA)
    PH like F, as in English
    TH like H in 'him' ; the aspirate washing out the *t*.

The Gaelic *verb* always precedes the noun or pronoun and is *not* declined ; it is the same for all persons and numbers, being very different from the English verb in form and structure.

All verbs (except 10) in the Gaelic language are regular and have only past and future time tenses.

As a matter of interest, I give the verb 'to be', and not being declined as I have said, is the same throughout :

THÀ MI (ha mee) I am   THÀ SINN (ha sheen) we are
THÀ THU (ha oo) thou art   THÀ SIBH (ha sheev) you are
THÀ E (ha ay) he is   THÀ IAD (ha eent) they are.

As THÀ ('is', 'are', or 'am') always precedes its nominative, we get the impression of a constant asking of questions. Example, 'it's a cold day' in Gaelic would literally be 'is the day cold ?'

There is no affirmative word corresponding to the English 'yes' ; nor a negative 'no'. A question is put by the interrogative form of the verbs, and the answer must be made by the affirmative or negative form of the verb ; its tense corresponding to the form used in putting the question. Very involved ? And certain idioms seem to 'rotate'. To translate 'I hate him', the literal Gaelic wording would be 'hate is at me to him'. Again, 'I remember' forms itself as 'it is memory with me'. And 'I love you', in Gaelic becomes, 'Love is at me on you'. (Far too long a sentence, I'm thinking, in English for an ardent lover !)

In English, posing the question 'Did you go to town ?', you would answer, 'I did'—not 'I did go', for the verb 'go' is understood. But in Gaelic, however, no such suppression as this can occur, and you must enunciate the whole verb ; thus 'I did go'.

Nouns such as the names of males, young of all animals regardless of sex, trees, vegetables, liquors, colours, metals, elements, seasons and days of the week are *all* masculine.

Usually feminine are names of females (including animals), countries, musical instruments and diseases.

The Gaelic *adjective* is immediately after the noun it qualifies. Thus CU (a dog), and DONN (brown)—and 'a brown dog' becomes CU DONN (a dog brown).

Regarding the points of the *Compass*, the observer—like the Druids and sun-worshippers of old—is supposed to face the rising sun. Thus, *East* is EAR (in front of) ; *South* is at the right hand, DEAS ; *North*, the left hand TUATH ; and *West*, *i.e.* where you are standing, is IAR (the land at the back of you).

Gaelic therefore is a very different make-up to other foreign tongues we hear. Each word seems to weave a story of its own composition to both the casual labourer and the learned don. As I have said earlier, those speaking Gaelic are getting fewer and fewer, although it forms a language subject in the Higher Leaving exams. In 1915 Gaelic was recognised as a subject for the Leaving Certificate (Lower Grade only). The following year, 1916, the Higher Grade paper was set. On the whole, it has been a neglected language.

The following words, phrases and meanings, taken at random, may be useful to visitors coming to these parts :

THÀ E BRÈAGH (ha breeah) : its fine
THÀ E FLIUCH (ha fluke) : it's wet
THÀ E FUAR (ha fooar) : it's cold
THÀ E GAOTHACH (ha guur) : it's windy
BLÀTH (bplah) : warm
MO GHAOL (moh voil) : my love
CÉILIDH (cayley) : a meeting for gossip and song.
CIA MARA THÀ-THU (Kamera-ha) : how are you ?
THÀ GU MATH (ha goo ma) : I'm well
STRUPAG (strupack) : cup of tea and a bite to eat
FÀILTE (faltchy) : welcome
GLÉ MHATH (gley va) : very good
ACHNASHEEN : field of storm
ÀIRD, or ÀRD : a height, promontory or headland
STRATH : a broad valley
GÀIRLOCH : short loch. Originally and more correctly spelt GEÀRR-LOCH, or GERLOCH. GEÀRR (short), spelt GHEÀRRLOCH in Gaelic
BADACHRO : BAD (clump), A (of), CHRÒ (trees, or nuts), might there-fore mean a 'clump of trees'
GLEN DOCHERTY : properly GLEANN DOCHARTIE, is believed to have been the name of a man ; in essence it means 'the glen of ex-cessive scouring'—indicating that its sides and base are scoured by spates
BEINN DAMH (or DAMPH) : mountain of the stag
CARN DEARG : red cairn
GRUINARD : in Gaelic GRUINAIRD ; origin vague, may be Norse. GRIAN, the sun ; AIRD, height
MELVAIG (or MOLVIG) : in Norse it would mean a shingly bay ; in Gaelic MEALL BHEAG, a little hill
MELLON UDRIGIL : Hill of Udrigil. Norse
OPINAN : little bays
SAINT MAELRUBHA : Maree, is a corruption from this saint's name.
SLIOCH, or SLEAGHACH : resembling a spear. From certain angles

this 3217 foot mountain on Loch Maree appears as a broad spear-head

ULLAPOOL : an old name probably from UILE (all) and POLL (pool) ; or a pool large enough for all.

DUBH : black
FIONN : white
BUIDHE : yellow
GORM : blue
DONN : brown
GLAS : grey (or green)
DEARG : red
BREAC : trout
BRADAN : salmon
FRAOCH : heather
EILEAN : island
INVER : mouth of river : (Gaelic, INBHIR)

UISGE : rain
GRIAN : sun
CAORA : sheep
UAN : lamb
CIOBAIR : shepherd
FANG : sheep pen
BÓ (BA) : cow
EACH : horse
BAINNE : milk
HAAR : Scotch mist (not Gaelic merely broad Scotch)
KINLOCH : head of Loch (Gaelic CEANNLOCH)
TIGH : house
KYLE : strait (CAOL, in Gaelic).

It is certainly very sweet and restful to listen to the Gaelic being spoken ; especially wondering what it is all about—if *you* are being talked of in terms good or bad !

The vocabulary of Gaelic is much greater, and less defiled, than most ; it is not a 'mongrel' language like English. Gaelic is a clear-cut, pedigreed language, with a subtle gradation of meaning in the words it employs.

The Gael's contribution is a valuable one ; his language, song, poetry and his story enhance the arts of the world. And it has been said by distinguished Gaelic scholars 'if Gaelic dies, then it is a loss to civilisation'.

Gaelic may be giving ground, but it is still as full of life up in the real Highland territory as a flowering hawthorn tree ; and at the Mods—well, Gaeldom runs riot ! Wherever possible, I see no reason at all, with such millions of pounds (about 500 million a year) being spent on Education today, why Gaelic should not receive more attention and prominence in all Scottish schools.

Going back over the years, the Education Act of 1872 ignored Gaelic, but in 1874 a concession was made whereby an inspector might allow pupils to express themselves in Gaelic if they had difficulty in doing so in English ! How different today.

It may be recorded with pride, I think, that Ross-shire has the highest percentage of Gaelic speakers of all the counties.

The very earnest speakers, and students, of Gaelic maintain that the Gaelic language will be spoken a thousand years from now. But people talked like that about the old Norn language which faded out in Shetland hundreds of years ago, as they did about Cornish which died out in Cornwall about the same time—in the mid-1700s.

In 1800 one Scotsman in five spoke Gaelic. In 1860 the ratio was one in ten. Today (1962) it is about one in seventy. For some generations now Highlanders have been brought up in the comfortable belief that they can preserve their character, customs and traditions and yet allow their language to perish. The decline in the number of Gaelic speakers is due in no small measure undoubtedly to depopulation. Many of the Western Isles carry less than a third of the population they had a hundred years ago ; and the same process is going on all over the Highlands today. Look at our own Gairloch parish census (given under Gairloch) 5000 in 1880 and only 1763 in 1961—a drop of some 3237 people in just over eighty years ; over 60 per cent less.

Generally speaking, apart from isolated pockets throughout the Highlands, the Gaelic-speaking communities are almost entirely confined to the islands and the districts along the north-west coast.

I am told that in some *truly* Highland homes, twittering budgies are taught to speak Gaelic ! and at any local District Council meetings, if there is anything the Council does not wish the Press to understand or report they drift into their secret language, Gaelic ; and that leaves the Press guessing ! *Abab!* (pshaw !)

Recently, I saw in the 'wanted' columns of a National newspaper the following : 'Wanted : a Gaelic teacher with an English accent to teach Spaniards'.—The post was offered by a journalist who is principal of a private school (interested in physical culture, outdoor life and camping) near Madrid, which teaches Spaniards to read and write in Gaelic. And the weekly salary was £12 plus ; and as the cost of living in Spain is low, this would be equal to more than double that money in England.

So someone wearing a kilt and keen on Highland games and dancing and tossing the caber, with a knowledge of playing the bagpipes, red-headed and with hairy knees, would surely fill the bill ?

Slàinte Mhath indeed !—or as one might retail it over in Spain '*Slanjer Vah*' señor and señora, accompanied, of course, with a few flicks of the castinets !

So therefore, I would say to all the young in heart, 'Forsake not the Gaelic'—*Na treig a' Ghàidhlig*—but instead 'Forward the Gaelic'—*Suas Leis a' Ghàidhlig*.

I might here explain how *Slàinte Mhath* (good health) came into existence. In the days after the 1745 rebellion, no Jacobite was allowed to mention the name of Charlie (Bonnie Prince Charlie) in any shape or form, under penalty of death, and whilst they always toasted his name in secret, in public it had to be otherwise. They had to toast the 'King of England'.

But the Jacobites got over this stigma.

In Gaelic, *mór* means 'big' ; and it can also mean 'Marion' ; and 'Marion' was the underground 'password' for Charlie—Bonnie Prince Charlie—and they composed many songs to 'Marion', unsuspected.

At all Hanoverian dinners, banquets and like occasions, they would get up and say *Slàinte Mhór*, and the authorities, Quislings and so forth thought it was Gaelic for 'Big Health' ; whereas, of course, they were drinking to the good health of Marion, alias Prince Charlie.

And so it has 'come to pass', down the years in history, corrupted as *Slàinte Mhath*, pronounced the same (*vhor*) as in those days of 1745.

Another corruption of *Slàinte Mhath* could very well be written as *Slanjy Vaa*, seeing that not so long ago the question arose of how the Island of Rum should be spelt ; should it be Rum, or as generally shown on maps as Rhum ? There are quite a few peculiarly named islands off the west coast, Rum, Eigg, Muck (reminding one of a new cocktail name !), Bottle Isle, Soyee, Wisy, Ensay, Isay, Coll, Soag, Bac Mor (or Dutchman's Cap), Canna and so on.

Dr. Eggeling, Conservation Officer of Scotland's Nature Conservancy, states it should be spelled Rhum ; but there is no 'Rh' in Gaelic and so 'Rhum', if Dr. *Eiggling* (to so spell his name if I may !) insists it should be, might appear to have come down from the days of old Queen Victoria, which were blessed in gentleness if nothing else. Or maybe the islanders at the time were engaged in wholesale illicit distilling ; and if they persisted in letting the world know their island was spelt Rum, like the beverage, it might dawn on the mainland's Excise officer that with such a name he had better pay more frequent (and incognito) visits, just to 'have a look-see' ; if it *were* rum that was the staple industry (and diet) his nose would no doubt stand him in good stead—better so than if it were whisky !

Many place-names in Scotland have been much hacked about —or should one say 'mucked' about (seeing the island of Muck has been mentioned). Altnacealgach, just over the Ross-shire border in Sutherlandshire, was originally 'Aultch-Tana-Garadh'; and Inchnadamph, near-by, 'Yard-an-dam-à' !

Another, and familiar tongue-twister, is to be found in Fife, namely 'Auchtermuchty', originally known as 'Uachdar-muc-Garadh', but referred to by the locals simply as 'Muchty'.

But Spanish, slangish, or 'rumish', I prefer *Slàinte Mhath!*

CHAPTER 15

MACBRAYNES

SINCE it was one of Messrs. David MacBrayne's steamers, the old *Claymore*, that gave me my first look at Gairloch in June 1914, I think it but fitting to devote a little space to this great undertaking.

The Company held its centenary in 1951.

Travel in the good old days at the beginning of the 19th century was an adventure, and there were few 'comings and goings' to and from the Western Highlands and Islands.

Henry Bell's *Comet* of 1812 was the first steamer to sail regularly between Glasgow and Fort William making calls on the way. This vessel was wrecked in Loch Craignish in 1820. Her successor, *Comet II*, started sailing in 1821 but had a short life, for she sank in 1825 after being in collision on the Clyde, between Gourock and the Cloch lighthouse.

Sailings on the Caledonian Canal, although incomplete, were started in 1820 by the *Stirling Castle*, from Inverness to Fort Augustus. The Canal was completed in 1822 and the sailings extended to Banavie and round to Glasgow.

In 1824 G. & J. Burns was one of the companies operating the West Highland trade. The year 1847 was a landmark in the history of the Highlands, for in that year Her Majesty, Queen Victoria, travelled through the Crinan Canal from Ardrishaig to Crinan, and there joined the royal yacht *Victoria and Albert*. The passage through this wee Canal was made in a track-boat (barge), the track-horses being ridden by postillions clad in brilliant scarlet uniforms. In 1873, after staying at Inverlochy Castle, Her Majesty sailed in the *Gondolier* from Banavie to Inverness. The lochs and waterways leading to the Highlands traversed by the Queen became known as 'The Royal Route' and the name clings to this day.

With Messrs. Burns's many other interests taking up more and more of their time, they handed over their West Highland trade in 1851 to David Hutcheson, their chief clerk, on condition that their nephew, David MacBrayne, became one of the partners.

The firm, David Hutcheson & Co., was founded, and the partners were David and his brother Alexander, and David MacBrayne.

That was the beginning of the Company as it is known today —David MacBrayne Ltd.

The new Company, inaugurated on 10th February 1851, started off with a promising building programme. New tourist routes were gradually opened up throughout the Highlands. The railway line from Callander to Oban was completed in 1880, and it was thought by many that this would be the end of tourist traffic so far as David MacBrayne was concerned ; but it turned out to be the reverse. Traffic expanded year by year, and Oban— the Charing Cross of the Highlands as it was known—also grew to be a favourite tourist centre.

In 1876 David Hutcheson's operated a steamer service between Glasgow and Islay. The company's *Iona*, 174 gross tons, was the crack vessel on the Clyde until 1877 when a competitor launched the *Lord of the Isles*. This compelled the company to build the *Columba* in 1878, and it was a vessel far ahead, in every respect, of any river steamer then in being, second to none in comfort and design and almost as fast as Clyde river steamers today. Its gross tonnage was 602 tons, a paddle-steamer. It was probably the best known river steamer in the world. There were several features about the vessel which were unique. She was the first floating post office in the kingdom and probably the world. It was the first of the Company's ships to be built of steel, which at that time was still in the experimental stage. She was then the largest of all the Clyde river steamers and to this day there has never been a river steamer of greater length, and it is not so long ago since she was exceeded in tonnage.

The *Columba* became a household name and many a trip I have had on her. She was only employed during the summer months on the Glasgow–Ardrishaig run. During the winter she was carefully docked and closeted in cotton wool ! She continued in service until 1936 when she was broken up, after nearly sixty years of service ; a great steamer to be sure. The name of the *Columba*—symbolic of Scottish history—is appropriately continued in her successor the *Saint Columba*—the former *Queen Alexandra* I mentioned earlier in this book.

The two brothers Hutcheson retired, one in 1877 the other in 1879, leaving David MacBrayne as the sole partner and owner of the fleet, and the name of the Company was changed to David MacBrayne.

The first ship built for the fleet after the business was being carried on in Mr. MacBrayne's own name was the *Claymore* in 1881 for the Glasgow–Stornoway run ; the vessel I shall always remember. In many ways the *Claymore* was the counterpart of the *Columba*, except, of course, she was a screw-steamer not a paddle.

In 1880 MacBrayne took over many steamer and mail contracts from the Highland Railway Company, and in 1888 steamers of the Highland Fisheries Company on the Island routes were taken over, and so the ramifications of the Company extended. By then they had over 100 ports of call throughout the West Coast and the Islands.

In 1902 Mr. MacBrayne's two sons, David and Laurence, who had spent all their business lives in the service, relieved their father of the more burdensome details of management, although Mr. MacBrayne always made a daily appearance at the office. He died at his Glasgow residence in January 1907, aged 93. Truly a wonderful man and a man to whom the Western Highlands and Islands owe most.

The firm was then converted into a Private Limited Liability Company in 1906, and it then commenced operating bus services. The first service was between Fort William and North Ballachulish with one bus. Today the fleet numbers about 120.

During 1929 the mail steamer operating between Inverness and Fort Augustus was withdrawn and road services substituted, satisfactorily catering for passengers, mails and parcels traffic. Goods and livestock were conveyed by goods vehicles. Parcels traffic has been conveyed by the buses since their inauguration, but as the volume of traffic expanded considerably, goods lorry services were started. Such services also operate on some of the Islands, their function being the collection and delivery of traffic for the Company's steamers.

A major change in the Company came in 1928 when Sir Alfred Read, Chairman and Managing Director of Coast Lines

Ltd. and, the late Lord Stamp, President of the L. M. & S. Railway Company acquired the fleet and business of David MacBrayne Ltd. and entered into a contract with the government for conveyance of mails to the Western Isles. The name of the new Company was David MacBrayne (1928) Ltd.

The next few years saw expansions and improvements equal to those which had taken place under the old régime, as routes were being opened by linking road and water transport in order to open up still more of the Highlands to the outside world.

In 1929 the *Lochness*, 777 tons, was launched for the Stornoway–Kyle–Mallaig mail service, and in the same year the cargo vessel *Lochshiel* was built, 208 tons.

In 1930 the building of the motor-vessels *Lochearn* and *Lochmor*, both 542 tons, furnished the Inner and Outer Hebrides with ships exceeding in comfort and convenience all previous mail boats.

Shipping history was made in 1931 with the building of the *Lochfyne*, 754 tons. She was the first diesel-electric coastal passenger vessel in the United Kingdom. In addition to the propulsion by electric power, all deck and auxiliary machinery, cooking and other services were operated by electricity.

This vessel proved so satisfactory that a ship with similar propulsion and machinery, the *Lochnevis*, 568 tons, was built in 1934 for the Mallaig–Kyle–Portree mail route.

During 1935 negotiations were completed for the taking over of the Turbine Steamers Ltd. fleet, the grand old ships *Columba* and *Iona* had made their last voyages in the MacBrayne fleet and were replaced by two turbines, the *King George V* and the *Queen Alexandra*.

In 1935 the *Queen Alexandra*, 851 tons, was renamed *Saint Columba* and underwent vast alterations. The boat deck extended well aft, two funnels replaced by three smaller ones and a mainmast added. As such she is now the only passenger coastal vessel in the U.K. with three funnels. Two years later she was converted to oil-fuel burning, with result that today, although nearly fifty years old, she is still amongst the fastest vessels operating in the Clyde estuary.

At the outbreak of the Second World War the MacBrayne fleet again began to play its part in war as in peace. The Western Isles now depended entirely upon MacBraynes.

Many ships, including the dear old *Queen Alexandra*, were requisitioned or acquired for government service. Two of their fleet were at Dunkirk, and one of the ferry-boats in the Normandy D-day landings. One of the fleet, the *King George V*, conveyed, on two occasions, Mr. Winston Churchill to the battleship when he was on his way to the other side of the Atlantic.

The war over, all the vessels emerged from their battleship-grey to their familiar livery—black hull, white superstructure and red funnel with black top.

There were no ships built or acquired during the war and so deficiencies had now to be made up.

The *Loch Seaforth* was built in 1947 for the Stornoway–Kyle–Mallaig route and is now *the* ship in the fleet, with the greatest tonnage (1090). She was also the first to be fitted with radar ; really a beautiful ship.

David MacBrayne Ltd. of Clyde House, Glasgow, C.2, are now the sole operators of regular steamer services, both passenger and cargo, to the Western Isles and Islands, and they receive an annual subsidy of about £250,000 pounds for so doing.

From the foregoing readers will have realised the tremendous part 'MacBraynes' have played (and are still playing) in those far-off Highlands and Islands.

Yes, the name MacBrayne runs like a slogan throughout the Western Highlands of Scotland. In the whole range of world transport, *Wells Fargo* (of the western states of America fame) is the only other title which can compete with it as a personal name applied to a transport tradition.

It is to be remembered that these far northern isles, the Hebrides, were in fact the southern isles of the Norsemen. Every loch and creek has seen the arrival of the pillaging Vikings, and on every headland and shore the Highlanders—ancestors of the very people with the same names who are here today—once stood to give them a welcome of steel.

See for yourself, for the first time, the blue peat smoke from a croft chimney, the indigo and foam of the young Atlantic, the endless golden and silver sands, the white clustered villages, the far purple promise of the Outer Isles. I believe it will all give you a sheer delight ; and I am sure my belief will not be wrong.

Earlier I mentioned Queen Victoria's sailings, which gave the name—The Royal Route. In 1902 Their Majesties, King Edward

and Queen Alexandra, cruised through the Highlands in the
Royal Yacht and visited most of the scenes of interest on The
Royal Route. In August 1956 H.M. Queen Elizabeth, accom-
panied by H.R.H. the Duke of Edinburgh, their children and
H.R.H. Princess Margaret, visited the Western Isles in the Royal
Yacht *Britannia*.

In 1961 the total number of passengers carried was 500,000,
freight nearly 100,000 tons and motor cars over 10,000. As
regards mail, there is no specific record kept of the quantity
handled, but it must be colossal.

When I went on board the *Claymore* that first time in June
1914, I was soon to learn the little ditty which went something
like this :

> The Earth unto the Lord belongs,
> And all that it contains ;
> Except the Western Highlands,
> They belong to the MacBraynes !

And very true it is.

CHAPTER 16

INVEREWE GARDENS

INVEREWE, the Highland Garden famed for its rare plants and superb background of loch and mountain ; situated at Poolewe, Wester Ross, 85 miles from Inverness, 36 from Achnasheen, and 7 from Gairloch.   Admission 2s. 6d. ; weekdays 10 a.m.–dusk ; Sundays 2 p.m.–dusk.

So reads, in generally accepted terms, the references one sees in many places as to these sub-tropical gardens.

In this book on Wester Ross, and Gairloch in particular, I do not propose to devote any time to giving readers a description of these gardens, for there are several books dealing with its history and trials in which any interested visitor can read a full and complete account of all that was involved ; but I would so like to mention these gardens as briefly as possible, for I feel the least any work (touching on any aspects of life and events near to Inverewe) could do is to pay solemn tribute to the fortitude and courageousness of the pioneering spirit displayed in this stupendous task ; and I am pleased in my own small way to salute all those associated with this veritable 'wonderland'.

Very briefly then.   The famous Inverewe Gardens and Estate situated on the Inverewe peninsula—so aptly described by its Gaelic name *Àm Ploc Ard*, the high lump, and a mass of red Torridonian sandstone—were commenced by Mr. Osgood Mackenzie in 1862, just on 100 years ago.   The big white house itself was built in 1865.

At that time the ground was a bare promontory on which were growing only stunted willows.   With the exception of the thin low line of the north end of Lewis, 40 miles away, there was nothing between its top and Labrador, and it was continually soused with salt spray.   Mr. Mackenzie planted trees and waited for 20 years.   He cut clearings and to their shelter carried earth and peat to make these gardens.   He filled them with rare and lovely things ; trees, shrubs and plants from China, Tasmania, Tibet, Central America, Chile, South Africa, New Zealand, the Himalayas, Australia and Japan. And today it is a paradise, a Garden of Eden. His daughter, Mrs. Mairi Sawyer, carried on her father's work until she died in 1953, shortly after formally handing over the Gardens the year before to the National Trust for Scotland, with an endowment for its upkeep. (It was only in 1950 that this N.T. for Scotland set up a Scottish Gardens Committee to act as an advisory body to the Trust and to guide policy concerning the administration of gardens connected with properties owned by the Trust.)

In respect of Inverewe the Trust is deeply indebted to the Pilgrim Trust who made a grant for the maintenance and development of the property, and to a Life Member of the Trust who contributes a generous sum annually from the income of a private charitable trust. By this combined effort the Trust is now in a position to ensure the preservation of the gardens in the years to come.

Mr. Osgood Mackenzie believed that the proximity of the Gulf Stream would provide the warmth for a garden at Inverewe and would be virtually free from frost.

There are exotic plants by the hundreds, and its charm lies in its naturalness and true magnificence of its setting.

In 1961 some 50,000 visitors paid to see these gardens, enjoying its quiet beauty ; sometimes as many as 600 or 700 visited it daily. All this could not have been accomplished without the most careful planning and it will for all time remain a monument and tribute to the enterprise and forethought of its original owner, who died in 1922.

In 1954 Dr. J. Macqueen Cowan, C.B.E., V.M.H., F.L.S., F.R.S.E. retired from the office of Assistant Regius Keeper of the Royal Botanic Garden, Edinburgh, and took up residence at Inverewe House to look after the gardens for the Trust, and when he died in 1960, his widow, Mrs. Cowan, carried on her husband's work.

The centenary of Inverewe Gardens was celebrated on 7th April 1962. When Mrs. Cowan relinquished charge of the gardens, the National Trust—early in 1962—appointed Mr. Allan F. A. Lamb, O.B.E., B.Sc. (Forestry) Edin., their representative ; and he is ably assisted by his wife who is a B.Sc. (Botany) St. Andrews, and Dip. Hort. (Swanley). Mr. Lamb was in the Colonial Forest Service for thirty-two years, in Nigeria, Sierra Leone, British Honduras and Trinidad.

The Secretary and Treasurer of the National Trust for Scotland (founded in 1931) is Mr. Stormonth Darling, M.C., W.S., of 5 Charlotte Square, Edinburgh.

One can become a member of the Trust—to all the properties under their care—at the following subscription rates : Annual, 10s. ; Life, £20.

There is a licensed restaurant attached to the gardens, managed by a young couple who obtained their training at Ross Hall, Glasgow, which is recognised as one of the finest 'catering' schools in the world.

The question is often asked, 'What is the best time to see Inverewe ?' Conditions vary from year to year, and so no definite answer can be given ; but there is plenty of interest to be seen at every season.

In a good rhododendron year the display of colour reaches its height *late April–early May*. The early rhododendrons flower in *February* and *March*, and towards the *end of March* daffodils are coming into bloom.

Azaleas enhance the coloured glory towards the *end of May*.

The Rock Garden is at its best *late May–early June*, apart from a host of other plants flowering throughout the whole season.

By the *middle of June* most rhododendrons have finished flowering.

All through *June* and *July*, colour is to be seen in the massed plantings of primulas and meconopsis.

The herbaceous border is at its best in *July* and *August*.

Hydrangeas begin to flower in *August* continuing through *September, October, November* and even into *December*.

In *September* heaths and heathers are at their best ; and in *October* and early *November* the leaves of maples and other trees and shrubs have turned to yellow, red or russet brown. Even in *December, January* and *February* a few plants will always be found in flower.

Inverewe is a 'must' for everyone who comes to Gairloch. It is an amazing accomplishment, an unknown quantity quite unbelievable in the far, far north of Wester Ross. Eucalyptus trees over 90 feet high, and a Eucryphia with a spread of over

80 feet give some idea of this isolated Paradise, or as another book terms it, an 'oasis of the North'.

Just before reaching the garden entrance gate, you pass on the seaward side a carefully made conical cairn to which a plaque has been fixed with the following inscription cast in bold lettering:

In memory of Alexander Cameron
The Tournaig Bard, 1848–1933
Who lived all his long, useful and highly respected life on
the shores of Loch Ewe and whose Gaelic poems and songs
earned for him a wide and an honoured reputation
throughout the North.

Here follows another eulogy to his memory in Gaelic. (*Tournaig* is a large house with a croft or two around, a mile out from Inverewe on the Aultbea road.)

Time was a few years ago when there were a larger number of gardeners working at Inverewe than today, and they were always willing to help those who were opening up any small new garden nearby—supplying plants and the like—but now I believe only three gardeners appear on the payroll and they cannot possibly give any aid to any newcomer.

However, I live west of Garve, and nobody hurries once you've passed there ; so I'm not worrying or even hurrying, for I have found a keen, clever, and above all, an interested expert in gardening and forestry locally, to whom I have entrusted my 'estate' with its planning.

A five-year plan no doubt ; but then, you see, we don't hurry west of Garve. Like the Inverewe Gardens we just enjoy the calm, unhurried ways of life up here, where privacy is respected and the long white beaches of shell sand remain unspoiled and, for the most part, forgotten.

As I have already said the gardens are a veritable tribute to those who undertook such a task. It clearly demonstrates that the labour put into any worthy conception is never wasted ; and after a thorough tour of these gardens you cannot but come away, closing the gates, thinking of those words written on Wren's tomb in St. Paul's Cathedral :

SI MONUMENTUM REQUIRIS CIRCUMSPICE
'if you seek his monument, look around'

Such words are so appropriate to Osgood Mackenzie and his daughter, who carried on her father's wealth of fortitude.

CHAPTER 17

CHRISTMAS AND NEW YEAR

TAKEN as a whole Scotland pays little attention to Christmas in relation to what it pays the New Year. You will remember in 'The Kirk', the Free and the Free Presbyterians do not recognise the 25th December as Christmas Day.

But it is safe to say that of all the days in the year, *Hogmanay* (New Year's Eve) stands out first and foremost ; the eve of Scotland's greatest feast. 'Hogmanay !', the very name savours of intrigue. One overseas person I heard ask, 'Is it something you eat or drink ?'

Scots are born with the conviction that New Year's Eve was the invention of their own native genius ; so it is well to bear that in mind when you go to a real Scots party in the Highlands, for you will doubtless be surrounded by strapping, six-foot, hairy-kneed Highlanders, and by buxom young lassies who can—if roused—fling you a resounding smack with their broad hands. Try to tell the party that other nations beside Scotland celebrate New Year and you will be asking for trouble right, left and centre ! Persist in your argument and you'll get properly 'clobbered' off and your head in your hands—shorn off, figuratively speaking, with a claymore as slick as Isobel's bacon-slicer !

So face up to it and join in ; that's your only salvation being an Englishman !

You need to learn up a few appropriate phrases in advance, in order to keep conviviality going your way, such as 'Och, hiv another wee nip' ; 'Shure a wee nippie won't harrrrm ye' ; 'Have a wee deoch-an-doris'—this comes at the end, the grand finale, of course—and if one of your party turns to you, raises his glass and says, 'Here's tae us,' you say, 'Wha's like us ?'— and at once you become the life and soul of the party ; an Englishman acknowledging Scotch superiority !

There are, of course, lots of other single words and asides you could mutter which would be helpful as the evening wore on, in claiming that you have *some* Scottish blood in you ; for instance, 'forbye'; 'Lang may your lum reek'; 'Aweel' (this said deeply and solemnly is always a winner !) ; and since it *is* New Year's Eve you are celebrating—in case you had forgotten, and doubtless you will forget as dawn comes along—there's always 'A guid New Year tae ane an' a'' of course ; and remember, it's always 'Rabbie Burns', never Bobby Burns !

If you should establish some Scottish ancestry in your family tree, you are well on the road to survival. I remember the story of a Red Indian who wished to find out if there was any Scotch parentage in his blood—for he had a shrewd suspicion there was— and going to an Edinburgh pedigree office, was told he was descended from one Cluny Macpherson. At a Hogmanay party over in Canada he was nearly scalped, for he went round telling everybody he was descended from 'Loony' Macpherson !

I have been at a few Hogmanay parties in England, but they have nothing on those up in the Highlands.

You start at one house party—the one that is to be, you think, the 'Kingpin' so to speak ; liberal supplies of wine (generally home-made damson wine ; damsons soaked in lump sugar and gin for over six months !) and whisky available, but doled out in the scullery so as to be on 'the quiet' ; extra specially made soup, from extra-special stock ; a choice of venison, chicken, or duck (mountains of it) ; dainty sweets like lemon meringue pie, pear condés, Trinidad trifle and so forth emblazoned with (again) mountains of real whipped cream, plum pudding, cheese ; 'whangs o' cheese', particularly 'crowdie'. Crowdie is the traditional skim-milk cheese of the crofts and farms of the North of Scotland. It is skim milk made into a curd. The whey is drained off, a little salt is added ; and there you have a white, fat-free spreading cheese. Then there are oatcakes made with fine (extra fine) oatmeal, that melt in your mouth, stacks of pancakes and scones in case you are still hungry ! In fact, not only the table but the sideboard is 'plastered' with food. 'Mother' has had her apron on and blouse sleeves rolled back at 'action-station' (the cooker) for days in advance, making certain that *this* was going to be a meal beating all former meals ! Then, as the hours slip by, Aunt Alice will 'phone up and ask everyone along to her house a few miles away down a narrow, dark, tor-tuous road ; and there you are assailed with more wine and food,

and your hostess most annoyed if you say 'no'. And this could
go on for hours, so long as you carried a box of indigestion
tablets with you ! A party and parties that put the old year to bed
with joy and splendour ; and finally you come away, still 'car-
conscious' if you have taken due care throughout the sma' hours—
saying *Ceud Mìle Taing*, 'a hundred thousand thanks', and 'my !
what a nicht wi' Burns we've had ! !' In fact it would be appropriate to recall here two verses from Burns, viz. :

> Some hae meat and canna eat,
> And some wad eat that want it.
> But we hae meat, and we can eat,
> And sae the Lord be thankit.

> We thank thee for these mercies Lord,
> Sae far beyond oor meerits ;
> An' noo let Margo clear the plates
> An' Wullie fetch the speerits.

The practice of 'first-footing', however, *i.e.* going the rounds
of friends' houses after midnight, taking something in (generally
a 'half') and wishing them a 'Good New Year', is still the custom
up in the Highlands as it is further south.

And so, at the close of a real good Hogmanay (with one's
tongue the next day like the bark of a dead tree and you feel you
have been drifting in an open boat for days beneath the parching
pitiless sun of Capricorn) you come out into the cold of the night ;
the cold air beating on your forehead which makes worse confusion of your befuddled mind ; and as very often is the case
when you leave the house that has befriended you in its wealth
of enjoyment, people and warmth, you find it has been snowing
heavily during the hours you have been indulging, and the world
outside is nothing but a white blanket—and your spirits sink like
a wet blanket, and you think of the extra work this will involve,
up here in 'cut-off' Wester Ross : sheep to bring in from the
moor ; water to carry to the hens in their distant huts ; maybe
cars and vans to dig out. Yet for all this, the country takes on a
magic of white wonderland : trees of rarest lace pattern ; sculp-
tures of strange beauty ; far-off glistening peaks ; and all a
'stilly quietness' of an uncanny nature.

It is nearly four o'clock in the morning, and if it had been
spring the only sound left would be that from an early-morning
lark high overhead, singing in a new day—a New Year ?

In the big cities, the gathering is not so intimate, so close, as in the Highlands, and the Highland families and crofts. There, the ordinary people come to tread under foot, as bitter ashes, their last hopes of the Old Year, its miseries they had survived, and to welcome the next year with hope and confidence that none could warrant, and none defeat. Bells ring loudly, little, flat, black bottles come out of hip-pockets as if by magic, and nips offered to friend and stranger alike ; hands then held in a circle (all this in the main streets mark you !)—unknown hands mostly,—songs are sung and then a boisterous dance or reel trodden. 'Another dram' ; 'Shure another wee dram will no' harrrm ye Andra' ?' 'Och, aye' ; and in the poor homes of the big cities, 'Another dram and another thick slice of black bun, ma lassie'.

And that's the end of another year ; and Scotland's motto carries on high 'NEMO ME IMPUNE LACESSIT' ; or, translated in Glasgow-Scotch, 'Wha' daur meddle wi' me ?'

The *very* old custom of 'first-footing' in the Highlands was that you gave the 'letter-in' a coin in exchange for something he or she brought in ; and after a drink and a bite—both wishing each other well—you then let the 'first-footer(s)' out by the back door !

In a sense this bears comparison with the New Year resolutions many of us are apt to make. We readily make a list only to find them gone soon enough. We let them in, and then let them out !

It is strange some of the folk up here do not acknowledge Christmas. I would have thought they would, even for the children's Santa Claus belief ; for to them, elsewhere, it is the Day of Days ; even though we grown-ups have become too old for such belief. For that day at any rate—for those twenty-four hours— some special benediction descends on fallow hearts ; for eyes that will see, for ears that will hear. The floodgates of affection and generosity are opened wide.

Of all the gifts of Christmas, the gift of the very day itself— 1440 minutes—is the most precious, and is a gift bestowed on all. Everyone, no matter what their creed or race, could spare five minutes of those 1440 to embrace its honest meaning ; to give a soft answer ; to turn the other cheek ; to do unto others as you would be done by ; to take the glibness out of 'Peace on Earth, goodwill towards men' ; and to exchange with one another—no matter (and I say it again) what religion you may hold—a right

'Merry Christmas', and that coming cheerily from the heart. For religion is surely meant to be a happy affair ; not dull, grave, dour, gloomy or cheerless ?

So Christmas and New Year come and go ; and with it again the age-old opportunity to begin anew ; to reach at least slightly beyond the usual barriers of SELF. For it is ineradicably written that the future belongs to the pure in heart.

At one of our village shops I picked up a pretty Gaelic Christmas card which I sent my English friends. I give the Gaelic first and the translation later—so although Christmas is not accepted by the majority here, there appears nothing wrong in displaying Christmas cards for sale? Canny, eh? Aye, and deep !

> NOLLAIG CHRIDHEIL . . . AGUS BLIADHNA MHATH ÙR
> GED THA 'BHLIADHNA SO A' DÙNADH
> IS TÉ ÙR A' TIGHINN 'NA H-ÀITE,
> 'SE AR GUIDHE IS AR DÙRACHD
> GUM BI 'N CÀIRDEAS MAR A BHÀ . . .

and the liberal translation :

> Hearty Christmas and a Good New Year
> Though this year is ending
> And a new one takes its place,
> It is our wish and our desire
> Our friendship will remain.

And so I hope it will remain, now and for many years to come ; here's 'health everlasting to you', *Slàinte Nach Teirig*, my ever good, hospitable and sincere folk.

As a pleasing postscript to this New Year chapter, it may not be out of place to record the following. In putting a 'phone call through locally on New Year's morning, the voice at the exchange wished me a Happy New Year. I asked who was speaking, and the operator said 'The Exchange'. But I said, 'Who is it ?' 'Oh ! it's Cathey', she said. 'I don't think we've met, but I often pass you on the road in your car.' How very nice indeed, and I felt like letting the Postmaster-General in London know of this pleasing gesture on the part of an ordinary telephone operator to an ordinary subscriber. You would not come across the like of this—except in Gairloch !

CHAPTER 18

RUI   H'
B   L   C —FRAGMENTS
'S   EA

THIS chapter is devoted to a few items that do not properly merge in with the general run of things embodied in all the foregoing pages, but which, nevertheless, are recorded, since they are of interest *en passant*.

1. ROADS

Many people you meet who plan a tour up North, ask 'What are the roads like ? Can we take the car without fear of the back axle dropping off, or springs being broken along "those terrible roads" and in such an "outlandish place" ?' And you will recall the verse I quoted as to General Wade in Destination Gairloch (2).

I hasten to state that the roads today are first-class; narrow, it is true, in some parts, but with ample 'passing places' to permit of overtaking or of allowing oncoming cars to pass you. You need to look well ahead, and not only keep to the left, but in some districts 'hug' the left; and of course there are many blind corners and bends.

This Major-General Wade was undoubtedly a great man for the Highlands, mending roads, opening up new roads, and generally bringing 'life' to the many isolated villages.

He received his commission as 'Commander-in-Chief of the Forces in North Britain' on 25th December 1724 ; his immediate objective being to make the roads better between garrisons and barracks—'for the better communication of His Majesty's Troops'; and in the middle of the next year he proceeded from Edinburgh to Inverness. By the end of 1725 he had begun the construction of his great military highway through the Great Glen from Fort William to Inverness ; this was followed by the making of the road southwards, Inverness to Dunkeld. In 1731 he commenced another gigantic job, the road from Fort Augustus, over Corrie-yairick across country to Dalwhinnie, and thence to Aberfeldy and Crieff. During a period of only eight years he constructed a total of 250 miles of major roadway. He certainly was a great guy !

In 1733 he constructed the Tay bridge at Aberfeldy, whereupon his work as a road and a bridge builder was completed, for he was relieved of his command in 1740, died eight years later (14th March 1748), aged 75, and was buried in Westminster Abbey.

A Major Caulfield was appointed Wade's successor and he continued in office for thirty-five years. Later on, we find the name of Thomas Telford, another great road and bridge builder, looming up in the early 1800's ; he opened up a road on the *north* side of the Caledonian Canal from Inverness to Fort Augustus, via Dores and Foyers, which then effected vast changes in the mode of travel throughout the Highlands. Thereafter Telford's name appeared prominently before the public.

In General Wade's day, the pay for masons and special labour was 1s. 6d. a day ! The general rough work was done by military parties under their own officer's command, privates getting 1s. a day.

Many of Wade's old military roads can be seen to this very day ; and of course you pass over many of those hump-backed bridges—Wade's bridges. Yes, if you'd seen these roads before they were made !

Truly a great pioneer and a great worker. So, to the memory of good old General Wade, I think we should—in a manner of speaking—say *Slàinte Mhath!*

2. SUPERSTITION

In quite a few instances in this book I have made reference to Highland superstitions and legends ; Culloden, Loch Maree, Mellon Udrigle, fisher folk, the Brahan Seer and so forth ; and it may be interesting to record a few more ; because in the old days, people in Wester Ross firmly held to the adage that 'Coming events cast their shadows before them' in the fullest of supernatural ways.

Some Highland rivers and lochs, still reported to be haunted by supernatural beings, were anciently sacred to the deities. The names *Ness* and *Nevis* are believed to enshrine those of goddesses.

A degree of sanctity likewise clings to many of the old standing stones and especially those referred to in Gaelic as 'stones of worship'. Until well into historic times, courts were held at groups of standing stones for the purpose of settling disputes regarding the ownership of land and such like. Vows were made at some stones; at others, curses were employed; some spat upon for luck; some visited by women who desired a child. The standing stones at Callernish, across from Stornoway, come to my mind as a definite meeting-place for prayers and courts. They are second only to Stonhenge. The circle is 62 feet in diameter. In its centre stands a boulder 15 feet high with an altar in front. Stretching north and south of the circle are two rows of upstanding stones extending nearly 400 feet; and east to west forming a cross, there is a single row over 140 feet in extent.

There are still a number of Highland folk in lonely parts who will not eat pork. Then there were the bull sacrifices as late as the 17th century at Loch Maree. The bulls were chiefly sacrificed on 15th August, the day dedicated to St. Maurie (St. Maelrubha), whose memory was associated with that of an old pagan deity— the bull god. In many old byres (cowsheds), a hallowed stone used to be kept and milk was spilt on it to ensure that cream would rise and the churn would yield a goodly quantity of butter.

A lucky turning is 'by the right', *i.e.* from the north by the east to the south; the unlucky turning was 'by the left'—the exact opposite.

There is an old Gaelic saying which translated means 'close the north window, close the south, close the west window, evil never came from the east'.

An east wind in May is supposed to augur a bountiful fruit crop.

In some old churchyards the eastern and southern aspects were reserved for the good and affluent; the western area for the poor. Criminals and suicides were allocated the north side. Funerals in some isolated districts still approach the grave 'by the right'. Fishermen setting out turn the boat 'by the right'. Housewives stir food in the pots 'by the right'. Omens can be pictured by flocks of birds wheeling right or left.

By now I think we should 'by the right, quick march!'

I have already mentioned the Tomnahurich cemetery in Inverness; another legend was that a poet once met and invited two Strathspey fiddlers who had been playing in the streets of the town, to come and provide music for a dance. He led them to the cemetery grounds and the fiddlers made merry there in the hall near-by. When they came out, it was discovered they had been in Fairyland for 100 years, although they themselves had thought they had only been in the dance room for one night. They returned to their native Highland village as Rip van Winkles and entered a church. When the priest spoke the name of God, they crumbled to dust.

A similar story is told of a midwife who lived at Kildonnan, near Ullapool; a place I have already named. She received a call to go to a case not far away at Keppoch. She left her home on Christmas Day. As she did not reach Keppoch a man was hurriedly sent for her, only to be told by her friends that she had left for Keppoch the previous day. Everyone became alarmed, but search as they did the midwife could not be found.

On Christmas Eve, twelve months later, she appeared back home quite spruce and jolly. Noticing everybody was surprised she asked what was amiss. They told her she had been missing for twelve months and they believed her dead. 'Oh, dear, fancy that,' she said, 'I only left home last night and on my way to the confinement I met some people at Chathair Bhan (the white knoll; the playground of the fairies) close by the famous Loch of Maoilan Tompain, who insisted I should go to their wee dance hall, where we ate and danced. At last I got tired and here I am back home again!'

Still another, and similar, tale is related around the Gairloch district. A father set out to have his child's name entered in the session books, and to bring home whisky for the christening. As he and his friends were returning they were weary and sat down on a hillock, from which they heard singing and dancing. The father, wanting to see what was going on, went a few steps into an opening and disappeared. His friends carried on home. A week went by and there was no sign of the father's return and the friends became accused of murder. They implored for a year and a day to confirm their tale and they often went back to the spot to look for the vanished man. On the very last day of the respite one of them went into the cave and stuck a knife in the door to prevent him being shut in. He saw the father and dragged him out. 'Mon, Andra',' he said, 'why on earth could not you let me finish the reel?', to which his friend remarked that surely he had had enough dancing the last twelve months! 'Twelve months?' said he, and would not believe he had been in the cave but for a short time. When he reached home he found his wife sitting by the fire holding a child in her arms, one year old!

In truth, time marches on!

There were olden beliefs which fastened themselves to all the changes in life, most of them connected with the wish to see into the unknowable future—life after death.

The hour of birth was significant; a child born at midnight was supposed to have the gift of second sight.

At baptism it was thought lucky if the child cried when water was sprinkled on it—originating from the fact that, according to the scriptures, unclean spirits cried out aloud when driven by our Saviour.

As to marriage, a Highland girl should adopt the Latin motto 'SI VIS AMARI, AMA'—if you wish to be loved, love! and at the same time try to find out all she could of her young man by various old-time means, such as counting the cuckoo notes when first she hears them in spring, to learn the number of years she would be single. Dreams, too, were respected. If after eating salt herring the lassie dreams of her lover offering her a drink, then her wedding day would be soon.

As to death, the howling of a dog was ominous; and a cockerel crowing more than naturally at night was an indication of death. Horses, when driven along a road and shying for no known reason, were supposed to see the phantom of a funeral. Laughter of an owl, another omen. Highland carpenters long ago used to say that when there was an unseemly rattle of wood in their workshop it was a sure sign that a coffin would soon be needed.

Some ordinary Hielan' folk are imbued with 'charm and skill'. A story is told of a woman working in the cornfield who got something in her eye which could not be removed by usual homely means. She then went to a married woman who possessed 'charm' and asked her help. The woman went to a near-by well opening to the north, uttered some words, lifted some water to her mouth, spat it out again and in that mouthful was the offending irritant of the eye.

For toothache it was said that carrying a cheek-bone of a

sheep in the pocket would charm away the pain. Similar to my Yorkshire home where carrying a potato in your pocket is a cure for rheumatism and gout! 'Aweel.'

Skye, of course, reeks of superstition and 'hauntedness'. You feel the spell of Skye on you as soon as you cross over from Kyle of Lochalsh. Skye stands almost alone in its wealth of magnificence and of the Cuillins, the Bens, the Glens and the Heroes.

Most Skye names are a mixture of Norse and Gaelic, for in the olden days it was a Viking land ; Norsemen colonising it. In the wintry months when everything is at its loneliest, you could imagine a Viking stepping out in front of you on the road or hillside, with his uplifted sword.

I have already mentioned the fairy flag at Dunvegan Castle ; the fuller story goes something like this. Long, long ago when the heir was born to MacLeod of MacLeod, the nurse left the room where the infant was sleeping to go down and join in the festivities. The Chieftain told her to go back and bring the baby down to be shown round to the clansmen. When she entered the room she found the child wrapped in the fairy flag ; and as she carried it downstairs, fairy voices were heard singing out that the flag would save the clan in three great dangers. It was to be waved three times, and three times only, in case of great need ; if waved for some trivial matter, a curse would fall on the clan.

So far, it is history that it has been waved twice ; the first against the invading MacDonalds who were all killed though the MacLeods were hopelessly outnumbered ; the second time the flag caused them to be saved from a cattle plague.

As to the curse, it was to involve the death of the heir, the rocks at Dunvegan would be sold to a Campbell, and when a fox had young in the castle, the MacLeods' glory would dwindle, and much of their estate be sold. In 1799 it is said, MacLeods' factor decided to test this curse and he took the flag out of an iron chest, waved it and put it back again. Shortly after that the heir was blown up in H.M.S. *Queen Charlotte* ; the imposing rocks near Dunvegan (called 'MacLeods Maidens') were sold to Angus Campbell of Ensay ; and they are still in possession of his grandson. A tame fox in possession of a Lieutenant MacLean *did* have its young in the west turret in the castle, and the MacLeod's riches declined. Strange indeed ?

Talking of superstitions, fairies and the like, someone asked me, 'What goes over the road and never touches it?' I said, 'A fairy? elf? leprechaun? hobgoblin?' 'No,' said my Highland friend as he moved his glass along the bar counter for another drink. 'Well, what?' said I, all tensed up. 'The County Council!' he said. 'Same again please, Alec.'

3. PEAT

A very large part of Wester Ross is covered by peat bogs, and to the casual visitor these bog-lands with their characteristic vegetable life seem uninteresting except for just a passing glance, to say to their friends 'back home', they had seen 'peat growing'! to say what a lovely smell pervades a room with a peat fire burning. 'Oh, we'd love to see an old-fashioned peat fire,' they say. But there is more to it than that.

It is the crofter's main—in fact only—fuel; and a real crofter has a hard life. Towards the beginning of March he begins to turn over the land with the foot-plough—the cas-chrom—quite a tricky, primitive implement to handle, and one in the Highlands which has never really been ousted by the spade and plough. By the middle of April most of the spring work is done and then 'the peats' have to be cut—this again with a special cutting tool—fences to be seen to; later on the crops have to be reaped, potatoes lifted, outhouses repaired for the winter, sheep looked after, drains 'sorted' and so on. The peat so cut is stacked on the bog for drying in the summer and then lifted and taken home for the winter fire. There is never any rest for the crofter, never a dull moment.

But to come back to peat. Peat is evidently a post-glacial deposit, and in the long ages past with the weather cool and wet, the growth of 'sphagnum' moss would be encouraged and this is the main formation of peat. So it grew and accumulated over the long, long years. Peat deserves to be classed among the most interesting natural phenomena of the Highlands; not only the peat itself but the many objects preserved in it. At some depth at the bottom of bogs, hazel, birch, alder and willow have been found in perfect state—after centuries of time.

In some bogs hazel-nuts have been unearthed deep below the ground, as perfect as the day they dropped off the trees; some peat fields are full of the rose-beetle wings, still glittering in metallic lustre, which must have lain there embedded in these black, airtight 'silos' long ago ; and from the masses discovered in many districts these beetles must have swarmed like the locusts in the old Egyptian days. It is very evident that in those far-off ages a different vegetation covered the earth when peat began to form and that the land was full of plants and insect life now extinct.

The usual impression of peat is that it is a very modern growth and quickly formed. Nothing could be further from the truth. Forest upon forest ; peat upon peat ; and so 'it came to pass'.

Peat is also found at the bottom of some lochs—submarine peat bogs ; and these too must be thousands of years old.

The Scottish Peat Committee have been investigating this peat problem for the last thirteen years, and in their early 1962 final report, state that a peat industry providing jobs for 4000 workers and reclaiming tracts of land for farming, could be developed in Scotland.

More than 1,600,000 acres in Scotland are covered with deep peat, and workable deposits are put at 600 million tons of peat solids, equivalent to some 500 million tons of coal. One of the attractions of large-scale peat utilisation is the prospect of agricultural reclamation of the basal soil after clearance of the peat. It is to be hoped—for the sake of the Highlands—this considered opinion will not lie dormant.

4. REGALIA

In 'The Stone of Destiny', where mention is made of the Coronation Stone, it may be worth while recording that the regalia of Scotland is older than that in the Tower of London ; for by the death of Charles I in 1649 most of the English regalia was destroyed ; and it was only after the re-establishment of the monarchy by the return of Charles II in 1660 that a new regalia came to be made—which is what we look upon today in the Tower.

As to Scotland, however, the Crown of Scotland is said to have been used at the Coronation of Bruce. The sceptre is 16th century work, and the great Sword of State was presented to James IV by Pope Julius II. So in this respect the honours go to Scotland !

5. ACCOMMODATION

From what I have detailed in 'Across the Bay', visitors should appreciate that in the season here, every available nook and cranny is full to capacity—even outhouses and spare hen-houses seem to spring to life with camp beds suddenly made up in them from May to September ; and unless one makes some advance bookings one is met with a steady reply, 'No room in the Inn' ; and many have to resort to sleeping in their cars on the roadside. Tourism is very buoyant in Scotland, in the north-west and Skye in particular. Each year Scotland has more holiday-makers than its native population of 5,223,000. Tourism is estimated to bring in at least £80,000,000 to Scotland in 1963 ; and it is thought this figure will reach £100,000,000 before long.

Gairloch Estate is very exclusive. Many of our wealthy London bankers and stockbrokers who visit here long to build so as to have a permanent little house for summer retreat ; yet they cannot buy a site for love or money. No sites are given for building, though there are acres upon acres of land of no arable or grazing use whatsoever.

Strange, yet it is so ; and the estate has rigorously held to this principle for years past, relaxing only on special grounds. Before I managed to secure my own little house, I felt very sore over this; but nothing (I repeat) nothing would change the old order. Now I have my domain, I am glad this is so, and in saying this I show, I suppose, great selfishness ; for if sites were granted *ad lib*. it would undoubtedly make this haven very urban and commercial and spoil the general tranquillity of life—for I know many, many houses would be built and so the hamlet would soon develop into a sort of 'new town' that we read of nowadays coming into being in other parts of Scotland and England.

No, it is fine—though selfish—to think this area is not to be spoilt ; that it is, in a way, protected. A case, may be, of 'I'm all right Jack !'

Of course here houses are handed down for generations and more often than not, the feu charters are never changed and made over to current owners. In one small place near by, the whole of the main street is occupied by local people who have no legal right to ownership. For instance, one man, who has raised his family throughout the years, is living in a house that is still in the name of his grandfather ; another, in the name of a cousin twice

removed ; another in the name of a distant relative living in
Canada, and so on, right down the line. And those who might
want to sell find they have no Title Deeds in their name that
legally allow them to sell ; and to have such deeds looked into
and altered would probably take four or five years ! But as I
have said before, once you pass Garve nobody hurries, let alone
cares about Deeds and such-like fancy-phrased documents of
'hereinbefores' and 'whereas and whereat'.

Readers may have drawn their conclusions from what I have
said here and there about hotels that I am not too enamoured
with the Highland fare sometimes put up at some recognised
star hotels *en route* from England, and that I incline towards the
smaller ones.

One reads in the Press quite often, of a traveller giving vent
to his, or her, disgust at either the food, service or high tariffs ;
and I think if one *did* complain there and then of any irregularity
it would be far better and carry more weight.

At one hotel, priding itself 'Highland', stopping for afternoon
tea, the half-full milk jug had a dirty, creamy ring round the
inside—obviously 'cream of yester year', stale scones, butter on
the turn, cups dirty. To crown all, the waitress came along
with no bill and merely said, 'That'll be four bob each, please'
(at least I think she said 'please'). Not even four 'shillings'—
just four 'bob' ! 'Bob' in a Highland hotel, whose manageress
is a Gaelic scholar ! Four shillings each for that ; eight shillings
for the two of us !

At another well-known hotel, calling in with five other
friends for coffee at 11 a.m., we were met by the porter saying in
no mistaken terms that we'd have to wait half or three-quarters
of an hour' because he was busy putting six suitcases in a car !
As though that would occupy him all that time ; and he just
turned on his heel and walked away.

Perhaps some of these hotels are so richly endowed they can
'afford' to play ducks and drakes with the travelling public ?
It is cases such as these that besmirch the general spirit of Highland
hospitality ; they throw a spanner in the works. Hotels and
guest houses are servants of the public ; that should be No. 1 in
their 'aims and objects' catechism. We are doing *them* a favour
with our patronage—a point sadly forgotten at times.

Then there is another point *re* prices ; the various handbooks invariably say weekly terms 'from' such and such a rate. But never, in my experience, can you get a room at the lower-priced tariff. You are told they are all taken. I often wonder if there *are* any such rooms ? Although in the Scottish Tourist Board's circular to all hotels, guest houses and so forth, there is clearly marked in bold black print, 'It is of the utmost importance to the good name of the Scottish Tourist industry that accurate prices be printed in *Where to Stay in Scotland.* Please give careful attention to the terms, etc.' So that the good name of the Scottish Tourist industry is upheld, constant investigations are very necessary.

In time you get to know the nice, homely, reasonably priced places to make for in travelling and you adjust your journey to suit ; and of course you tell your friends not to stay at this or that hotel. In due course it should react favourably ; let's hope it does. But there are many people who, liking a place, must come and spend a fortnight in it not 'because of' but 'in spite of'. 'Aweel.'

For myself I like things done nicely, and all in keeping with the locality ; pleasant smiles, helpful comments and, especially, smart service. All this pays a handsome dividend, which many hotel managers might note.

There are some publications you can buy which give lists of 'selected' hotels for you to stay at ; chosen by their representative spending a night there and favourably reporting. You don't need to tell me the management does not know to expect such a V.I.P. and so puts up good food, good attention and so forth accordingly !

It is the same when a couple of Directors come up for a day's visit to their manager in the Highlands, just to 'look around', so that at the Shareholders' Annual Meeting held in a town office, the Chairman can rise and say, 'I, and another of my co-directors, visited your hotel during the year under review and, we are pleased to report, found everything in first-class order, the food and service *par excellence*'. What a laugh ! I have seen and heard it said at more than one shareholders' meeting. And the quaint part is, these City Directors—'City Slickers'—think they are ungullible. Mon ! mon !

And if in the ordinary course of events, you should complain to the management about having to wait over one hour to have your breakfast of cereal, bacon and egg and coffee, the retort could be, 'Well, you haven't a train to catch, have you?' It reminds me of Ireland, where the trains—in Eire—go as and when they please and stop as and when they please. On one short journey, taking so long and staying ages at wayside stations, I got out and said sarcastically to the guard—who was having a heart-to-heart talk over nothing to the engine-driver—'Have I time to pick a few flowers on the bank here before you blow your whistle?'; and he rather gruffly and sarcastically too, no doubt, said, 'Sure, but there aren't any flowers that I can see'; to which I said, 'No, but I've some bulbs in my pocket!' *Slàinte!*

6. GOLF COURSE

The Gairloch golf course briefly alluded to in Chapter 4 (Gairloch), is of such a picturesque nature that I feel it is deserving of more space in this book. It is only a 9-hole course, but as sporting holiday-courses go, there is no better or more beautiful one in Britain—and that is a sweeping statement. The 9 holes cover 1975 yards and the bogey is 31; the longest hole, the 8th, is 360 yards. This, to a really good golfer is child's play, and I suppose many with handicaps around the 3 or 4 mark would take only 27 or 28 strokes to go round in, as against 31 printed on the Club's card. But, then, this is Gairloch; not St. Andrews or Sunningdale.

The course was planned and laid out by a Captain Burgess, and much ingenuity was displayed in the placing of the greens in the positions they are today. So much has been made out of so little ground available.

The ground on which the course was laid out was granted for that purpose by Sir Kenneth Mackenzie, Bart., of Gairloch, and during his lifetime he, as well as his wife, took a keen interest in the Club's welfare and finances.

There is a nicely built wooden club-house with all con-veniences, and a wee shop—but no 'post orfice'! The greens are beautifully kept because some few years ago the finances enabled the club to purchase a large-size petrol-driven green-cutter; very different from the old days when Angus, the green-keeper I knew for many a long year, had to cut the grass with an Old-Father-Time's scythe; and for the greens, a small hand-mower he had to pull around up hill and down dale. And he kept it well-night perfect.

Old Angus, in his early 70's now, retired in 1950, being green-keeper since 1923. He used to journey daily from his Strath croft on a bicycle carrying his wee cairn-terrier ('Chappie') in a basket in front of the handle-bars ; and the wee fellow would follow him lovingly around the course.

Angus is leading a very quiet life now as he is none too strong ; but when I saw him recently in his little croft he was bright and cheerful—the same old Angus I knew in those restful days prior to the Second World War. I trust he will be spared for many more years to come. From his croft he can see 'his' golf course a few miles away with thoughts of yesterdays. From the club-house steps one can see the mountains towering in the distance—Boisbhein and Ben Alligin ; great landmarks, and from some of the tees (particularly the high one, No. 6, reached by steps cut in the earth) there are magnificent views. You need to go round this small pocket-edition course to appreciate its fascinating attractiveness. In the season naturally it is crowded, but not too crowded ; out of season—well it is Heaven, real Heaven. And as you amble round slowly and with no attempt at lowering any records, and look around and admire the majesty of nature, the complete peace—utter and absolute—the stillness of life and of all that is about you, you stand and pause, and if you are religiously inclined you thank God you are alive and able to 'take in' the beauties of the earth ; if you are not, well then you can just 'take off your hat' and bow to the almighty Universe.

Yes, to play over the golf course of Gairloch when everything is quiet is a privilege that money cannot buy ; a privilege to look upon the firmaments made by One unseen Power, when I am sure you will be drawn to quote words from the Song of Solomon: 'How fair and how pleasant art thou, O love' to gaze and feast upon. If the poet Omar Khayyám could say, 'There was a Door to which I found no Key ; there was a Veil past which I could not see', I would say you need no key to this door opening wide to natural grandeur ; and there is no veil hiding this landscape's alluring beauty.

Viewing this wonderful panorama, it may not be out of place to quote the Biblical saying, 'If thou wouldest believe, thou shouldest see', and one feels constrained to bend one's knees in adoration ; for the trees, rocks and mountains are before one's eyes—as witnesses.

7. 'FRAGMENTARY'

I am often intrigued by various idioms the womenfolk in the Highlands come out with at times. Tea-time in particular. They always talk of 'infusing' the tea ; whereas in Yorkshire 'mask' is the word for 'infusing'! Another pet saying, 'Is your cup out ?' and 'Will you take a cup in your hand ?', meaning just a casual cup of tea taken, well—just anyhow, to which you could quite well reply, 'A mouthfu' o' tea in ma haun' will dae me fine !' Och aye.

Young folk coming up to these wondrous beaches *must* get sun-tanned, come wet, come dry. It would never do to go back to the office without some natural colour on you when you had told all your other office pals you were going to the far, far north ! One day when it was quite cold and wet—in fact it had been like that all week—and passing along the road by a beach, I saw a girl lying full length on the sands on a bathing towel in scanty costume. Being of an inquisitive turn of mind, I went down and said jokingly, 'Are you thinking of getting sun-tanned in this weather ?', to which she said, 'I've been promising myself this holiday all the year so I could get some colour on my pale face and body, and I'm going to get it—even if it's blue !'

And for the story of 'the pipes' ; of a young Scot who, returning from a holiday in London, telling his friends back home how funny the folk were down south. 'How come ?' they enquired. 'Well,' he said, 'one night, very late, perhaps two o'clock in the morning, a man came banging and shouting at my door, and was obviously in a rage ; and at two o'clock in the morning, mind you!' 'And what did you do, Alex ?' his pal asked. 'Oh, me, I didna do anything at a' ; I just went on quietly playing ma pipes !'

News. Although we are far removed from Central Africa and the land of the tom-toms and bush fires, news travels just as fast—if not faster. Every whisper overheard in the long grass, stampedes someone into action ! Many keep a telescope handy, so that if anything is happening at a body's house a few miles away up the hill, the lens comes in awfu' handy like ! 'Aye, that's the District Nurse right enough ; she's gone into Mistress Mackenzie's house. I just wonder? Ah! well; and they were only married last Lammas! Still it's no business o' mine!' With so many telescopes in the Highlands you need to keep a watchful eye on yourself and your movements.

Of course the mail van, the carrier's van, the bread van, the butcher's van, the local bakery van, the traveller's van, and any other van on the road connecting one village with another is a grand means of 'conveyance'; and all concerned are not slow in keeping their eyes open and their ears to the ground!

And should you have a big car—a foreign one for preference, that is easily distinguishable and different from an ordinary black Austin or Ford—well! I mean to say! Sometimes I think it might be a good idea to paint one's car a different colour each side; so that 'parking' one way it would appear cream; another way, red. Just to puzzle some folk! Still, it all helps to make life brighter—this 'ever-watchfulness'. For is not variety the spice of life? And if you are told any gossip the party will tell you not to mention it for they will say, 'I don't want to put my tongue in it'. Another Highland idiom?

Highland Wedding. A Highland wedding is a never-to-be-forgotten event; not only by the bride and groom, but by all the villagers; in fact I think the latter get more 'kick' out of it than the happy couple.

I have been present at a few, and at one—in the Free Church long years ago—I remember being an onlooker from the balcony at the back of the kirk, and when the ceremony was over and the bride and groom came down the aisle, we showered confetti and rice down on them from 'the Gods'. This time-honoured practice has now disappeared—disallowed I think is the term—and so I come to 'this modern age'.

Prior to 'the day' it is the custom to waylay the intended bride (we will call her Mairi) and her young man Johnny; and this is done in a manner far excelling any English custom. The lassie is kidnapped, smeared all over with black boot polish, hair saturated with wet flour and sticking up like an O-Cedar mop, and carefully guarded by her 'friends' whilst being driven on a fish lorry up and down the village several times to the tooting and blasting of the horn so that all but the bed-ridden could not fail to see all the fun of the fair. Her Johnny is also waylaid, held down and rolled in the mud along the street, or square, his face and legs being similarly given a sun-tanning. In some cases, he is gradually bereft of his clothes, and when it comes to his under-pants being torn off, the womenfolk rush indoors and draw the blinds! And if either or both events were deemed not to be 100 per cent successful, then the ritual is repeated.

Comes the day : as I have said, one not readily forgotten. Cars of every vintage appear, taking young and old to the church; the one chosen being generally that to which the bride belongs. After the service guests are whisked away to the local hotel for drinks and the cake-cutting ceremony ; and then the 'feed', washed down with whisky galore ; telegrams read and speeches with stories that sometimes are tinged blue—the colour of the bridesmaids' dresses—but what does that matter, west of Garve ! A local band is engaged to provide Scottish music from concer-tinas ('boxes') and piano, with a piper thrown in if possible to lead the bride and groom to the floor, whereupon everyone follows suit and trips the light fantastic. Sets are arranged for eightsome reels, and as the evening wears on, the whole 'ensemble' becomes wilder and wilder, the drams being knocked back in routine fashion, for 'reeling' is thirsty work, and thereon 'reeling' becomes the operative word. Young and middle-aged, and even the not-so-middle-aged are almost lifted off the floor by the energy displayed by the manly men in kilts. The band is kept oiled by a special brew and their feet tapping in unison with those on the slippery floor ; and the 'Road to Stornoway by Oronsay' gets rougher and rougher !

Some of those in the inner circle repair to the corridor outside the rooms where the bride and groom are changing, and when ready both are lifted shoulder high and borne downstairs preceded by the piper into the hall, where an avalanche of confetti is awaiting them, and finally both are 'plonked' into the waiting going-away car. Sometimes they are brought back again, just in case somebody has missed seeing them off !

With the principals away, more music, more drams, and for those who get peckish, tea and helpings from the mountains of cake and sandwiches laid by ; a means of steadying one up tem-porarily for further sessions of drams and singing and dancing. Towards midnight a thinning-out is noticeable as signs of weari-ness and 'unreliability' gain ground (or lose ground might be more apt!). Then it is that a real problem presents itself; the journey home? Fortunately the local P.C. is kept engaged in conference, so he cannot hear or notice the cars being plunged into gear as they make their attempt at a special 'reel' over the hills and into the darkness of the glens. Perhaps he too, next morning, was feeling the strain and responsibility weighing heavily on his shoulders, for a wedding is not to be taken lightly by Her Majesty's guardian of the Law. 'Tis a serious affair if taken in the right spirit. Chust that. Better to wait till you see five roads ahead of you before saying goodnight, for if you then take the middle road you're sure of having two others on either side of you to help keep you straight!

Yes, I came away from my last Wester Ross Highland wedding hearing 'myself' saying to 'myself'; if it's 'myself' that's getting married 'tis a Highland wedding for 'myself'; for there is every chance of the groom driving off with the prettiest bridesmaid instead of the pretty bride! and no one would know much about it, till next morning! Och aye!

Posting Letters. I have already referred to the strictness of keeping the Sabbath up in the Highlands; as to the unrighteousness of arriving and departing on a Sunday; the reading of Sunday newspapers and the like.

Strangers may care to know that it is not considered proper to post any letters on the Sabbath, even though they had been written on Saturday night and you would be passing the P.O. on your way to Kirk; despite the fact that the post box is not cleared till Monday morning's outgoing mail.

CHAPTER 19

IN THE END

THE first chapter of this book is termed 'In the Beginning'. Most, if not all beginnings, have an end of some sort or another; and so the time has come now to draw these lines to a close and come to a full stop.

The north-west coast of Scotland has been etched by the sea into innumerable attractive inlets. It is a country of rocky bays and trout streams, of golden sands and peat, and Ross-shire itself is a county of remarkable contrasts. Dingwall is the county and market town, and serves some of the richest farmland in Scotland; yet 10 miles as the crow flies to the west you are at Garve, where you are in a different world of vast moorlands with only an odd croft dotted here and there, but with mountainous splendour; and of the whole of Ross-shire I rank Gairloch as the No. 1 gem. Like St. Paul, Wester Ross has the gift of being all things to all men, and for those who seek natural beauty, then here around Gairloch is a world of warmth and seas embroidered with many islands.

From 1914 onwards I had wished to end my days in this parish and that small acorn of passion and desire has, after close on fifty years, grown to be a rooted tree in Strath, Gairloch. There is a Chinese proverb which says, 'If I keep a green bough in my heart, the singing bird will come'. Though not a bough, I kept a wish long enough in my heart for its fulfilment to come along. Many of those I saw romping about the pier that June of 1914 when I first touched at Gairloch and who are today my friends in their 50's, were but 3 or 4 years old then. Time marches on, to be sure.

There is a strange, peculiar charm that envelops Gairloch and the districts one passes through to arrive here. Whenever I have been away from Strath for a month or so, or even for day, and I get to Garve which, as I have said, is the real start of the Wester

234

Ross Highlands, I experience a certain glow within me as the car bounds and purrs along. I feel myself scuttling through the bends and glens with the pleasurable assurance of a homeward-bound squirrel, and saying to myself, 'Life is now beginning'.

Artists and renowned writers have in their own ways extolled the beauty of the North of Scotland, but by no amount of reading or flights of imagination can one appreciate, let alone absorb, the real atmosphere until, and only until, one has been in the Highlands and come to know the place and its people, and live amongst them all.

It takes a long, long time to really know them as they are ; certainly not just a fleeting week's holiday ; and even after long years it is difficult to define just what it is that wakes within one the irresistible yearning to come back.

This is not, mark you, a land of luxury living by any means. But who wants that if there are so many, many other compensating factors which you simply cannot get elsewhere ? Luxury ? It is too often a let-down ; for the more you acquire the more acquisitive you get.

There is another old Chinese saying, 'Possessions are like a drug ; the more you have the more you want'.

A washing-machine may be a woman's heart's desire. If only you had that, you'd be perfectly happy. You get it. And then ? The machine is heaven but you still have to hang out the clothes on a biting cold day or festoon them around the kitchen grate when it rains. So you begin to have, deep down, an aching desire for a spin-drier to make life perfect. This you get from your fond husband's pay-packet ; then a dish-washer, and a potato peeling machine for your hands get so rough and red peeling potatoes and washing-up day in and day out !

There is no luxury in the world that can be said to be the last ; each new gadget breeds another new gadget ; and no money can buy enduring contentment and happiness. That comes only from within ; and that 'within' can be abundantly satisfied by the glory of nature seen here in its ever-changing moods across the bay and to the mountains far beyond—and with the people who inhabit this great corner of Scotland, Wester Ross.

Both Gairloch bay and near-by coastal waters are supposed to be swept by the Gulf stream which may account for the winters being mild (we are about the same latitude as Labrador). Whether that be so or whether it is the presence of such large masses of water, frosts have not the same keenness here as in many parts further south. Changeable weather, however, is a frequent drawback to those who cannot stay long for a chance improvement, but then, in this country, we can have all four seasons in one day! From March to September the nights are much shorter than in England. In June and July there might only be a matter of an hour's darkness; and if clear weather, no darkness at all. In winter, of course, it is the reverse. In autumn and spring the Aurora Borealis, or Northern Lights, often make their grand appearance, but this is apt to forecast stormy weather. Fogs are practically unknown in this humid region. Towards the end of the winter with frost and snow away, the heather takes on a grey tint. Larches are the first, and then the birches, to herald spring. Towards the end of May nature has begun its revival. By June the heather is growing and by late August to September it is every shade of lilac and purple and the bracken coloured red, yellow and brown.

There is in truth no season of the year when nature stands still or does not please the eye in Wester Ross.

I have long known and loved this part of Ross-shire and have seen it in every month of the year, and yet even now I find a new delight each day springing up in some shape or form. Search where you will in Britain you will not come across such a rugged attractive coast-line with so uncrowded beaches on such limitless golden stretches of sand; a friendly people with old-world Highland courtesy, charm and unbridled hospitality—an unspoiled way of life.

Yet many English folk have the picture of northern Scotland as a wild remote place inhabited largely by uncouth people who are 'crafty' and 'cunning'. I think if you are searching for an adjective, a more suitable one would be 'deep'. And, I ask, should that be held against one? I am deep myself at times and why not?

Many think the Highlands are just around Stirling and the Trossachs; an hour's run or so from Edinburgh or Glasgow. You are not in the Highlands of Scotland until you pass Garve, 30 miles west of Inverness, which city is 180 miles from Edinburgh; and then Garve to Gairloch, another 45 miles, takes almost two hours.

So up here, it is a long, long journey from, say, Yorkshire and the Midlands—some 500 miles.

But once here, you are in a world apart ; you have left the fast-moving traffic of the broad motorways, the large and numerous heavily-laden diesel-engined commercial vehicles, struggling up a bit of a rise with clouds of black and evil-smelling smoke belching out from their exhaust pipes—far too common a sight on many of the main roads today. You have left all that pollution for an atmosphere charged with ozone, an air of absolute purity where you may drink freely from almost any burn or loch you come across.

This is a land of crofts and crofters, some 20,000 of them— little fields adjoining a wee dwelling-house ; agricultural small-holdings in fact—who for many ages past seemed to have had lots of troubles of their own. A Crofters' Commission was set up some years ago to help them out of their difficulties. It is said crofters are making as good use of their land as the men on the bigger upland farms. But they cannot make a living on present-day standards from crofting alone, and the economists say the reason is the majority of crofts are too small. Their resources are far too limited to give an adequate volume of output.

A year or so ago this Commission set about seeking powers to 'rationalise crofting agriculture', which of course obviously meant dispossessing crofters, who by reason of absence, disability or age, were not working their land to advantage ; throwing crofts together and so on. Throughout the years, the crofting system has survived all these rigours and pitfalls to a remarkable degree. In social terms it is very effective ; it gives inner joy and satisfaction to the people in their gaining happiness from the produce of their soil ; and all told is more efficient than even scientific farming.

Of course, in some crofting districts one sees many patches of reeds and thistles in the land, and if the Commission has its eyes on such, it should also examine the reasons for them. I think the two wars would be the answer, for the menfolk had no reserved protection on returning. A man may not work his croft now because, whilst he went off fit to fight for his land, he came back disabled with, say, tuberculosis.

The result of all this has been a new Crofters Act which came into force on 27th August 1961, in which provisions are made for sub-letting, but which will not affect their tenure in any way. The main change provided in this new Act is to get more crofting land under cultivation by reorganising the township and sub-letting crofts to create bigger holdings, but no such reorganising of any township would be attempted without the majority consent of the members. It is estimated that about two-thirds of the crofts are not now being cultivated or are under-cultivated, or have been informally turned over to neighbours for grazing.

I am glad to think the crofters are getting a promise of security and of a proper and fair deal, for they serve the country well—very well ; and they are not ashamed of their heritage. I have yet to meet a crofter who is not a most likeable character. A number of them may be poorly off, living in wee cottages through whose doors luxury has never entered. But they still live in *Tìr nan Òg*—'the land of the ever-young'. They are worthy, if not a wealthy, folk.

I have said this is a land of crofts and crofters ; and I may say too, this is a land of Games, with a capital G——and at such Games, 'the Tartan'.

The Highland Games held nearest to Gairloch is in Skye, at Portree, and take place on the last Thursday in August in a hollow—a natural amphitheatre—only five minutes' walk from the square. The brae to the hollow is generally lined on both sides with tents put up by gypsies professing to tell you your fortune and selling also many odds and ends. You sit around the hillside looking down on the hollow where platforms have been built for the Highland dancing contests. Nearby, in the specially reserved seats, sit the 'gentry'—the judges—all bedecked in their full Highland regalia, sashes and kilts, the whole setting a verit-able colourama ; an afternoon that will remain long in your memory.

I have seen some athletes of wonderful 'frame' at these games ; some who can lift and throw a 28-lb weight as far as 70 feet or so, as though it were but a small stone ; nae bother at a'. I think some of the porridge-makers must have photographed these giants for their carton covers ; Tarzans of the Tartans we could rightly call them.

Thousands attend these games and the contestants come from far and near.

Of course, Braemar on Royal Deeside, miles away from here,

is the 'hub' of the Highland games, and with Royalty present, it dominates the world in such sports. 'Cabers and capers', a wonderful day of events, personalities and splendour, the like of which you will never see in any other realm of sport. August and September are the most colourful months in Scotland when all the various clans foregather and wage war in the tossing of the caber, putting the weight, throwing the hammer, dancing the Highland flings, in the tug-of-war, playing the pipes, and in so far as Portree is concerned the 20-odd mile marathon race up the mountains and down the glens.

A great deal of these Highland games date back to the days of Queen Victoria, who used to spend many happy months at Balmoral and who so loved the Scottish country.

I have read of one great barrel-chested Highlander—a veritable Hercules—who turned professional and during his long career all over the world amassed 11,000 prizes and some £30,000 in cash. Brawn combined with Brain ? Truly up in the north, magnificently built men match their magnificent mountains.

Games and the Tartan ? It seems these days tartan is much to the fore ; in fact in some districts it is becoming the rage ; tartan kilts, scarves, ties, rugs, carpets, shirts, waistcoats, slacks, pyjamas ; and as I remark further on, my Charlie Boy's lorry ! On some of these labelled 'Scottish Tartan', should you look closely, you may see on another smallish tag 'made in Switzerland'. But let it be here stressed ; the kilt is the dress of the Highlander ; it is not the national dress of the Scots. 'The Kilt is for Hielan' men !'

In Edinburgh you can often go into a tartan store shop in Princes Street and hear an American woman asking for a certain clan tartan, explaining that her grandmother, or great-grandmother, had some Scottish blood in her and therefore she herself must also surely have Scotch blood surging through her veins and thus can legitimately wear 'the tartan' ; and as all this is good for trade—whether it be Festival trade or not—Mrs. Hap J. Hazard gets her tartan skirt, and maybe a suitable kilt for 'junior' —a wee brainless looking boy with heavy-lensed glasses.

It was not so long ago that a White Russian woman arrived at the Duke of Fife's home wearing a skirt of his own Carnegie tartan, which she said she had bought at an Eiffel Tower shop in Paris ! However, being a gallant Scot and a staunch upholder of his clan, he ordered her to put on something different whilst she was his guest ; whether it were a MacLinsky or a Buccanoski tartan, he didn't mind.

Of course, as I have said many times, once you pass Garve, nobody hurries ; Time is dissolved in the clear air and scenic beauty. Why hurry yourself? *Avrio* is the Greek word for tomorrow ; *mañana*, the Spanish for tomorrow also ; as is *narliki* in Ceylon ; *am maireach*, the Gaelic for tomorrow.

A Spaniard may perhaps mean tomorrow when he says '*mañana*' ; a Greek may mean next week in saying '*avrio*' ; in Ceylon, an Indian Tamil when he says '*narliki*', keeps on saying '*narliki*'—but a Highlander ? Well, he may mean next year, maybe aye or maybe och aye.

Friends of mine asked a relative to do a wee bit cement job at their house which would take him a couple or three days ; and he said he would start the next week. He finished it three years later they told me!

Major alterations to my wooden bungalow in Strath were undertaken by men from Beauly ; contractors working on their own, known to each other and who formed a grand team. They toiled hard at it, through five dreary, wet, stormy, wintry months by floodlight to finish. Incoming travellers wondered if the Fleet was in ; such bright lights in the dead of winter in Gairloch!

There was Colin the mason and Colin the plasterer ; there was Donald the plumber and Donald the electrician ; not forgetting Hughie the painter ; and at the end, no, *not* Uncle Tom Cobley an' a', but the leader himself, the 'gaffer', bachelor 'Charlie Boy'—woodwork's master craftsman! What a boy! What a team! and what superb workmanship, and above all, everything done on time. When all was finished Charlie's fame had spread around. People were literally queuing up to get him to do work for them ; and of course the County officials at Dingwall soon heard and gave him contracts. Charlie Boy ; a case of from 'Log Cabin to White House' surely ? And so well-liked by all the girls at the céilidhs! Am sure many a heart fluttered as his lorry sped on its rounds, and perhaps he would get lots of 'phone calls, for he had both his name and 'phone number graphically painted on his lorry against a gaily tartan-sash-designed background, that any girl could fall for! And if he had toothache, he would go over 70 miles to his dentist at Inverness, who had a specially attractive receptionist! Och aye! nae bother.

Maybe, however, it is the easy view of time that is one of the hidden charms here. All the same, they are all a grand community. They have a quality that has characterised Scotsmen throughout the ages—VIGOUR—and what a quality that can be. The Highlands still supply the cities with policemen, bar-tenders and domestic servants ; all second to none. And how many Highlanders have gone abroad—even from such a poor, lowly township as this—to play the part in the old days of Empire builders ? More than you might ever imagine ; and what builders they were ; fine, stout fellows all. People are rated higher than possessions with a Highlander. One should remember that. To convince a Scotsman they say you must give him a long argument. To convince an Englishman you must give him plain facts.

Yes, a great people ; and half the charm of living here is in one's dealing with them. If you endear yourself to them, they will endear themselves to you. It is senseless to come amongst them with any degree of superiority or braggadocio. We, here, have known a few of this calibre. Their lives become not worth living, believe me. And for the tourist, what would a Highland holiday be, if it were not for the personal contacts of the daily visit to the general stores for groceries or haberdashery ; and to the post office for letters and fish ! And if you keep your ears open, hear some gossip on the way. Their English is spoken with an exquisite intonation ; they have a courtesy and hesitant grace of manner peculiar to themselves that you never find in any other part of Britain. You never find a bombastic, loud-mouthed Highlander. But, alas ! the Highlands are not a progressive area or community as we think of the term 'progress' in England. The population tends to dwindle away ; fewer and fewer speak the Gaelic tongue despite schooling efforts and the various Mods held about the country which lead to great (but only temporary) excitement. But no matter what part of the Highlands you visit, no matter what religions they keep, Catholic, Free Presbyterian, Free Church, Church of Scotland, they have all held together in their trials and tribulations through the years ; and of course their records in the two World Wars cannot be surpassed.

I have mentioned the Mods (a yearly festival of Gaelic music, song, dance, oral competitions, and the like) which is held for a week at different centres each year and to which all Gaelic-lovers (gentle Gaels with true speech on their lips) wend their way, young (even the very young) and old ; for music is a universal language—a language which all the world understands, be it Gaelic or otherwise.

In October 1961 it was held at Stirling and was the 58th Gaelic Mod, and was so well attended by participants and visitors from home and abroad, that it was said to have been the biggest Highland invasion since Prince Charlie's forces marched in, in 1746 !

Invariably on the Sunday before 'the week' commences there is a traditional Gaelic service held in the town's main church and is attended by the Provost, Magistrates and members of the Town Council.

The first of such Mods was held in Oban in 1898 and such foregatherings have taken place ever since (war years excepted). People who want to meet others similarly imbued, people who want to sing and dance in the old traditional way, attend ; for to such folk their songs draw strength from their wild hills and bitter misty moors ; warm and fragrant from the heather ; and in the whole assembly kith and kin are woven and knitted together like the strands of wool in the Fair Isle jerseys still made by old knitters in out-of-the-way places.

At such assemblies the songs of the isles delight all ears (even English ears), the gaily-coloured kilts (with hues like the tint of heather, the greens resembling moss) swing and swirl, and the women wear the brooches of their respective clans. Tartan is uppermost, everywhere ; even the shops make it their special display in all manner of forms ; and generally the Council 'goes to town' in stretching a banner across the main street emblazoned with the slogan *Ceud Mìle Fàilte* (100,000 welcomes) ; a cheering thought even if it is pouring with rain. I suspect many English visitors will enquire of the first Highlander in kilt they meet in the street as to what these foreign words mean ; and if the six-foot tall, hairy-kneed kiltie is the usual Highland wag, he will tell them in all seriousness it literally means, 'I can't give you anything but love'. And so the world wags on ; and I raise my glass to all these merry indefatigable Highland folk, who over the centuries, and I am sure for many yet to come, will never lose their heritage.

But each year the number of Gaelic-speaking persons diminishes owing to constant 'depopulation' of the Highlands. It is recorded that during the last 100 years the population of the counties of Argyll, Inverness, Ross and Cromarty, and Sutherland has fallen by nearly 62,000. There is little opportunity for those growing up to find employment at home, and so they have to leave for the south. In one of the islands in the Outer Hebrides, 22 per cent of its population were forced to leave during the past ten years. Surely this makes one, as the French say, 'furiously to think'.

I have remarked before on the great strains and hardships the Highlanders endured during the bygone famine years and the 'clearances'; and one may ask why the Highlanders did not offer more resistance to the inhumanity of those clearances. One factor was their God-fearing nature; many of their ministers told them that it was the Will of God. And another cause was that the young active males were away in the Napoleonic wars, fighting for the very people and government that was clearing them away; and when they returned, they found their homes and people gone.

Everything is, of course, much better today as I have hinted before this, but money is still required to be spent constructively, and legislation to accompany same. Hitherto the central government has generally given but a niggardly amount of money to carry out a 'rebirth' of the land economy of the Highlands.

Nothing is really possible without money. In the past the Highlands must have been the most expensive area in Britain from the point of view of money given in Public Assistance, poor relief and unemployment benefits. Unproductive money is money down the drain and the Highlands have been dubbed an area of a receiving character; a subsidised land.

The Highlander will put forward his whole effort if a reasonable profit is at the end of his labours. If there are no proper roads, no transport, no steamers calling to create life and prosperity —well, he can't build or make them himself; so logically in the far-away spots he says, 'I'll let the world go by'. After all, will the peats dig themselves; will the fish jump ashore?

It makes gloomy reading those terrible days when a people were forced by poverty and sometimes by other men's greed to cross the seas to a new home. But as I have said before, those men were ready to adapt themselves to a new living in the rigours of pioneering in Canada, New Zealand and Australia. History tells us it was the women who put up the greatest fight against evictions at the time of the Highland Clearances. The Battle of the Braes in Skye is notable for them.

But to return to the Mod and its adherents. Most of the elderly women who steadfastly attend, and who come from all quarters of the Highlands and Islands—mayhap bereft of their menfolk—are of a shy, retiring disposition ; but the memories of song and laughter still abound in their bosoms. And as these women and wives listen to the young performers ('the young in heart'), they smile happily to the speech and to the tradition which, to them, is a sure and living force ; for there are things which can be expressed only in Gaelic ; truths in life that can only be put to Gaelic verse. For life in the Highlands is hard, as hard and as dreary as the barren rocks that surround them and their crofts ; yet all the same, the love of life lies lightly on their chiselled faces. Young farmers have left their crofts for the week of the Mod, and whilst they are away their cattle will be roaming the hillside at leisure crushing back the old invader—the bracken. Some of the youngsters only have enough money saved to come for the one day they are 'performing' ; and then back they must go to their homes which may be in one of the far-away islands of the Outer Hebrides. A hard existence, but 'stocky' people to be sure.

Yes, young and old come to town ; junior choirs, assiduously coached by their Gaelic teacher, come to re-live, to revitalise one part (and to them *the* part) of Scottish home life which, to these young boys and girls, spells contentment of their own wee Highland homes. Until they grow up—and there's the rub !

A few pages back in connection with these crofter-folk, I said they still live in the 'Land of the Ever Young'. And verily, so they do.

In order to extend the Mod idea and stimulate interest—and incidentally finances—I think it would be a good idea if 'Festivals' in the near future embraced Gaelic, Welsh and Irish songs and music ? 'What say all of us ?' If that 'came to pass', what a 'do', what a 'draw', what publicity and what drams would go down the hatch, and cash-registers in the towns would need a general overhaul the following week having been working 24 hours each day ; for the 'bell' would be worn out !

I have already mentioned Highland hospitality being unequalled anywhere. Let me give but a small example. It was a dark, wet and stormy night when I went up the hill to call on my neighbour's farm. My house was not quite completed and I was staying at the hotel. I begged the 'Chieftain' to come down with a torch and see the latest developments, for he was keenly interested in all the long five months' work. We went and returned, blown and battered, and shoes soaked through. Despite my protests, there was nothing for it—the Chief's wife loudly proclaimed—but for me to take off my shoes and put on grandpa's slippers (three sizes too big of course!) whilst my own wet uppers were put near the kitchen range to dry out whilst we had the evening meal ; and then later I was able to go off with dry soles. Where else would you find such kindly thoughtfulness ?

And then there is the Scotch cooking, which I have touched on previously ; Highland cooking. Simplicity marks the answer to its goodness I think ; that, and the ingredients. Foreign cookery with French names (for the simplest of dishes ; really absurd) does not appeal to the Scots ; but more, the clean 'oaty' taste of pinhead porridge, bubbling on the hob and taken with salt, a horn spoon you *must* have, and a cup of milk beside you to keep dipping into with each spoonful of oatmeal. Then newly baked pancakes, oatcakes and warm white flowery scones you want to cuddle ; and shortbread made with butter, *real* butter. Haggis, the lordly dish, so often on the menu at St. Andrew's Night celebrations abroad, when it is religiously 'piped in' and carried, burning, aloft and around all the gathered tables. Haggis and roast chicken is a grand mixture ; and if you should have a dram of unblended Highland Malt Scotch Whisky (Glenlivet, Strathspey, 100° proof, 8 years old) to pour over it, then and then only will you begin to believe me when I say this is God's own country.

Truly it has been said that Scotland is the best place to take an appetite ! Scots halesome farin' is hard to beat.

Then, as I have said previously, up here religion plays a major part in the life of the community ; and so remembering that 'when in Rome do as the Romans do', I have always 'Kept the Sabbath' ; the term so frequently used up here. Not that down in England I made Sunday any other than a day of rest ; but up here the Sabbath takes on a different sense and feeling. There is a general stillness in the air which can almost be seen and touched ; and you feel everyone else is keeping the day Holy. *That*, I think, is the key to the difference experienced in England where people make Sunday a holiday outing in the car, or cut the grass ; buses run and coaches make up Sunday so-called 'mystery tours'. There is none of that here, except in the season, the coming and going of visitors' cars ; and here I should make a point—it is considered quite wrong to either arrive or depart on the Sabbath. Indeed many houses would not take you in on that day. Have I not recalled the days when posts were put across some minor roads, 'No motors on Sundays' ? Even today the ferries at Strome and Kyle do not operate on the Sabbath ; nor at the Mallaig–Armadale, nor Glenelg–Kylerhea (both South Skye) ; nor Kylesku on the north-west of Sutherland, except under special circumstances.

Yes, I am sure *that* is the key ; everyone else is keeping the day Holy ; and you, dear reader, would surely not care to be out of step ? Which reminds me of the story of the First World War, where a mother was watching her son—a very raw, awkward recruit, drilling with his unit on the barrack square. He couldn't keep in step at all. But his mother, loving him as she did, turned to a friend saying, 'There goes ma Jock ; everyone out of step but ma Jock !'

The Sunday paper van from Inverness that supplies the various hotels *en route* to Aultbea, is barred from entering into some areas on his 'Wells-Fargo' dash through !

This Scottish Highland heritage of keeping the Sabbath could very well be extended beyond the Highland boundaries. A complete day of rest, relaxation and thought enables one to start the week with a calm confidence. It is to be envied and copied. The difference between the Sabbath here and the Sundays down in England cannot be realised until you live here . . . 'Keeping the Sabbath'.

This, then, is the end.

I may not be in Ceylon, looking at the holiest mountain in the world, Adam's Peak.

I may not be in Naples watching the mighty Vesuvius erupting.

I may not be in Hong Kong's peak gazing down on the twinkling fairyland of the harbour and Kowloon.

I may not be in Singapore sitting drinking on the verandah at Raffles hotel, watching the world go by.

I may not be in Aden pondering over the age and workmanship of Solomon's biblical water-tanks.

I may not be in Egypt—awestruck by the Pyramids.

I may not be in Tangier, darting furtively through the
native Kasbah.

No ! none of the above places that I know so intimately—and that
are in their own way singularly wonderful—can in the main
compare with Gairloch, where I am looking south 'across the bay'
2 miles to Badachro, and 20 miles beyond, mighty big Beinn
Bhan towering in the Applecross Forest region ; and still further
on, the Cuillin Hills in Skye some 45 miles away ; and in the
early mornings to see from one's bedroom, whisps of misty cloud
rolling and wrapping themselves around the hills of Torridon,
skirting the valleys as though they were angel's robes trailing and
floating upwards. Yes, truly on a crisp, frosty spring morning the
sun, rising over the eastern hills so close at hand, bursts wide open
a new day ; travels over the snow-capped Torridon, Applecross
and Cuillin ranges—'Kilimanjaro white'—then drops into the
sea behind Skye like a red-hot ball of fire—'Trinidad Red'—
ready to start on its orbit through space again the following day ;
and the next day ; and the day after that : as has been the pattern
since these mountains were created. Truly Wester Ross and
Skye present a differing picture day in and day out ; year in and
year out. The scenery and the gentle atmosphere is captivating ;
and I cannot reason why there is such a craving for 'holidays
abroad' with so much grandeur offering itself on one's own
doorstep, so to speak. Seeing is believing ; pity is, there are so
many disbelievers. The power and faithfulness on which the
successive changes of day and night and of the seasons of the year
depend—and which uphold the stars in their orbit—are equally
engaged to support His people. To see all this and the ever-
changing colours and hues cast upon these 'up-lifting' mountains
by the rising or setting sun and which seem near enough at times
to touch in the clear air, can you wonder one's wish to interpret
the title as being 'and it came to happen' ; not, that 'and it came
to pass ; away '?

As in the song of songs, which is Solomon's, the winter is past,
the rain is over and gone ; the flowers appear on the earth ; the
time of the singing birds is come, and the voice of the turtle is heard
in our land.

This indeed is a great land, as well as a great people.

Here, one meets the *real* Highlanders, dwelling in the homes of their fathers and their fathers' fathers. Here are nonagenarians, octogenarians, and a few youthful septuagenarians! Friends all ; and surely friends—such good friends—make the latitude and longitude of life ?

I have mentioned Queen Victoria more than once. She and her consort loved Scotland ; to quote but one instance, she wrote in her diary at Balmoral, 'Alas, the last day. I wished we might be snowed up and unable to move'. . . .

In living a full life out East, enjoying it and the world in general—for is it not said, 'Life was meant to be lived ?'—when I left, my friends (flatteringly of course!) said I was far too young to retire, cutting myself away from public service ; that I would 'peter out' and go to seed doing nothing. However, one's imaginations, plans and memories over the span of years—which so help one to take life in its stride—have resulted in creating the Dream of that Day in 1914, in living these closing years amongst a wonderful country of mountains, lochs and glens ; amongst a people as wonderful as their land ; a people that, in a way though, are backward in unbridling their emotions, or in giving rein to their imaginations in this life : but a people so rich in sincerity—so very, very rich—that feeling so much one of their family, when it does 'come to pass', I trust I may be remembered as someone who loved their ways, and above all, themselves.

> Until the rivers run up stream
> Until lovers cease to dream
> I would feign be here. . . .

But of course that cannot be. As the years multiply, the milestones become gravestones ; 'and under each a friend'. And whilst we are squeezing more and more years into life, there is yet no sign of the Elixir of Youth—and the eternal search goes on.

'In the End', with the kiss of rain and wind, and the contentment of an unfettered mind, I shall say to Gairloch and its great and noble folk, 'Farewell, thou art too dear for my possessing'.

So ; *vive vale; slàn leat; Slàinte Mhath;* and on this final page *Slàinte Nach Teirig!* which being interpreted is 'Here's health everlasting to you'.

THE END